EASY CRAFTS FOR HOME & FAMILY

EASY CRAFTS FOR HOME & FAMILY

Sterling Publishing Co., Inc.
New York

Library of Congress
Cataloging-in-Publication Data Available

10 9 8 7 6 5 4 3 2 1

Published in 1999 by Sterling Publishing Company, Inc
387 Park Avenue South, New York, N.Y. 10016

© in this collection, Australian Consolidated Press, 1997

Distributed in Canada by Sterling Publishing
c/o Canadian Manda Group, One Atlantic Avenue, Suite 105
Toronto, Ontario, Canada M6K 3E7

Printed and bound in China

Sterling ISBN 0-8069-9830-X

STERLING PUBLISHING CO., INC.

Contents

Treasures for Tots 6

Charming for Children 36

Gorgeous Gifts 72

Great Gardeners' Goods 86

Hearth & Home 98

Fête Favourites 130

Nicest Knits and Classic Crochets 140

Festive Flair 174

Perfect Pastimes 194

Knitting and Crochet Notes 212

Embroidery Stitches 213

Pattern Pages 215

Stockists 225

Index of Projects 226

Treasures for Tiny Tots

Heirloom Shawl

*A truly wonderful heirloom,
to be passed from
generation to generation.*

MEASUREMENTS

Approximately 50″ diameter.

MATERIALS

Patons 3-ply Baby Wool (25g/1oz):
20 balls. One set No.3 needles.
One short and one long No.3
circular needle. One No.3/D
crochet hook.

TENSION

31 sts to 4″ in width over st st.

SPECIAL ABBREVIATIONS

M2: make 2 sts by working (K1, P1) into
next st; M3: make 3 sts by working (K1, Pl,
K1) all into next st; M5: make 5 sts by
working (K1, P1, K1, P1, K1) all into next st.

METHOD

Using set of needles, cast on 10 sts, placing 3
sts on first needle, 3 sts on second needle,
and 4 sts on third needle.

1st rnd. *yfwd, K1; rep from * to end.

2nd rnd. Knit.

3rd rnd. *yfwd, K2tog; rep from * to end.

4th rnd. *M3, K1; rep from * to end.

Knit 4 rnds.

9th rnd. As 3rd rnd.

10th rnd. As 4th rnd.

Knit 6 rnds.

17th rnd. *K1, yfwd, K2, yfwd, K1; rep from
* to end.

18th rnd. *K1, M2, K2, M2, K1; rep from *
to end.

19th rnd. *K2tog, yfwd, sl 1, K1, psso; rep
from * to end.

20th rnd. As 18 rnd. Rep last 2 rnds 3 times
more.

27th rnd. As 19 rnd.

Note. When number of sts will not fit com-
fortably on set of needles, transfer sts to circular needle.

28th rnd. *K1, M5, K2, M5, K1; rep from * to
end.

Knit 2 rnds.

31st rnd. *yfwd, st 1, K1, psso, K10, K2tog;
rep from * to end.

32nd rnd and alt rnds. Knit.

33rd rnd. *yfwd, K1tbl, yfwd, st 1, K1, psso,
K8, K2tog; rep from * to end.

35th rnd. *K1, yfwd, K1tbl, yfwd, K1, sl1,
K1, psso,K6, K2tog; rep from * to end.

37th rnd. *K2, yfwd, K1tbl, yfwd, K2, sl1,
K1, psso, K4, K2tog; rep from * to end.

39th rnd. *K3, yfwd, K1tbl, yfwd, K3, sl1,
K1, psso, K2, K2tog; rep from * to end.

41st rnd. *K4, yfwd, K1tbl, yfwd, K4, sl2,
K2tog, psso; rep from * to end.

43rd rnd. *K5, yfwd, K1tbl, yfwd; rep from *
to end.

45th rnd. *sl1, K1, psso, K9, K2tog, K1,
yfwd, K1tbl, yfwd, K1; rep from * to end.

47th rnd. *sl1, K1, psso, K7, K2tog, K2, yfwd,
K1tbl, yfwd, K2; rep from * to end.

49th rnd. *sl1, K1, psso, K5, K2tog, K3,
yfwd, K1tbl, yfwd, K3; rep from * to end.

51st rnd. *sl1, K1, psso, K3, K2tog, K4, yfwd,
K1tbl, yfwd, K4; rep from * to end.

53rd rnd. *sl1, K1, psso, K1, K2tog, K5,
yfwd, K1tbl, yfwd, K5; rep from * to end.

55th rnd. *sl1, K2tog, psso, K6, yfwd, K1tbl,
yfwd, K6; rep from * to end.

57th rnd. * yfwd, K1tbl, yfwd, sl1, K1, psso,
K11, K2tog; rep from * to end.

59th rnd. *yfwd, K3, yfwd, sl1, K1, psso, K9,
K2tog; rep from * to end.

61st rnd. *yfwd, K1, yfwd, sl1, K2tog, psso,
yfwd, K1, yfwd, sl1, K1, psso, K7, K2tog; rep
from * to end.

63rd rnd. *yfwd, K3, yfwd, K1tbl, yfwd, K3,
yfwd, sl1, K1, psso, K5, K2tog; rep from * to
end.

65th rnd. *yfwd, K1, (yfwd, sl1, K2tog, psso)
3 times, yfwd, K1, yfwd, sl1, K1, psso, K3,
K2tog; rep from * to end.

67th rnd. *(yfwd, K3, yfwd, K1tbl) twice,
yfwd, K3, yfwd, sl1, K1, psso, K1, K2tog; rep
from * to end.

69th rnd. *yfwd, K1, (yfwd, sl1, K2tog, psso)
5 times, yfwd, K1, yfwd, sl1, K2tog, psso; rep

from * to end.

71st rnd. *K3, yfwd, K1tbl, yfwd; rep from * to end.

73rd rnd. *sl1, K2tog, psso, yfwd; rep from * to end.

75th rnd. *yfwd, K1tbl, yfwd, K3; rep from * to end.

77th rnd. *yfwd, sl1, K2tog, psso; rep from * to end. Rep last 8 rnds twice, ending with 77th rnd.

94th rnd. *M3, K1; rep from * to end...640 sts.

Knit 2 rnds

97th rnd. *K14, K2tog, yfwd; rep from * to end.

98th rnd and alt rnds. Knit.

99th rnd. *sl1, K1, psso, K11, K2tog, yfwd, K1tbl, yfwd; rep from * to end.

101st rnd. *sl1, K1, psso, K9, K2tog, K1, yfwd, K1tbl, yfwd, K1; rep from * to end.

103rd rnd. *sl1, K1, psso, K7, K2tog, K2, yfwd, K1tbl, yfwd, K2; rep from * to end.

105th rnd. *sl1, K1, psso, K5, K2tog, K3, yfwd, K1tbl, yfwd, K3; rep from * to end.

107th rnd. *sl1, K1, psso, K3, K2tog, K4, yfwd, K1tbl, yfwd, K4; rep from * to end.

109th rnd. *sl1, K1, psso, K1, K2tog, K5, yfwd, K1tbl, yfwd, K5; rep from * to end.

111th rnd. *sl1, K2tog, psso, K6, yfwd, K1tbl, yfwd, K6; rep from * to end.

113th rnd. *yfwd, K1tbl, yfwd, K7; rep from * to end.

115th rnd. *K1, yfwd, K1tbl, yfwd, K1, sl1, K1, psso, K13, K2tog, psso; rep from * to end.

117th rnd. *K2, yfwd, K1tbl, yfwd, K2, sl1, K1, psso, K11, K2tog; rep from * to end.

119th rnd. *K3, yfwd, K1tbl, yfwd, K3, sl1, K1, psso, K9, K2tog; rep from * to end.

121st rnd. *K4, yfwd, K1tbl, yfwd, K4, sl1, K1, psso, K7, K2tog; rep from * to end.

123rd rnd. *K5, yfwd, K1tbl, yfwd, K5, sl1, K1, psso, K5, K2tog; rep from * to end.

125th rnd. *K6, yfwd, K1tbl, yfwd, K6, sl1, K1, psso, K3, K2tog; rep from * to end.

127th rnd. *K7, yfwd, K1tbl, yfwd, K7, sl1, K1, psso, K1, K2tog; rep from * to end.

129th rnd. *K8, yfwd, K1tbl, yfwd, K8, yfwd, sl1, K2tog, psso, yfwd; rep from * to end.

131st rnd. *sl1, K1, psso, K15, K2tog, yfwd, K1, M2, K1, yfwd; rep from * to end.

133rd rnd. *sl1, K1, psso, K13, K2tog, yfwd, K6, yfwd; rep from * to end.

135th rnd. *sl1, K1, psso, K11, K2tog, yfwd, K2, (M2) 4 times, K2, yfwd; rep from * to end.

137th rnd. *sl1, K1, psso, K9, K2tog, yfwd, K2tog, K1, yfwd, (yfwd, K2, yfwd) 4 times, yfwd, K1, sl1, K1, psso, yfwd; rep from * to end.

138th rnd and alt rnds. Knit, purling into second loop when two yfwds lie tog.

139th rnd. *sl1, K1, psso, K7, K2tog, (yfwd, sl1, K1, psso, K2tog, yfwd) 6 times; rep from * to end.

141st rnd. *sl1, K1, psso, K5, K2tog, (yfwd, sl1, K1, psso, K2tog, yfwd) 6 times; rep from * to end.

143rd rnd. * sl1, K1, psso, K3, K2tog, (yfwd, sl1, K1, psso, K2tog, yfwd) 6 times; rep from * to end.

145th rnd. *sl1, K1, psso, K1, K2tog, (yfwd, sl1, K1, psso, K2tog, yfwd) 6 times; rep from * to end.

147th rnd. *(yfwd) twice, sl1, K2tog, psso, yfwd, (yfwd, sl1, K1, psso, K2tog, yfwd) 5 times, yfwd, sl1, K1, psso, K2tog; rep from * to end...1080 sts.

148th rnd. Knit to end, then knit first st of rnd again.

Rep last 2 rnds 14 times more, dec 8 sts evenly spaced around last rnd...1072 sts.

Rep rnds 97 to 148 incl once, noting that st totals will differ. Cast off loosely.

To make up

With a slightly damp cloth and warm iron, press lightly. With right side facing, using hook, work one row sc evenly around outside edge. Fasten off.

Project by Coats Patons

Bright Boots

These cute, comfortable boots can be made in next to no time and for very little cost. Stitched from bright velveteen or corduroy and lined with a vivid print or tartan, any child will find them irresistible. You could use a rubber- or acrylic-coated fabric for a non-slip sole.

MATERIALS

8″ x 45″-wide corduroy or velveteen; thread; 16″ x ¼″-wide elastic; 8″ x 45″ printed cotton fabric, for lining.

FINISHED SIZE

6 months and 18 months.
Note: ¼″ seam allowance is included.

METHOD

Enlarge pattern ❖. Using pattern, cut two of front, sole and side pieces in main fabric. With right sides together, stitch front to side, matching center front (CF) dot. Stitch center back seam. Pin and stitch sole to side.

Cut elastic to fit ankle. Stitch in position marked on side, by stretching elastic and oversewing with a zigzag stitch.

Cut out and stitch lining as for boot, without elastic. With right sides of boot and lining together, stitch around top edge leaving an opening. Turn right side out, stitch opening closed. Topstitch close to edge.

❖ *indicates pattern on pattern pages*

Project by Betty Smith
Photography by Andrew Elton

11

Angel Birth Memento

Commemorate baby's birth date with this embroidered heirloom. Worked in satin stitch with backstitch details, the finished work can be framed.

MATERIALS

10″ square of cream muslin; soft lead pencil; crewel embroidery needle; DMC stranded embroidery thread in the following colors: cornflower blue 3807, cream 3823, crimson 321, flesh 407, auburn 3830, brown 3826.

FINISHED SIZE

4½″ x 3½″ (embroidered area).

METHOD

Transfer design to center of muslin using pencil.

Use colors indicated on diagram. Work the blue ribbon area using 2 strands of thread and satin stitch, then outline the bow with backstitch. Use 1 strand of thread for the remainder of the design, working in backstitch for the angel bodies and for words; satin stitch for the heart, brown hair and wings; colonial knots for the lips and red hair. Write baby's name and date of birth and stitch it in backstitch.

Note: Pattern below is half actual size. Enlarge on photocopier set to 200%.

*Stitched by Judy Newman,
based on a design by Deborah Kneen
Photography by Ross Coffey*

Christening Bonnet

Delicate and silky, this charming bonnet is perfect for a christening. It's quick to make, crocheted in soft rayon thread and has flower motifs on each side.

MATERIALS
1 ball rayon crochet thread (known as crochet silk); No.5 crochet hook, or hook to achieve correct tension; 36" x 1"-wide ribbon; thread.

FINISHED SIZE
Newborn.

TENSION
First 3 rows should measure 2" in diameter.

Bonnet

Make 6ch, join with a sl st in 1st ch made to form a ring.

1st rnd. 3ch, 11dc in ring, join with a sl st in 3rd ch made at beg. (12dc altogether counting the 3ch as 1dc throughout.

2nd rnd. 3ch, 1dc in same place as sl st *2dc in each dc to end, join with a sl st in 3rd ch made at beg...24dc.

3rd rnd. 3ch, 1dc in same place as sl st *1dc in next dc, 2dc in next dc; rep from * to last dc, 1dc in next dc, join with a sl st in 3rd ch made at beg... 36dc.

4th rnd. 3ch, 1dc in same place as sl st *1dc in each of next 2dc, 2dc in next dc; rep from * to last 2dc, 1dc in each of next 2dc, join with a sl st in 3rd ch made at beg...48dc.

5th rnd. 3ch, 1dc in same place as sl st *1dc in each of next 3dc, 2dc in next dc; rep from * to last 3dc, 1dc in each of next 3dc, join with a sl st in 3rd ch made at beg...60dc.

6th rnd. 3ch, 1dc in same place as sl st *1dc in each of next 4dc, 2dc in next dc; rep from * to last 4dc, 1dc in each of next 4dc, join with a sl st in 3rd ch made at beg...72dc.

7th rnd. 3ch, 1dc in same place as sl st *1dc in each of next 5dc, 2dc in next dc; rep from * to last 5dc, 1dc in each of next 5dc, join with a sl st in 3rd ch made at beg...84dc.

8th rnd. 3ch, 1dc in each dc to the end, join with a sl st in 3rd ch made at beg.

Proceed as follows:

Next rnd. 1ch, 1sc in same place as sl st, 4ch, *miss 2sc, 1sc in next sc, 4ch; rep from * to end, join with a sl st in first sc made...28 loops.

1st row. Sl st in first 4ch loop, (1sc, 1ch, 2dc) in same loop, 3ch, 1sc in next loop, *3dc in next sc, 1 sc in next loop, 4ch, 1 sc in next loop; rep from * till 2 loops remain, 3dc in next sc, 1sc in next loop, 3ch, 3dc in last loop, turn, and continue to work in rows.

2nd row. 1ch, 1sc in each of next 3dc, 3ch, *1sc in center dc of next 3dc, 4ch, 1sc in next loop, 4ch; rep from * 11 times, 1sc in center dc of next 3dc, 3ch, 1sc in each of next 2dc, 1sc in turning ch.

3rd row. (1sc, 1ch) in first sc, 1dc in each of next 2sc, 3ch, 1sc, in 3ch loop, *4ch, 1sc in next loop, 3dc in next sc, 1sc in next loop; rep from * 11 times, 4ch, 1sc in next loop, 3ch, 1dc in each of last 3sc.

4th row. 1ch, 1sc in each of next 3dc, 3ch, *1sc in next 4ch loop, 4ch, 1sc in center dc of next 3dc, 4ch; rep from *11 times, 1sc in next loop, 3ch, 1sc in each of next 2dc, 1dc in turning ch.

5th row. (1sc, 1ch) in first sc, 1dc in each of next 2sc, 3ch, 1sc in 3ch loop, *3dc in next sc, 1sc in next loop, 4ch, 1sc in next loop; rep from *11 times, 3dc in next sc, 1sc in 3ch loop, 3ch, 1dc in each of last 3sc.

Rep 2nd to 5th rows incl 3 times.

Next row. 1ch, 1sc in each of next 3sc, 2sc in 3ch loop, * 1sc in each of next 3dc, 2sc in next 4ch loop; rep from *11 times, 1sc in each of next 3dc, 2sc in 3ch loop, 1sc in each of next 3sc...73sc.

Next row. 1ch, 1sc in each sc to end.

Next row. 1ch, 1sc in each sc to end.

Next row. 1ch, 1sc in each of next 2sc, *3ch, sl st in last sc made, 1sc in each of next 3sc; rep from *to last 2sc, 3ch, sl st in last sc made, 1sc in each of last 2sc. Fasten off.

Rose

(make 2)

1st rnd. 6ch, (1dc, 3ch) in 6th ch from hook, 5 times, join with a sl st in 3rd of 6ch made at beg.

2nd rnd. 1ch, (1sc, 3dc, 1sc) in each 3ch loop, to end, join with a sl st in 1ch made at beg...6 petals.

3rd rnd. Working behind petals, 1ch, 1sc around turning ch of 1st rnd, 5ch, *1sc around next dc in 1st rnd, 5ch; rep from * to end, sl st in 1ch made at beg.

4th rnd. 1ch, (1sc, 5dc, 1sc) in each 5ch loop to end, join with a sl st in 1ch made at beg.

5th rnd. Working behind petals, 1ch, 1sc around 1st sc worked in 3rd rnd, 7ch, *1sc around next sc in rnd, 7ch; rep from * to end, join with a sl st in 1 ch made at beg.

6th rnd. 1ch, (1sc, 7dc, 1sc) in each 7ch loop to end, join with a sl st in 1 ch made at beg.

Fasten off.

Stitch ribbon to bonnet, stitch rose securely over the ribbon.

Project by Margaret Metcalfe
Photography by Andrew Elton

Quick-Knit Shawl

This classic shawl is a wonderful, quick and easy pattern in 3-ply, which features a design of squares with a crocheted, scalloped edge. Knitted shawls such as these are handy for many situations, such as for snuggling baby in the pram or in the car seat, and, unlike fabric quilts, they stay in place.

MATERIALS

500g/1lb of 3-ply pure wool; No.6 needles (a circular needle can be used to accommodate a large number of stitches — work in rows not rounds); No.4/E crochet hook.

FINISHED SIZE

44" x 38" approx.

METHOD

Cast on 238 sts.

**1st row. Knit 46, (K2tog, yrn, K46) 4 times.

2nd row. K1, purl until 1st rem, K1. Rep 1st and 2nd rows 27 times...56 rows.

Next row. *K2 tog, yrn; rep from * until 2 sts rem, K2.

Next row K1, purl until 1st st rem, K1** Rep from** to** 3 times, then rep 1st and 2nd rows 27 times. Cast off.

Edging. With crochet hook, join yarn to edge and work sc evenly all round edge of shawl, join to beginning then work 4 more rounds of sc, working 3sc into corners on each round to keep edge flat.

Scalloped edge. Work 4ch, 3dc into same space, miss 2sc, *1sc, 2ch, 3dc into next sc, miss 2sc, rep from * to * until end of round. Join to top of 1st scallop and fasten off.

Project by Betty Newman
Photography by Cath Muscat

Flannel Edging

Bathtime is also a time for pampering. Dress up a plain facecloth with a crocheted edging. This pattern looks lovely on bibs too.

MATERIALS

1 flannel; 1 ball rayon yarn — 3-ply; No.8 crochet hook.

METHOD

Work with right side facing.

1st round. Work sc evenly around the edge of flannel working multiples of 4 plus 1.

2nd round. 1sc in first sc, *miss 1sc, 5dc in next sc, miss 1sc, 1sc in next sc; rep from * to end.

3rd round. 1sc in first sc, 1sc between next 2dc, *(3ch, 1sc between next 2dc) three times, 1sc in next sc, 1sc between next 2dc; rep from * ending with 1sc in last sc.

Fasten off.

Projects by Margaret Metcalfe
Photography by Ross Coffey

Edged Bib

Inexpensive bibs, available from chain stores, can be transformed into something special with touches of delicate crocheted edging.

MATERIALS

1 bib; No.10 crochet cotton; No.8 crochet hook.

METHOD

With right side facing, work 1sc into bib edge, *4ch, 2dc in 4th ch from hook, 1sc into bib; rep from * to end. Fasten off.

Cot Sheet Set

These cot sheets and pillowcase are made lovelier with the addition of a delicate appliquéd bow. Choose fine, silky ribbon and simply tie it in a generous bow, then stitch in place.

MATERIALS

120″ x 45″-wide white fabric; thread; 80″ x 60″-wide soft, fine ribbon.

FINISHED SIZE

Pillowcase 16″ x 12″ plus frill; sheets 43″ x 33″.
Note: ¼″ seam allowance is included in instructions.

Sheets

Cut two fabric pieces 45″ x 36″. Stitch a narrow hem on sides of each sheet. Stitch a 1″ hem on top edges and a ¼″ hem on bottom edges.

Tie 40″ of ribbon into a soft bow, press flat and arrange in center of top edge of top sheet. Pin and handstitch in place.

Pillowcase

Cut one 17″ x 13″ piece for front and two 13″ x 12″ pieces for back. Cut and join a strip for frill 112″ x 7″.

Appliqué a ribbon bow in center of front at top edge as for sheet.

Stitch a 1″ hem on one 13″ edge of each back piece. Overlap the hemmed edges to form a 17″ x 13″ piece, tack together. Join ends of frill strip, press in half along length. Gather raw edges to fit around front, pin and stitch in place.

Place back over front, with right sides together, encasing the frill, stitch in place. Trim edges and neaten, turn out and press.

Project by Betty Smith
Photography by Andrew Elton

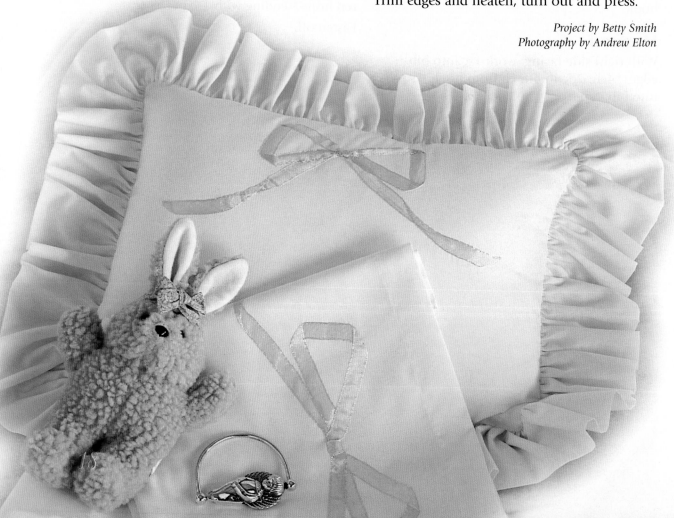

**pattern for wrist rattle
actual size**

Wrist rattle

This little piggy ... is a wrist rattle. Bright, with a friendly face, it makes an entertaining tinkle. And if you ever have retraced your steps trying to find a toy that's been dropped over the side of the stroller, you'll appreciate one which is attached to baby's wrist!

MATERIALS

Scraps of pink and purple felt; water erasable pen; 6-stranded embroidery thread in pink, black and blue; thread; 3 bells (from craft or pet stores); 2 small Velcro squares or dots.

METHOD

Using pinking shears, cut two 3"-diameter felt circles (one pink and one purple) and two 6" x 1" strips of purple felt. Trace pig face pattern and cut in pink felt. Stitch to purple felt circle. Draw face using water erasable pen and embroider in colors using backstitch for lines and satin stitch for fill-in areas. Stitch felt circles wrong sides together securely around edges, leaving a small opening. Insert bells, stitch opening closed. Place two strips together and stitch around edges to make wrist strap. Stitch embroidered circle onto center of wrist strap. Stitch Velcro to ends of strap.

*Project by Judy Newman
Photograhy by Cath Muscat*

19

Teddy Frame

If you have basic folk art skills, you'll enjoy painting this picture frame. Teddies tumble around each corner, between delicate floral bouquets.

MATERIALS

Tracing paper; sticky tape; 7″ square wooden frame; artist's acrylic paints in the following colors: Light Cream; Brown; Raw Sienna; Medium Red; Yellow Oxide; Norwegian Orange; Medium Olive Green; Jo Sonja's Rich Gold Paint; base coat and varnishing brushes; No.2 round brush; No.6 or 8 flat brush; liner brush; grey graphite transfer paper; stylus or empty ballpoint pen; waterbased matte or satin varnish; sandpaper.

METHOD

Base Coat

Sand frame and wipe clean. Base coat the frame with two smooth coats of Light Cream, allowing the paint to dry thoroughly between each coat. Trace the patterns for the bears and bouquets onto tracing paper. Note that the top and bottom bear patterns are reversed for the right side of the frame. To do this, simply turn the tracings over. Position each motif on the frame, using the photograph as a guide, and secure with magic tape. Slip a sheet of grey graphite transfer paper underneath the tracing and lightly transfer the motif, using a stylus or empty ballpoint pen to trace over the pattern lines.

Gold Trim

Take the flat brush and paint the outside molded edge of the frame in watery Rich Gold paint. Allow to dry. With the same brush, float Brown along the edges of the molding. Side load the flat brush with Rich Gold and float a shadow around the inner edge of the frame.

General Tips

The bears and bouquets are colored in with a No.2 round brush. Use watery paint to give a transparent, watercolor effect. If the color looks too strong, blot it with a cotton bud. When dry, fine details and outlines are added with a liner brush.

Bears

Base with Raw Sienna. Outline with Brown, using tiny broken lines. Eyes and nose are also Brown. Color the ribbons using Medium Red or Yellow Oxide.

Project by Deborah Kneen
Photography by Andrew Elton

Butterfly Rug and Crib String

Colorful butterflies and flowers will hold baby's attention for hours — appliqué them onto soft flannelette and embroider a garden of flowers to make the sweetest blanket ever. Make the matching garland for a cot or pram, or to hang in baby's room, with the same motifs tied onto bright ribbon. Choose floral fabrics with small, colorful prints for the prettiest effect.

Butterfly Rug

MATERIALS
80" x 36"-wide flannelette (choose one with a non-flammable finish); scraps of floral cotton fabrics; 8" square of fusible webbing; dressmaker's pencil; stranded embroidery thread to match fabrics and two shades of green; 160" satin binding for blanket.

FINISHED SIZE
40" x 36".

METHOD
Cut flannelette into two 40" lengths, for front and lining.

With dressmaker's pencil, mark a circle onto the center of front using a large dinner plate as a guide.

Trace butterfly shapes. Using a hot iron, fuse webbing to wrong side of floral fabrics, then cut out eleven small butterflies, one medium and three large. Remove paper backing from webbing and position ten small butterflies around marked circle. Fuse butterflies in place.

Arrange remaining butterflies in one corner of blanket, fuse in place.

Using two strands of embroidery thread and colors desired, blanket-stitch around edge of butterflies. Embroider flowers and leaves between butterflies, working lazy daisy stitches for petals and leaves and French knots for centers. Work a few flowers and leaves between remaining butterflies.

Pin front and lining fabrics, with wrong sides together, matching edges. Machine stitch over the marked circle to hold fabrics together. Encase blanket edges between the fold of the satin binding, zigzag stitch in place.

Butterfly Crib String

MATERIALS
Five 12" x 4" squares cotton fabric; thread; polyester fiber filling; 120" x ¼"-wide satin ribbon.
Note: Trace pattern for butterfly, adding ¼" seam allowance to pattern.

METHOD
Cut out two large butterfly shapes from each of five fabrics. With right sides together and using small stitches, sew around each butterfly leaving opening between dots. Turn right side out, fill lightly with fiber, stitch openings closed.

Tie ribbon around each butterfly, leaving 28" of ribbon at each end and looping ribbon around center of each butterfly before tying a bow. Hand-stitch bows.

Project by Lisa Johnson
Photography by Andrew Elton

For blanket, use small, medium and large shapes. For crib string, use large shape and add ¼" seam allowance.

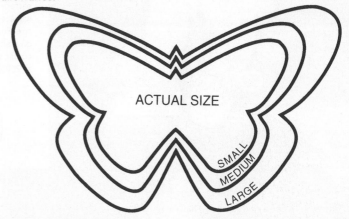

ACTUAL SIZE

SMALL
MEDIUM
LARGE

Teddy Blanket and Bear

Round and round the garden... appliquéd felt bears and embroidered flowers tumbling around this pure wool blanket make it pretty and practical. It's backed with cotton fabric.

MATERIALS

48" x 36" wool blanket fabric; beige felt; thread; polyester fiber filling; embroidery thread in brown for bear details and cream for over-sewing and backstitching; embroidery needle; chalk; DMC Perle embroidery thread in pale green, yellow and pink; tapestry needle; 48" x 36" fabric for backing; 8" narrow ribbon.

FINISHED SIZE

Blanket: 47" x 35"; Toy bear: 4" long.

METHOD
Blanket

Make a 16" circle in the center of blanket fabric. Trace pattern for bear and cut 6 in felt; set 2 pieces aside for bear toy. Position four bears around the circle and overstitch in place using cream embroidery thread, inserting a small amount of fiber filling in center to give bears rounded tummies. Using the same thread, backstitch a line to define arms and legs. Using brown embroidery thread, satin stitch eyes, nose and mouth. Make 3 colonial knots for buttons on bear front.

Using chalk, mark positions for the words, 'Round and round the garden, Like a teddy bear' spaced evenly between the bears, as pictured on our rug.

Embroider the lettering using whipped running stitch. Use green for the letter outlines, then whip each stitch in yellow. Between each bear, work lazy daisy stitch flowers (5 stitches per flower) in yellow. Add groups of 3 colonial knots to fill gaps between flowers.

Place backing fabric right side together with blanket, machine stitch around edges, using a ½" seam allowance and leaving an opening to turn through. Trim corners, turn through, slipstitch opening closed and blanket stitch around edge of blanket using yellow thread.

Toy bear

Pin remaining 2 bear shapes together and oversew edges using cream embroidery thread, stuffing with a small amount of fiber filling. Complete in same way as for blanket. Tie a ribbon bow around neck.

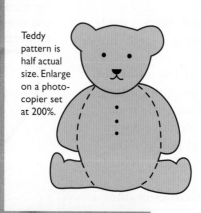

Teddy pattern is half actual size. Enlarge on a photocopier set at 200%.

Project by Judy Newman
Photography by Ross Coffey

Teaser and Squeakers

Heart, star and moon shapes in brightly colored felt will keep baby amused and happy.

MATERIALS

Felt in various colors; contrast color DMC Perle embroidery thread; tapestry needle; non-toxic craft glue; 1"-wide ribbon to fit across cot 4 times, for teaser only; ½"-wide elastic; to fit across cot; 36" of ¼"-wide ribbon; small foam squeakers (available from craft shops); thread.

METHOD

Make patterns ❖ for heart, star and moon shapes.

Teaser

Cut out 2 felt pieces for each shape required. For teaser, you will need 6 finished shapes. Stitch 2 shapes together using running stitches with Perle embroidery thread and tapestry needle. Cut out spots of contrasting colored felt, glue onto shapes.

Cut 1"-wide ribbon in half. Stitch ribbon lengths together along edges, with wrong sides facing. Cut elastic to fit across cot, insert into ribbon casing, gathering ribbon and stitching to secure at each end. Cut ¼"-wide ribbon into 2 lengths, fold each piece in half and stitch the fold to each end of ribbon casing, for ties. Position shapes across ribbon casing and stitch in place.

Sqeakers

Stitch 2 shapes together for each squeaker, inserting a foam squeaker between the pair of shapes as you stitch. Cut out spots of contrasting colored felt and glue onto shape.

Project by Chris Moss
Photography by Ross Coffey

quilt center); 64″ of 45″-wide green checked cotton fabric; fusible webbing; 40″ of 36″-wide thin wadding (for quilt).

FINISHED SIZES
Sheet: 65″ x 60″.
Quilt: 40″ x 32″.

METHOD
Jingler

Enlarge pattern for animals. Cut two of each animal in pink, purple or green. Place right sides together and stitch using ¼″ seam and small stitches, leaving an opening for filling. Trim seams and clip curves, turn right side out. Fill with fiber and stitch opening closed. Stitch eyes in colonial knots and ear detail on elephant in running stitch, using 3 strands of embroidery thread. Cut two 24″ lengths of ribbon, place wrong sides together and stitch along edges. Insert elastic, pull up to gather and stitch ends of ribbon and elastic together securely. Cut two 36″ lengths of ribbon, fold each in half and stitch the fold of each to one end of the gathered ribbon for ties.

Stitch animals to gathered ribbon, evenly spaced. Stitch bells securely, at each end of animals.

Sheet

Cut one 65″ x 60″ piece of sheeting fabric. Stitch narrow hems on long edges (sides). Stitch a 2″ hem on one short edge (bottom edge). Cut one 60″ x 5″ piece of green checked fabric. Place checked strip and top edge of sheet, right sides together and stitch. Press and turn under raw edges of

Jungle Jingler, Sheet and Quilt

Friendly jungle animals make a wild theme for cot linen. The matching jingler fits across the cot or pram and will entertain. If you want to co-ordinate the nursery, use our shapes to stencil walls, change table or other nursery furniture.

MATERIALS

8″ of three 45″-wide fabrics in pink, purple and green; fiber filling; 120″ of 1″-wide ribbon; 16″ of ¼″-wide elastic; 4 bells (from craft or pet stores); thread; 6-stranded embroidery thread in yellow, green, purple and pink; 90″ of 60″-wide cotton sheeting fabric (for one sheet and

checked strip, fold strip in half and stitch to make a contrast border. With three strands of yellow thread, work herringbone stitch along edge of checked border. Using three strands of green, work running stitch next to herringbone stitch.

Apply fusible webbing to wrong side of pink, purple and green fabric scraps. Cut out three elephants, two rhinos and two giraffes in colors desired. Remove paper backing and fuse to sheet with feet next to border. Work straight stitches around each animal using three strands of contrasting embroidery thread.

Quilt

Cut 28″ x 20″ rectangle of white sheeting for quilt center. Cut two 28″ x 7″ checked strips for side borders and two 30″ x 7″ checked strips for top and bottom borders. Cut 40″ x 32″ checked rectangle for back and same size piece for wadding.

Fuse webbing to pink, purple and green fabric for appliqués. Enlarge animal pattern and cut out each animal in each of the three

fabrics (9 in total). Mark 4″ from top and bottom edges of central rectangle of quilt. Within these marks, position animals in three evenly spaced rows. Fuse in place and zigzag or handstitch around each animal. Cut two strips 20″ x 3″ in checked fabric, press raw edges under and stitch across top and bottom of quilt center, 2″ from each end. Stitch side borders in place then stitch top and bottom borders in place; press.

Work herringbone stitch in yellow and running stitch in pink on horizontal seams of quilt center; press from wrong side.

Place quilt back on quilt top with right sides together and place wadding on top of quilt back. Stitch around entire quilt, leaving an opening. Turn right side out and stitch opening closed. Machine or handstitch quilt as desired to secure wadding between fabrics.

Project by Judy Newman
Photography by Cath Muscat

For sheet: enlarge on photocopier set to 200%
For quilt: further enlarge by 122%
For jingler: further enlarge by 160%

Traditional Pompom Hat

Any baby will look lovely in this cute pull-on hat.

MEASUREMENTS
To fit: 3(6, 12, 24) months. Fits head 16(18, 19, 20)″.

MATERIALS
Baby wool in 4-ply (25g/1 oz): 1 ball each of lemon (MC), mint (C1) and lilac (C2); one pair each No.2 and No.3 knitting needles; tapestry needle.

TENSION
32 sts and 42 rows to 4″ over patt, using No.3 needles.

Hat

Using No.2 needles and MC, cast on 122 (134, 146, 158) sts. Work 22 row stocking st. Change to No.3 needles.

Beg patt. 1st and 3rd sizes only.

Using C1, 1st row. Knit.

2nd row. K5, P4, *K8, P4; rep from * to last 5 sts, K5.

3rd row. P5, K4, *P8, K4; rep from * to last 5 sts, P5.

Rep 2nd and 3rd rows once, then 2nd row once.

All sizes. (This is the 7th row for 1st and 3rd sizes, but 1st row for 2nd and 4th sizes.) Using C2, **7th row.** Knit.

8th row. P3, K8, P4, *K8, P4; rep from * to last 11 sts, K8, P3.

9th row. K3, P8, K4, *P8, K4; rep from * to last 11 sts, P8, K3. Rep 8th and 9th rows once, then 8th row once.

Note: For all sizes, return to 1st row as given for 1st and 3rd sizes for patt.

Using MC, rep rows 1 to 6 incl once.

Using C1, rep rows 7 to 12 incl once.

Using C2, rep rows 1 to 6 incl once.

2nd, 3rd and 4th size only. Using MC, rep rows 7 to 12 incl once.

3rd and 4th sizes only. Using C1, rep rows 1 to 6 incl once.

4th size only. Using C2, rep rows 7 to 12 incl once.

All sizes. Shape crown. Using MC (C2, C2, C1), **1st row.** K3, K2tog, *K4, K2tog; rep from * to last 3 sts, K3...102 (112, 122, 132) sts.

2nd row. P3, K6, *P4, K6; rep from * to last 3 sts, P3.

3rd row. K3, P6, *K4, P6; rep from * to last 3 sts, K3.

Rep 2nd and 3rd rows once, then 2nd row once.

Using C1 (MC, MC, C2), **7th row.** K2 *K3, K2tog; rep from * to end...82 (90, 98, 106) sts.

8th row. K3, P3, *K5, P3; rep from * to last 4 sts, K4.

9th row. P4, K3, *P5, K3; rep from * to last 3 sts, P3. Rep 8th and 9th rows once then 8th row once.

Using C2 (C1, C1, MC), **13th row.** K1, K2tog, *K2, K2tog; rep from * to last 3 sts, K3... 62 (68, 74, 80) sts.

14th row. P2, *K4, P2; rep from * to end.

15th row. K2, *P4, K2; rep from * to end.

Rep 14th and 15th rows once, then 14th row once.

19th row. K2tog all across... 31 (34, 37, 40) sts.

Break off yarn, run end through rem sts, draw up and fasten off securely.

Pompoms

Make three small pompoms, one in each color yarn, and attach to the crown with a length of twisted yarn.

TO MAKE UP
Join seam, noting to reverse seam for first 12 rows of stocking st. Allow stocking st to roll onto right side of hat to form purl fabric brim.

Photography by Ross Coffey

Eye-Catching Pompom Hat

Any baby wearing this gorgeous hat will be greeted with lots of friendly smiles. Make it by knitting two squares worked in a simple striped design, topped with bright pompoms. Our instructions are for sizes from three months to two years.

MEASUREMENTS

To fit: 3(6, 12, 24) months. Fits head: 16(18, 19,20)".

MATERIALS

Baby wool 4-ply (25g/1 oz): one ball Main Color (MC), one ball Contrast Color (CC). One pair each No.2 and No.3 knitting needles. Tapestry needle for sewing seams.

TENSION

28 sts and 36 rows to 4" over stocking st, using No. 3 needles.
Using No.2 needles and MC, cast on 57 (65, 69, 73) sts.

1st row. K2, *P1, K1; rep from * to last st, K1.

2nd row. K1, *P1, K1; rep from * to end.

Rep last 2 rows 3 (3, 4, 5) times.

Change to No.3 needles.

Beg patt. Using CC, work 6 rows stocking st.

** Using MC, **7th row.** Knit.

Note: Do not weave colors in Fair Isle patt but carry colors not in use loosely across on wrong side of work.

Always carry colors to ends of rows and catch it in at side edge. Carry MC above CC.

8th row. P2MC, P1CC, *P3MC, P1CC; rep from * to last 2 sts, P2MC.

Using MC, work 2 rows stocking st.

11th row. K1CC, *K3MC, K1CC; rep from * to end.

Using MC, **12th row.** Purl.**

Using CC, work 6 rows stocking st.

Using MC, work 6 rows stocking st.

Rep from ** to ** once, using CC in place of MC and MC in place of CC.

Using MC, work 6 rows stocking st.

These 36 rows form patt.

Cont in patt until work measures 5(5½, 6, 6½)" from beg, working last row on wrong side.

Cast off. Make another piece in same manner.

TO MAKE UP

Join side and top seams. Using MC and CC tog, make 2 small pompoms and attach one to each corner of hat.

Photography by Andrew Elton

Socks and Singlet

MATERIALS

1 pair cotton socks; 1 ball rayon crochet cotton (known as crochet silk); No.7 crochet hook; 1 singlet with holes in neckline ribbing.

Socks

Work both socks in the same way.

1st rnd. With inside of sock facing, sc evenly around the top of sock, making sure you can still stretch the sock and having an even number of sc when finished, join with a sl st in first sc made.

2nd rnd. 1ch, 1sc in same place as sl st. *3ch, miss 1 sc, 1 sc in next sc; rep from * to last sc, 3ch, miss 1 sc, join with a sl st in first sc made.

3rd rnd. Sl st in first 3ch loop, (1 sc, 3ch, 1sc) in each loop to end, join with a sl st in first sc made. Fasten off.

Singlet

1st rnd. 1 sc in each hole around the neck edge of singlet, making sure you can still stretch the singlet at neck edge, join with a sl st in first sc made.

2nd and 3rd rnd. Work as for socks. Fasten off.

Project by Margaret Metcalfe
Photography by Andrew Elton

Touch-and-Feel Playmat

Small babies will love this textural treat — there's something soft, slippery, ribbed and fluffy to touch, and a feast of color. It's easy to make — we cut shapes from brightly colored fabrics and stitched them to a padded felt backing. Great for ages three to six months.

MATERIALS

90" of 36"-wide felt; 48" of 36"-wide thin wadding; six 36" lengths of ribbon or ric-rac braid in various colors and widths; fabric scraps of fake fur, felt, cotton, corduroy and suede (see below for exact details or use your own scraps as desired); lace motifs; matching and contrasting threads; non-toxic fabric glue.

FINISHED SIZE

45" x 36".

METHOD

Prepare Appliqués

(Use colors desired. We have listed our colors to assist you with assembly.) Cut three 3" x 2" rectangles of cotton and stitch them in the center of three 6"-diameter circles of pink felt. Take two of the circles and stitch them onto two 10" squares of fur fabric.

Cut three 3"-diameter orange felt circles and stitch lace motifs on two pieces and a 3" x 2" suede rectangle on the other. Cut two 5" squares of yellow cotton. Cut two 5" squares of red fur and cut each diagonally to make four triangles. Cut two 6" squares of green corduroy and two 3"-diameter circles of either cotton or fur; stitch circles in the center of the square. Cut one 6" square of grey fur and stitch a 3" green corduroy circle in the center.

Arrange Appliqués

Cut two 45" x 36" pieces of felt and one 45" x 33" piece of wadding. Arrange the appliqué pieces in the same order as listed above. On one piece of felt, position them as follows: across the width, place a length of braid 2" from one end, secure it with a little glue. Place a length of ribbon and two lengths of braid next to it. Then place the 10" squares of fur at each side of the felt, with remaining pink circles in the center. Lay four lengths of ribbon and braid next to them.

Continue positioning appliqués using our photograph as a guide and using glue to keep pieces in place or secure with pins. Stitch on all pieces using zigzag stitch.

Assembly

Place remaining felt piece wrong sides together with appliquéd felt piece with wadding sandwiched between. Stitch around the mat to secure layers. Trim edge with pinking shears.

Project by Judy Newman
Photography by Cath Muscat

Country Friends Mobile

Friendly farmyard animals will be welcome in any child's room. Simple shapes come alive with felt ears and a touch of embroidery and, when made from checked or plaid fabric they have a country feel. Threaded on cord with a tinkling bell on the end, they can be hung from a cot or curtain rod.

MATERIALS

For each mobile: 4" x 12" fabric for each animal; thread; polyester fiber filling; 40" cord; embroidery thread, for eyes and other features; scraps of felt, for sheep ears; craft glue; 1 bell.

METHOD

Enlarge patterns ❖ and add ¼" seam allowance. Using patterns, cut out two fabric pieces for each animal. With right sides facing, stitch fabric pieces together, leaving openings between dots marked on pattern. Clip curves and turn right side out. Fill with fiber and insert cord through top and bottom openings. Space animals evenly along the cord, then stitch openings closed. Stitch eyes, tails and chicken combs using embroidery thread and stitches desired. Cut out two felt ears for each sheep, glue in place. Tie a bell to cord end.

Project by Betty Smith
Photography by Andrew Elton

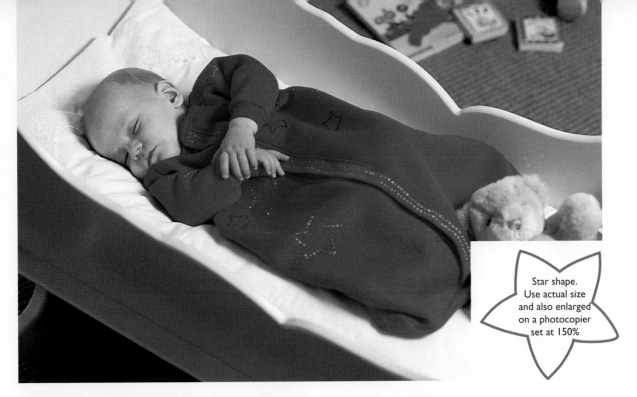

Star shape. Use actual size and also enlarged on a photocopier set at 150%

Twinkle, Twinkle Little Star Sleeping Bag

A sleeping bag makes a lot of sense because it saves parents from getting up in the night to replace thrown-off covers. Ours is stitched in fleecy stretch fabric and decorated with simple running stitch stars. For warm weather, use a lightweight fabric.

MATERIALS

36″ of 56″-wide fleecy-lined fabric; 12″ of 36″-wide ribbing; thread; Velcro dots or pop fasteners; water erasable pen; gold and blue embroidery threads; embroidery needle.

FINISHED SIZE

To fit 6 months approx.

METHOD

Enlarge pattern ❖ and add ½″ seam allowances. Check length, adjust if needed. Cut two sleeves, two fronts and one back from fleecy fabric. Place sleeves and back right sides together, at sleeve seam, stitch and press open. Stitch fronts to sleeves in same way. Stitch side seams and clip underarms.

Cut one 16″ x 3″-wide strip of ribbing for neck. Fold in half lengthwise and cut ends into curves. Place raw edges together along neckline and stitch in place, stretching ribbing and using small zigzag stitch. Turn allowance towards fleecy fabric and topstitch. Cut two 6″ x 3″ ribbing strips for cuffs. Stitch 3″ edges of each piece, right sides together, then fold in half. Place raw edges together with right side of sleeve and stitch in place as before.

Cut two 22″ x 3″ strips of ribbing for center front. Fold each in half lengthwise and stitch to center front edges. Press towards fleecy fabric and topstitch. Overlap front ribs and tack in place at bottom edge.

Cut one 16″ x 5″ fleecy fabric; this forms a rectangular base between front and back bottom edges. Trim corners into curves. Place right sides together with bottom edge of front and back, stitch in place. Attach Velcro or pop fasteners along front rib. Trace star pattern, enlarge and transfer actual size and enlarged stars at random using water erasable pen. Stitch over outlines in running stitch in gold or blue. Work two rows of running stitch in gold on the front rib.

Project by Judy Newman
Photography by Cath Muscat

Charming for Children

Rabbit in Liberty Duds

A really appealing toy for all ages.

Size

16″, approximately.

Materials

8″ x 36″ muslin; 12″ x 36″ printed fabric (for overalls); polyester padding; two eyes or buttons; pink embroidery thread; sewing thread; press stud; two small buttons (for overalls).

Method

Enlarge pattern ❖ pieces to correct size on paper and cut out.

From print, cut two each of strap and overalls.

Cut all other pieces from muslin, including two lining pieces for overalls. Cut two ears from padding.

Sew leg and arm seams, leaving tops of each unsewn. Clip curves and turn out to right side. Fill arms and legs with filling.

Sew back head seam from large dot to star. Sew seam on front face from nose to star.

Place right sides of ears together then position padding over the top. Sew seams leaving straight lower edge open. Turn out to right side and press.

Stitch small pleats in ears as indicated on pattern, then pin to seamline on front face at ear position, as indicated. Sew front face to front body at neckline. Repeat with back head to back body.

Sew darts in back where indicated on pattern. Sew back seam to dot, leaving an opening above dot.

Fold leg tops, dot to dot, matching seams. Stitch across tops of legs to hold.

Pin arms to right side of front body at position marked. Keeping arms, legs and ears to inside, place right sides of body pieces together and pin. Sew around seamline, clip curves and turn out to right side. Fill body, then stitch back opening closed.

Using embroidery thread, sew mouth and satin-stitch nose.

Using strong thread, sew button eyes.

Overalls. Sew center front seams of overalls and lining. Stitch hem on lining. Sew center back seam of overalls from crotch to dot.

Sew straps, turn out and topstitch.

Pin strap ends to front at position marked. With right sides together, pin and sew facing to overalls, clip curves and turn out. Topstitch around top edge.

Pin and sew leg seams, matching crotch. Turn up leg hems and sew. Sew small hems at center back.

❖ *indicates pattern on pattern pages*

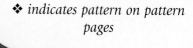

Teddy with Embroidered Vest

This soft, cuddly teddy is easily made with a just a few pattern pieces. We used inexpensive muslin fabric, but wool blanketing or flannel could also be used.

MATERIALS

16" x 36"-wide muslin fabric; thread; polyester fiber filling; six-stranded embroidery thread in desired colors.

FINISHED SIZE

15" in length.
Note. ¼" seam allowance is included.

METHOD

Make pattern ❖ from graph.

Cut fabric using pattern. Mark vest outline on fabric pieces. With right sides facing and using a small machine stitch, sew pairs of ears and arms together, leaving bottom edges open. Turn out and stuff with filling; set aside. Stitch center front seam and center back seam of body to dots, leaving opening as indicated. Pin the front and back of bear together, pinning ears and arms in the positions marked.

Stitch side seams, then reinforce seam at crotch and neck. Clip curves, trim seams and turn through carefully. Stuff legs with filling and stitch across dotted lines at top of legs. Stuff remainder of bear with filling; stitch back opening closed.

Using 2 strands of embroidery thread, sew the vest outline in running stitch. With 3 strands of thread, satin stitch 3 buttons on center front seam. Using 3 strands of thread and mixing colors as desired, lazy daisy stitch inside the vest fronts.

Using 3 strands of thread, satin stitch eyes and nose, then backstitch a mouth.

❖ *indicates pattern on pattern pages*

Project by Christine Moss and
Judy Newman
Photography by
Andrew Elton

Calico Cat

This cute toy with a patchwork skirt will delight.

MATERIALS

20″ x 36″ muslin; 8″ x 36″ of three fabrics with small prints; pink patches for cheeks; buttons; thread; padding; 80″ ribbon for trims.

METHOD

Make pattern from graph. From muslin, cut head, upper body and lower body pieces. From one print, cut upper body for bodice, shoe top and sole of shoe. From second print cut out five skirt sections 5″ x 7″. From third print, cut out five skirt sections 5″ x 7″.

Sew face patches in place using zigzag stitch and machine embroider face features. With right sides of head together, sew around head, leaving neck opening. Turn out. Fill with padding. Set aside.

Sew tucks in bodice front, press in sleeve hems ¼″, pin wrong sides of bodice over muslin upper body, stitch sleeve hems. With right sides together, sew upper body seams leaving neck and waist unsewn; turn out.

Join skirt sections, with right sides together, along 7″ lengths of alternating fabrics. Sew a ½″ hem, gather waist.

With right sides facing, sew lower body pieces together, leaving open at waist and ankles.

Clip curve, turn out. Pin skirt to waist, adjusting gathers evenly.

With right sides together, pin and sew upper body to lower body at waist, taking in skirt.

Fill body not too firmly.

Turn in neck edge and sew on head by hand. Make shoes and fill with padding, turn in ankle edges and sew, by hand, to muslin legs.

Sew on buttons and trim ankles, wrists and neck with ribbon bows.

Project by Betty Smith, photography by Andrew Elton

Country Cousin

This delightful doll is a treasure who brings a touch of country charm wherever she's displayed. She's made of wooden cotton reels.

MATERIALS

One large wooden bead; 4 smaller wooden beads; 5 cotton reels; 40″ fine ribbon; 24″ x 16″ fabric; 20″ ribbon to co-ordinate; raffia for hair; black marker pen; rouge.

METHOD

Tie largest bead (head) to center of

ribbon with double knot. Push knot to bottom (neck).

Separate both remaining ends of ribbon, add to each, first one spool then one round bead. Pass ribbon back through each arm spool.

Thread both ends together through one spool.

Separate ends again and add two spools and one round bead to each end. Thread ribbon back up both leg spools and tie at waist. (See diagram.)

With right sides together stitch dress side seam along 16″ length. Turn under and stitch hem top and bottom, leaving small opening in top hem to form casing for ribbon. Thread ribbon, and pull up dress to fit doll's body. Tie and stitch to hold tie in position. Bunch and glue raffia hair in place, add black dots for eyes and a blush of rouge for cheeks.

Photography by Andrew Elton

Three Bears

Not Mama, Poppa and Baby, but three equally adorable bears.

KNITTED BOBBY BEAR

MEASUREMENTS
Approximately 20″ high.

MATERIALS
Patons 8-ply (50g/2oz.): 6 balls (approximately). One pair No.9 knitting needles. Tapestry needle for sewing seams and embroidery. Purchased crystal eyes. Ribbon. Bells for ears. Polyester fiber filling. Black yarn for features.

TENSION
17 sts and 24 rows to 4″ over st st, using yarn double. To achieve the desired soft effect, this pattern has been designed to be worked on larger needles at a looser tension than usually recommended.
Note. Bear is worked in st st throughout, using two strands of yarn tog throughout.

Body Back

Cast on 12 sts.

Working in st st, inc one st at each end of next and foll alt rows until there are 32 sts.

Dec one st at each end of foll 4th rows until 24 sts rem. Work 5 rows st st. Cast off.

Body Front

Cast on 12 sts.

Work in st st, inc one st at each end of every row until there are 52 sts.

Dec one st at each end of next and foll alt rows until 24 sts rem.

Work 3 rows st st. Cast off.

Arms

(make 2)

Cast on 15 sts.

1st row. Inc in first st, K6, inc in next st, knit to end.

2nd row. Inc in first st, P7, inc in next st, purl to end.

3rd row. Inc in first st, K8, inc in next st, knit to end.

Cont inc in this manner in every row until there are 25 sts.

Work 15 rows st. st.

21st row. K2tog, K10, sl1, K1, psso, knit to end.

22nd row. P2tog, P9, sl1, P1, psso, purl to end.

23rd row. K2tog, K8, sl1, K1, psso, knit to end.

24th row. P2tog, P7, sl1, P1, psso, purl to end.

Cast off.

Legs

(make 2)

Cast on 40 sts.

Work in st st, inc one st at each end of next and foll alt rows until there are 48 sts.

Dec one st at each end of alt rows until 36 sts rem.

Work 13 rows st st.

Next row. K17, K2tog, K17.

Purl one row.

Dec one st at each end of next 4 rows.....27 sts.

Cast off.

Ears

(make 2)

Cast on 16 sts.

Work 4 rows st st.

Dec one st at each end of next and foll alt rows until 8 sts rem.

Inc one st at each end of alt rows until there are 16 sts.

Work 4 rows st st.

Cast off.

Head Piece One

Cast on 20 sts.

Work 4 rows st st.

Inc one st at beg of next row and at same edge in every row until there are 26 sts.

Work 4 rows st st.

Cast off 2 sts at beg of next and foll alt rows 3 times in all...20 sts.

Work 5 rows st st.

Dec one st at beg of next row and at same edge in every row until 12sts rem.

Cast off.

Head Piece Two

Work to correspond with Head Piece One, reversing shaping. When making up, Body Front must be eased to fit.

Gusset

Cast on 8 sts. Inc one st at each end of 3rd and foll 4th rows until there are 20 sts.

Work 13 rows st st.

Dec one st at each end of next and foll alt rows until 8 sts rem.

Work 11 rows st st.

Next row. *K2tog; rep from * to end.

Next row. (P2tog) twice.

Cast off.

TO MAKE UP

With a slightly damp cloth and warm iron, press lightly. Sew Back and Front Body pieces tog, leaving neck edge open and easing Front into Back with cast-on edges at bottom; fill. Ease Gusset to fit Head pieces, noting that the tip of Gusset ends at the snout and Head pieces are sewn tog to form a chin. Leave neck open and fill. Sew eyes to Head, embroider nose and mouth in black yarn. Join Head to Body. Fold Arms and Legs in half lengthways and join seams, filling as you go. Stitch Arms and Legs to Body. Fold Ears in half so that cast-on and cast-off edges are tog, place bell in center, join seams and sew to Head. Tie ribbon in a bow around neck.

BETSY BEAR

MEASUREMENTS

Height approximately 18″.

MATERIALS

Patons 8-ply (50g/2oz.); 5 balls. One No. 6/G crochet hook. Tapestry needle for sewing seams and embroidery. Polyester fiber filling. Purchased crystal eyes. Bells for ears. Length of ribbon. Black yarn for embroidery.

TENSION

17 sts and 20 rows to 4″ over sc.

Special abbreviation

Dec one st: draw up a loop in each of next 2 sts, yarn over hook and draw through all 3 loops on hook.

Body

(make 2 pieces, beg at lower edge)
Make 17ch.

1st row. Miss 1ch, 1sc in each ch to end.....16sc.

2nd row. 1ch, 2sc in first sc, 1sc in each sc to last sc, 2sc in last sc.

Inc one st (as before) at each end of every row until there are 42 sts.

Work 8 rows sc fabric.

Next row. Dec one st, 1sc in each sc to last 2sc, dec one st.

Dec one st (as before) at each end of foll 4th row until 36 sts rem, then in alt rows until 30 sts rem.

Fasten off.

Left Side Head

Make 23 ch.

1st row. Miss 1ch, 1sc in each ch to end......22sc.

Inc one st (as for Body) at end of next and foll alt rows until there are 30 sts.

Tie a colored thread at end of last row.

Dec one st at each end of every row until 8 sts rem.

Fasten off.

Right Side Head

Work to correspond with Left Side Head.

Top Head

(beg at nose)
Make 4ch.

1st row. Miss 1 ch, 1sc in each ch to end....3sc.

Inc one st at each end of 3rd and foll alt rows until there are 23 sts.

Work 3 rows sc fabric.

Dec one st at each end of next and foll alt rows until 17 sts rem, then in foll 5th rows until 7 sts rem.

Fasten off.

Arms

(make 2)

Make 34ch.

1st row. Miss 1ch, 1sc in each ch to end....33sc.

Inc one st at each end of next 3 rows....39sc.

Work 5 rows sc fabric.

Dec one st at each end of every row until 31 sts rem then in alt rows until 23 sts rem. Cont in sc fabric until work measures 5″ from beg. Fasten off.

Legs

(make 2)

Make 49ch.

1st row. Miss 1ch, 1sc in each ch to end......48sc.

Inc one st at each end of next 3 rows.....54sc.

Work 5 rows sc fabric.

Dec one st at each end of every row until 46 sts rem then in alt rows until 38 sts rem.

Cont in sc fabric until work measures 6″ from beg.

Fasten off.

Ears

(make 2)

Make 13ch.

1st row. Miss 1ch. 1 sc in each ch to end...12sc.

Dec one st at each end of next and foll alt rows until 6 sts rem.

Work 3 rows sc fabric.

Inc one st at each end of next and foll alt rows until there are 12 sc.

Fasten off.

To make up

Do not press. Using a flat seam, join Body pieces, leaving top edge open and filling as you go. Fold Leg and Arm pieces in half, sew around edges using a flat seam and filling as you go. Join Side Head pieces tog to colored threads. Sew in Top Head from colored threads around rem edges of Side Heads, leaving lower edge free; fill Head with filling. Fold Ears in half and sew seams tog (do not fill), enclosing bells. Sew Head to Body, joining top edge of Body around lower edge of Head. Stitch Arms and Legs to Body. Sew Ears to Head. Sew on eyes. Embroider features as photographed. Tie ribbon around neck.

Bobby and Betsy Bear by Coats Patons

McTeddy Bear

Measurements

Seated bear is approximately 13″ high.
Note: The instructions and materials listed are for the teddy bear only and not for beret and scarf.

Materials

Cardboard for pattern pieces (lightweight cardboard such as that used for cereal boxes is ideal); 20″ x 60″ fur fabric; 6″ of contrast fur fabric for muzzle, ears, paws, feet and nose; matching thread; lead pencil or vanishing marker; polyester fiber filling; tool, such as a wooden spoon handle or a piece of dowel, to aid stuffing; tapestry needle and dark wool to embroider mouth; darning needle and strong thread to attach head and limbs; purchased safety crystal eyes; purchased plastic nose.

Method

Enlarge pattern ❖ pieces to correct size on cardboard, including relevant details such as the arrows indicating the direction of the pile and the 'letter' markings.

Cut out pattern pieces.

Pin pieces to fur fabric ensuring the grain and pile of the fabric run in the same direction as the arrows on the patterns. Note that a ¼″ seam is allowed on each piece so there is no need to add a seam allowance.

Cut out each piece separately to ensure the pile is running in the right direction. Using a pencil or vanishing marker, write the relevant letters on the wrong side of each piece.

Head

Placing right sides together, pin and sew two head pieces to head gusset, matching letters. Sew seam from C to D to E. Pin nose G into a fold. Sew seam from F to E and to G; turn out.

Note: If pile is caught between seams, pull out with the point of the knitting needle.

Place eyes in position and stitch. Fill head firmly. Gather neck edge and sew opening closed.

Body

Placing right sides together, pin then sew seam around curved body sections A to B; turn out. Fill body firmly. Gather neck edge and close opening. Sew head to body — C-F to A-B.

Arms

Sew contrast paws to two arm pieces (inner arms) as indicated. J across to K. With right sides together, pin and sew arms together, M around to N, to make two arms; turn out. Fill arms, close small openings. Sew arms to shoulder sides of the body.

Legs

Pin and sew legs Q to H and R to I. Sew contrast foot pads around I to H to I; turn out. Fill legs and sew openings closed. Sew legs to body, making a seated or standing bear, as desired.

Ears

Two fur pieces and two contrast fur pieces are required to make the ears. Using one piece of each color, pin right sides together to form two ears. Stitch around edge from O to P; turn out. Turn in raw edges, sew with running stitch, and pull up slightly to curve ears. Sew securely to head.

Contrast Muzzle

Fold muzzle, right sides together, from S to S. Sew seam through both thicknesses of fabric from S to T. Hand-stitch muzzle to face, turning the raw edge to the inside and stuffing with filling as you go. Secure nose in position. Use wool to embroider mouth. If pile covers features, carefully trim away with scissors. If desired, make a beret and scarf as pictured, or dress teddy with a bow tie.

SPECIAL NOTE: IF THE BEARS WILL BE HANDLED BY VERY SMALL CHILDREN, THEN DO NOT SEW ON BUTTONS FOR EYES, BUT EMBROIDER EYES, AS THE SMALL BUTTONS MAY BE DANGEROUS.

Hello Dolly

Dolls are always popular and, as ever, need just the right clothes to look their best. We've made an old-fashioned outfit — dress, country pinafore, bloomers and straw hat.

MEASUREMENT
To fit a doll 16″ tall and 13″ around the chest. The patterns can be scaled up to fit a larger doll or down to fit a smaller doll.

MATERIALS
20″ x 45″ of floral cotton fabric; 16″ x 45″ striped cotton fabric (for pinafore and lining); 5yds of 1″-wide broderie edging with holes for insertion of ⅛″ ribbon; 6yds of ⅛″-wide ribbon; 32″ of ⅛″-wide elastic; 8″ hat elastic; hook and eye; 2 press-studs; matching thread; raffia and large darning needle for hat.

METHOD

Enlarge pattern ❖ pieces from graph onto paper and cut out paper.

Note. Front and back of pinafore bib are represented on the same pattern piece. For pinafore bib back, cut two fabric and two lining pieces. For pinafore bib front, cut one from fabric and one from lining on the fold.

Dress bodice back and front are also represented on one pattern piece. For dress bodice back, cut two fabric pieces. For dress bodice front, cut one fabric piece on foldline shown on pattern.

Cut out other paper patterns as indicated.

From fabric, allow for 6″ x 36″ for dress skirt; 2″ x 45″ for skirt frill; 5″ x 36″ for pinafore skirt; 3″ x 45″ for pinafore sash. Arrange paper patterns on remainder of fabric, then cut out all pieces.

Cut out lining pieces.

Dress

Placing right sides together, sew broderie edging to lower edges of sleeves and one long edge of skirt frill. Press seams towards edging, then neaten seams with zigzag stitch and trim.

Join frill to form circle, then sew gathering along remaining raw edge. Sew CB seam of skirt leaving 2″ open at top of seam for CB opening. Sew frill to hem edge of skirt, easing the gathers evenly; neaten seam. Gather waist edge of skirt.

Thread ribbon through broderie edging on skirt; tie a bow at center back.

Turn under raw edges at CB seam opening on skirt to form placket.

Place right sides of dress bodice together, then sew shoulder and side seams; neaten.

Pin, sew and neaten bodice to skirt waist, easing gathers evenly. Trim off raw edge of broderie edging, retaining insertion section, to make narrower. Stitch edging to neckline, press seam and neaten with zigzag stitch.

Sew lace casing on right side of each sleeve where indicated on pattern piece. Sew, then neaten sleeve seams. Gather tops of sleeves between dots marked on pattern. Pin, then sew, sleeves to bodice. Matching shoulder and side seams, thread hat elastic through casing to fit doll's arms, and stitch to hold. Thread ribbon through edging on sleeves and stitch to hold. Tie two small bows. Stitch one to side of casing on each sleeve. At back of dress sew press-studs at waist and at back opening of bodice. Thread a ribbon through neckline broderie edging, leaving enough to tie a bow at back for closure.

Bloomers

Sew broderie edging to bloomer legs, as for dress. With right sides together, sew then neaten front and back seams of pants. Match seams together and sew legs through crotch. Turn in waist casing and sew. Insert elastic to fit waist. Thread ribbon through edging, starting at side of each leg and leaving enough ribbon to tie a bow at each side of doll's legs.

Pinafore

Cut rounded corners on the lower CB corners of skirt. Stitch broderie edging along this edge, as for dress, easing at rounded corners. Sew edging on shoulder flounces. Thread ribbon through skirt and flounce edging.

Gather top edge of flounces. Sew shoulder seams of pinafore bib to lining. Pin and tack flounces to bib, matching dots and easing gathers evenly. Pin right sides together of pinafore bodice and lining, then sew around neckline and armholes, keeping flounces inside between layers. Clip curves, turn out and press. Topstitch close to edges of armholes and neckline.

Placing lining sides together. Pin, then sew side seams of apron bib; press open. Placing wrong sides together, sew bib to skirt, easing gathers evenly. Press seam up to bib.

To make sash, fold right sides of fabric strip together in half along length. Sew seams, leaving one end open. Turn out, stitch opening closed and press. Pin sash at sash stitchline, as indicated on pattern leaving ends for ties. Topstitch sash to pinafore, enclosing waist seam.

Sew hook and eye at CB neckline.

Hat

Make a three-strand continuous plait using six threads of raffia per strand. (Begin stitching hat as follows. Thread in more strands of raffia to make plait as long as needed.)

Make a spiral for center crown and, with a single strand of raffia threaded through needle, stitch spiral edges together. Continue coiling braid around spiral and stitching, easing the braid into a curve and ensuring it remains flattish until it is about 2" in diameter.

Slope sides gently as you stitch to form rounded crown. Using the doll's head as a block, stitch and shape crown to fit, then begin curving braid outwards for brim, which is stitched flat in as many rounds as desired.

Project by Betty Smith, photography by Andre Martin

Fairyland Fantasies

Bring the magical world of fairies and elves to life in just a couple of hours with these super simple costumes.

Fairy Garland for her Hair

MATERIALS

28″ x 56″ net fabric; 10 metallic pipe-cleaners (we used Tinsel Strands, available from craft stores); 3 silk flowers; 1″ x 8″ lengths of curling ribbon.

METHOD

Cut net into triangles 7″ long and at least 2″ wide at the base. Twist 2 pipe-cleaners together at one end. Tuck a piece of net between the pipe-cleaners so it is held at the midway point. Twist pipe-cleaners around each other to hold the net in place. Continue in this way, joining in extra pipe-cleaners as needed until you have only 3″ free. Twist ends together to create a circlet, then fill the rest of the circlet with net and eventually fasten off by twisting the pipe-cleaner ends around each other. Press ends with pliers to make them safe. Twist flower stems onto the garland and tie on lengths of curling ribbon.

Fairy Wings

MATERIALS

3 metallic pipe-cleaners (we used Tinsel Strands); 32″ x 56″ net fabric; 1 pinfitting brooch back.

METHOD

Twist 2 pipe-cleaners together. Bunch the net together at the midway point and twist the pipe-cleaners around it to hold the gathers in place, keeping gathers flat and leaving 4″ of the pipe-cleaner ends free. Thread pipe-cleaner ends through 2 holes in the brooch back, twist ends together to secure. Cut the remaining pipe-cleaner into 2 lengths. Fold over a corner triangle at the top of each wing. Push one pipe-cleaner through the net at each corner triangle and twist ends together to form a small loop. With pliers, press all ends flat to make them safe. Pin the wings to your fairy's back and slip index fingers through the loops on the corners of the wings.

Fairy Skirt

MATERIALS

88″ x 56″-wide net fabric; 88″ x 4″ strip of gold fabric, for waistband; thread; elastic to fit child's waist; small silk flowers; star sequins; craft glue.

SIZE

Fits 3 to 8 years old.

METHOD

From net fabric, cut three 88" lengths: one 14" wide, one 12" wide and one 10" wide. (Skirt length will be approximately 14". Adjust width of fabric panels to alter skirt length.)

Separately fold each piece widthwise, into 3, pinning top edges together. Cut the bottom edges into sharp zigzags, taking care not to cut within 4" of the top edge.

Open out the pieces and place them in layers starting with the widest and placing the narrowest piece on top. Align top edges (which will be the waist edge). With right sides facing, and edges even, pin waistband piece to skirt, then stitch with ½" seam allowance. Pin ends of the waistband and side seam of skirt, with right sides facing; stitch. Turn ½" seam allowance of waistband to wrong side, then turn it over to form a 1"-wide casing. Pin and stitch in place, leaving an opening for elastic. Thread elastic through casing, check fit, stitch ends together. Stitch or glue star sequins and flowers to skirt.

Magic Wand

Cut out star shape in cardboard. Use craft glue to fix star to 12"-long small dowel or plastic stick, gluing 2" of the stick to one side of the star. Cover both sides of the star with glue and sprinkle generously with gold glitter; stand wand in a jar until dry. Lay wand flat and apply glue to one side. Drop beads, sequins and stars onto glue and allow

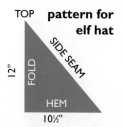

to dry before repeating on other side. Seal the surface by spraying with hair spray or gloss sealer.

ELF COSTUME

Cut sharp zigzags from the hem and sleeves of a long-sleeved, emerald green T-shirt to make our elf shirt. Team it with a pair of leggings and perhaps a wide leather belt.

Elf Anklets

Cut two 15" x 6" pieces of stretch fabric. Stitch narrow ends together and stitch a 1" casing around one long edge, leaving a small opening. Cut zigzags from the raw edge. Insert 8" of elastic into casing, check fit and stitch ends together.

Elf Hat

Cut one piece of stretch fabric on the fold, following diagram. With right sides facing, stitch the side seam. Hem raw edge and stitch a bell to the top of hat.

TOP **pattern for elf hat**
SIDE SEAM
12" FOLD
HEM
10½"

Elf Bells

Glue curling ribbon to one end of a thin 15"-long dowel, wind ribbon around to the other end and glue in place. Tie and glue a few lengths of ribbon to one end and tie bells onto the end of ribbon. Glue silver pompoms and star sequins to the top of the dowel.

Project: Skirt, garland, wings and wand by Multi-Plys
Elf costume by Christine Moss
Photography by Ross Coffey

Paper Beads

Recycle paper to create fabulous jewelery! These colorful beads are made by rolling triangles of paper cut from magazine pictures.

The size of the triangle will determine the bead shape and size. If you want all the beads to be the same, experiment with different sizes then, when satisfied, use one triangle as a pattern from which to cut out the others.

When triangles are cut, roll each one around a knitting needle. Trim the point off and glue the end in place. Then ease the bead off the needle and allow glue to dry. Thread beads onto strong thread and knot ends together to make a necklace. Bracelets can be made by threading beads onto shirring elastic.

Project by Christine Moss
Photography by Andrew Elton

Priscilla Pig

Découpaged in pretty rice paper, Priscilla has a lovely gold neck bow to match her nails. She'll make an attractive companion for an admirer of her obvious charms

MATERIALS

Bisque fired pig; black and gold acrylic paints; small paintbrush; patterned rice paper; PVA glue; flat plate for glue; ½" firm paintbrush; clear gloss Estapol (spray or can); gold ribbon.

METHOD

Paint eyes of pig black; nose, feet and inside of ears gold. Tear rice paper into pieces about 1" in diameter, ignoring pattern on paper. Tear, rather than cut, paper as torn edges blend more easily. Pour glue onto plate and, using dampened, firm paintbrush, begin painting glue onto a small section of pig. Apply a piece of paper to glued area and continue working with next piece of paper in the same way, overlapping each piece slightly so pig is completely covered. Take extra care around painted areas and, if any little gaps remain, simply tear tiny pieces of paper and fill gaps. Allow pig to dry completely. Apply a coat of Estapol; allow to dry. Tie gold ribbon bow around neck of pig.

Project by Dawn Andra
Photography by Andrew Elton

Projects by Christine Moss
Photography by Andrew Elton

FINISHED SIZE

28″-diameter circle.

METHOD

Cut two 29″-diameter circles in fabric. Place circles right sides facing and raw edges even, stitch around circles leaving an opening to turn through. Trim seam and clip curves. Turn right side out and stitch opening closed; pin and topstitch around edge. Make 18 buttonholes evenly spaced around edge of circle. Insert cord through buttonholes, knot ends.

BEACH BAG

MATERIALS

40″ of 45″- or 56″-wide heavy cotton fabric; 40″ of 45″-wide muslin, for lining; thread; 3yds cord.

FINISHED SIZE

38″-diameter circle.

METHOD

Cut two 40″-diameter circles, one in heavy cotton and one in muslin. Make as for toy bag, but stitch 24 evenly spaced buttonholes around circle edge.

Drawstring Bags

Circles of fabric drawn up with cord make great easy-sew bags for storing kids' toys or carrying all the essentials to the beach.

TOY BAG

MATERIALS

60″ of 45″-wide heavy cotton; thread; 3yds cord.

Double Delight

Knit this cute jumper with matching doll for the special little girl in your life.

MEASUREMENTS
To fit size: 2 (3,4,5) years. Fits chest: 22(23,24,25)". Actual measurement: 23½(25,26½,28)". Length to shoulder: 14½ (15,16,17)". Sleeve length: 9 (10,11,12½)". Doll: Height: 9".

MATERIALS
Jumper: Cleckheaton Country 8-ply (50g/2oz): 7(8,8,9) balls Main Color (MC — mauve). 1 (1,1,1) ball 1st Contrast (C1 — red). 1 ball each of 2 contrasting colors (C2 — bone, C3 — black) and small quantity of 4th Contrast (C4 — cream) for embroidery. **Doll:** 1 ball Main Color (MC — bone). 1 ball 1st Contrast (C1 — red). 1 ball 2nd Contrast (C2 — black). 1 ball 3rd Contrast (C3 — cream).

One pair each of No.3 and No.6 knitting needles; No.5/F crochet hook; 3 stitch-holders; 3 buttons for back opening and 2 small buttons for dolls on Jumper; No.4/E crochet hook. Polyester fiber filling and 3 small buttons for Doll. Tapestry needle for sewing seams and embroidery.

TENSION

22 sts and 30 rows to 4″ over stocking st, using No.6 needles for Jumper and 24 sts and 34 rows to 4″ over stocking st, using No.3 needles for Doll.

Back

Using No.3 needles and MC, cast on 67 (71,75,79) sts.

1st row. K2, *P1, K1; rep from * to last st, K1.

2nd row. K1, *P1, K1; rep from * to end.

Rep 1st and 2nd rows 3 (4,4,5) times [8(10,10,12) rows rib in all].

Using C1, **next row.** Knit.

Next row. As 2nd row.

Change to No.6 needles and MC for rem.**

Beg patt. 1st row. Knit.

2nd row. Purl.

3rd and 4th rows. Knit.

Rows 1 to 4 incl form patt. Cont in patt until work measures 9(9½,10,10½)″ from beg, ending with a 2nd row.

Shape Armholes and Divide for Back Opening. Next row. Cast off 3 (3,4,4) sts, knit until there are 29 (31,32,34) sts on right-hand needle, cast off center 3 sts, knit to end.

Cont on last 32 (34,36,38) sts for Left Back.

Keeping patt correct, cast off 3 (3,4,4) sts at beg of next row...29 (31,32,34) sts. Dec one st at end of next and foll alt rows until 26 (28,29,30) sts rem.

Work 40 (44,48,48) rows patt.

Shape shoulder. Cast off 6 (6,6,7) sts at beg of next row and foll alt row.

Work 1 row. Cast off 5 (7,7,6) sts at beg of next row, patt to end.

Leave rem 9 (9,10,10) sts on a stitch-holder.

With wrong side facing, join yarn to rem 29 (31,32,34) sts and work to correspond with other side, reversing all shapings.

Front

Work as for Back until there are 10 rows less than Back to beg of armholes.

Work 8 rows stocking st.

Shape armholes. Cont in stocking st for rem, cast off 3 (3,4,4) sts at beg of next 2 rows...61 (65,67,71) sts.

Dec one st at each end of next and foll alt rows until 55 (59,61,63) sts rem.

Work 19 (21,23,23) rows stocking st.

Shape neck. Next row. K22, (24,25,26), turn.

Cont these 22, (24,25,26) sts and dec one st at neck edge in alt rows until 17 (19,19,20) sts rem.

Work 3 (3,1,1) row/s.

Shape shoulder. Work as given for Back shoulder shaping, noting to cast off rem sts.

Slip next 11 sts onto stitch-holder and leave. With right side facing, join yarn to rem 22 (24,25,26) sts and work to correspond with other side of neck, reversing all shapings.

Sleeves

Using No.3 needles and MC, cast on 37 (37,39,39) sts.

Work as given for Back to **, noting to inc 4 (4,4,6) sts evenly across last row...41 (41,43,45) sts.

Work in patt as given for Back, inc one st at each end of 5th and foll 8th (8th,10th,10th) row/s until there are 45 (47,53,49) sts, then in foll 10th (10th,12th,12th) rows until there are 53 (55,57,59) sts.

Cont (without further inc) until work measures 9 (10,11,12½)″ from beg, ending with a 2nd row.

Shape top. Keeping patt correct, cast off 2 sts at beg of next 2 rows...49 (51,53,55) sts.

Dec one st at each end of next and foll alt rows until 23 sts rem, then in every row until 9 sts rem. Cast off.

Neckband

Join shoulder seams. With right side facing and using No.3 needles and MC, knit up 57 (57,63,63) sts evenly around neck, incl sts from stitch-holders.

Using C1, 1st row. Purl.

2nd row. K2, *P1, K1; rep from * to last st, K1.

Using MC, rep 1st and 2nd rows once.

5th row. K1, *P1, K1; rep from * to end.

Rep last 2 rows 0 (0,1,1) time/s.

Cast off loosely in rib.

Right Back Band

With right side facing and using No.3 needles and MC, knit up 39 (43,47,49) sts evenly along end of neckband and right side of back opening.

Next row. K1, *P1, K1; rep from * to end.

Next row. Rib 3, yrn (to make a stitch), rib 2 tog, [rib 11 (13,15,15), yrn (to make a stitch), rib 2tog] twice, rib 8 (8,8,10)...3 buttonholes.

Work 3 rows rib.

Cast off loosely in rib.

Left Back Band

Work to correspond with Right Back Band, omitting buttonholes.

Skirt

(make 2)

Using No.6 needles and C1, cast on 26 sts.

Work 5 rows stocking st.

6th row. P1, (P3tog) 8 times, P1...10 sts.

7th row. Knit.

8th row. P1, (P2tog) 4 times, P1...6 sts.

Cast off loosely.

With right side facing and using No.5/F crochet hook and C1, work 1 row crab st evenly along cast on edge.

TO MAKE UP

Mark center stitch at lower edge of stocking st of Front yoke. Using center stitch as a guide for doll placement, embroider dolls from Graph using knitting-stitch embroidery and working dolls 7 (11,13,15) sts apart between lower edge of arms. Using backstitch

and C3, embroider strap on shoes and V-shaped mouth on face. Using French knots and C3, embroider eyes. Sew dolls' skirts in position. Sew 1 small button to center of bodice on each doll. Using bullion stitch and C3 embroider hair to dolls as illustrated, winding yarn around needle 3 times for each stitch and drawing up firmly as this determines length of each curl. Join side and sleeve seams. Sew in sleeves. Sew on buttons. Sew end of Right Back Band to 3 cast off sts at center back, then slip st end of other band underneath.

TOY DOLL

Beginning at feet and using No.3 needles and C2, cast on 28 sts, marking center of cast on edge with a colored thread.

1st row. (wrong side). Purl.

2nd row. Inc knitways in each st at end...56 sts.

Work 3 rows stocking st, beg with a purl row.

Using C3, work 4 rows stocking st.

Shape feet. Next row. K6, (K3tog) 6 times, K8, (K3tog) 6 times, K6...32 sts.

Work 7 rows stocking st, beg with a purl row.

Using MC, work 6 rows stocking st, marking center of last row with a colored thread.

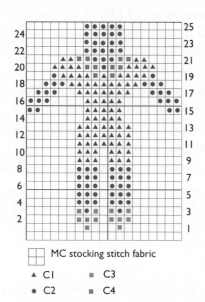

MC stocking stitch fabric

▲ C1   ■ C3
● C2   ■ C4

Using C1, work 18 rows stocking st.

Shape shoulders. Next row. K7, (K2tog) twice, K10, (K2tog) twice, K7...28 sts.

Work 1 row.

Using MC, work 2 rows stocking st.

Shape head. Next row. K8, inc once in each of next 12 sts, K8...40 sts.

Work 23 rows stocking st, beg with a purl row.

Next row. *K2tog; rep from * to end...20 sts.

Break off yarn leaving a long end, thread end through rem sts. Do not fasten off.

Arms

(make 2)

Using No.3 needles and MC, cast on 7 sts.

1st row. (wrong side). Purl.

2nd row. Inc knitways in each st to end...14 sts.

Work 10 rows stocking st, beg with a purl row.

Using C1, **Next row.** Purl.

Next row. K4, inc knitways in each of next 6 sts, K4...20 sts.

Work 6 rows stocking st, beg with a purl row.

Next row. (P2tog) 10 times...10 sts.

Cast off.

Skirt

Using No.3 needles and C1, cast on 80 sts.

Work 15 rows stocking st.

16th row. *P2tog, P3tog; rep from * to end...32 sts.

Cast off loosely.

Collar

Using No.3 needles and C3, cast on 32 sts.

Work 3 rows garter st (1st row is wrong side). Cast off.

TO MAKE UP

Join ends of rows tog on legs, body and head piece to form center back seam. Oversew cast on edge, carrying colored thread at center front through to center back seam. Stitch inside leg seam, beg and ending at colored threads and working through back and front tog, thus making 2 legs. Fill toes, legs, body and head firmly. Draw up length of yarn tightly at top of head and fasten off securely. Using backstitch and C2, embroider mouth. Using French knots and C2, embroider eyes, working each eye 5 sts apart. Using C2 double attach straps to shoes as pictured. Join arm seams filling lightly as you go. Oversew top of sleeves and attach to body just below shoulder shaping. Join center back seam of skirt. With right sides facing and using No.4/E hook and C1, work 1 row single crochet evenly along cast on edge of skirt, then 1 row crab st. Sew skirt on doll, 8 rows down from beg of head. Attach cast off edge of collar to neck, leaving 2 sts of C1 showing at center front. Sew 3 small buttons to center of bodice on doll. Using bullion stitch and C2 embroider hair to doll as illustrated, winding yarn around needle 5 times for each stitch and drawing up firmly as this determines length of each curl.

Project by Cleckheaton
Photography by Ross Coffey

Tie-Dyed Casual Clothes

It's easy to get hooked on this creative technique! Tie-dyeing produces colorful one-off patterns and enlivens plain white clothes. We show how to scrunch, wrap, pleat and tie the fabric for dyeing success!

MATERIALS

Rubber bands; string or fine rope; rubber gloves; cold water dye; plain white clothes (cotton gives best results); stainless steel or plastic container or large glass bowl; 4 tablespoons salt.

Note. Read manufacturer's instructions before using the dye.

METHOD

Prewash and dry clothes to be dyed. Tie fabric in desired pattern using rubber bands or string (for some possible patterns, see photographs).

Wearing rubber gloves, add contents of

one tin of cold water dye to 1 pint of hot tap water. Mix dye with enough cold water to cover clothing for dyeing in container. Dissolve contents of one sachet of dye fix in 1 pint of hot tap water, stir in 4 table-spoons of salt then add the mixture to the dyebath.

Immerse tied clothing in dyebath and swirl gently for 5 minutes to distribute dye evenly. Leave for 1 hour, turning clothing over occasionally. Remove clothing from dyebath and rinse under cold water until water runs clear. Remove bands or string and hang clothing to dry.

TIPS

- Avoid stains to hands and clothing by wearing rubber gloves and protective clothing.

- Pure cotton gives best results. Mixtures of natural and man-made fibers such as cotton/polyester and cotton/Lycra give color variations or paler shades.

- Pale-colored clothing can be dyed, but remember the original color will add to the final effect. For example, pale yellow dyed with red will give an orange result.

- If a printed fabric is dyed, the original pattern will still be visible.

Patterns

CIRCLES

Pick up points of fabric and secure with rubber bands. A dyed ring will form wher-ever the band masks the fabric. Add extra bands for concentric rings.

SCRUNCHING

Bundle the entire garment into a ball and wrap with rubber bands or string. This will produce an uneven, marbled effect.

SUNRAYS

Pick up a point of fabric and tie with string. Wrap string around the fabric, tying it in place regularly.

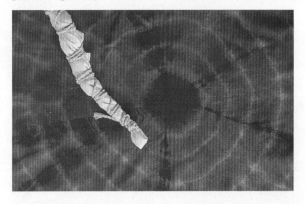

PLEATING

Fold fabric into even pleats and tie at inter-vals with rubber bands or string to give a striped effect.

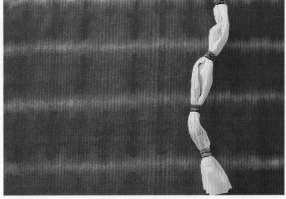

Project by Judy Newman
Photography by Andrew Elton

Kiddy's Indoor Cubby

Choose a cheerful kid's print and a stable table and build a cubby that's good for indoors or out. We've sized ours, with its roll-up window blinds and tied-back opening, to fit a card table, but making instructions also apply to table cubby-houses of other dimensions.

SIZE

To fit 30″ square card table.

Note. Although the measurements and materials listed are to fit a card table, with some adjustment, the tent is perfect to fit over a dining table for indoor games in poor weather. Adjust materials and measurements for a custom fit.

MATERIALS

5yds x 45″ cotton fabric; 12″ x 45″ contrast fabric (for blinds); 4yds of 1″-wide bias binding; thread.

METHOD

From cotton fabric, cut a 32″ square to fit card table top; ½″ seams are allowed. (For a different-sized table, measure the area and add seam allowance.)

The sides are cut in one whole piece. For card table, cut 125″ x 28″ for sides.

Cut two front facings, each 15″ x 26½″.

Cut facings for windows later, when windows have been cut out from sides. Save remaining cotton fabric to cut strips for binding blind edges. From contrast fabric, cut two blinds, each 12″ x 24″.

With right sides together, pin and sew front facings along 28″ ends of the 125″ length. Continue stitching around lower corners. Trim excess facing fabric at hem edge. Turn out to right side and press.

Turn up a hem to fit along lower 125″ edge; sew and press.

Pin the center front faced edges to the center of the 32″ square top. Pin, then sew sides around the top square.

Cut out windows, 10″ wide and 11″ deep, on the left and right sides, 2″ down from top seam.

Cut out facings to fit windows, then sew facings in place.

Fold window blinds in half to measure 12″ x 12″. Bind the three raw edges with strips of the main fabric. Sew folded edge of each window to side of tent, below top seams.

Fold bias binding in half along length and stitch.

Cut to make ties on each side of windows and front flaps.

Novelty Number Knits

Celebrate children's birthday with these figures of fun! There are five easy pieces to choose from, featuring big, 'age' numbers and cute little creatures.

MEASUREMENTS

To fit size. 1 (2,3,4,5). Fits underarm. 21 (22,23,24,25)". Garment measures. 24 (26,27,29,30)". Length. approximately 14½ (15,16,17,17½)". Sleeve fits 8½ (9,10,11,12½)".

MATERIALS

Patons 8-ply (50g/2oz): 5 (6,6,7,7) balls Main Color (MC). One pair each No.3 and No.6 knitting needles. Two stitch-holders. Small amounts of Patons 8-ply in colors as indicated on desired Graph. ❖

Tapestry needle for sewing seams and embroidery.

TENSION

22.5 sts and 30 rows to 4" over st st, using No.6 needles.

Note. We suggest knitting in large areas of color from desired Graph when knitting Front, then working smaller areas of color in knitting-stitch embroidery after Front is knitted. When changing colors in the middle of a row, twist the color to be used (on wrong side) underneath and to the right of the color just used. Use a separate ball of yarn for each section of color. Wind colors into smaller balls where necessary. If preferred, entire motif from Graph may be worked in knitting-stitch embroidery after knitting Front.

Back

Using MC and No.3 needles, cast on 70 (74,78,82,82) sts.

1st row. K2, *P2, K2; rep from * to end.

2nd row. P2, *K2, P2; rep from * to end.

Rep last 2 rows 4 (5,6,6,7) times, inc 1 (1,1,1,3) st/s evenly across last row...71 (75,79,83,85) sts, 10 (12,14,14,16) rows rib in all.

Change to No.6 needles.

Knit 4 rows garter st.

Work 62 (62,62,66,66) rows st st.

Shape armholes. Cont in st st, cast off 5 sts at beg of next 2 rows, then dec one st at each end of next and foll alt rows until 53 (57,61,63,65) sts rem.**

Work 29 (31,35,35,39) rows st st.

Shape shoulders. Cont in st st, cast off 5 (5,6,6,6) sts at beg of next 4 rows, then 5 (6,6,6,6) sts at beg of foll 2 rows.

Leave rem 23 (25,25,27,29) sts on a stitch-holder.

Front

See note. If knitting-in motif, count the number of sts and rows on the Graph of your choice and mark the position of it with pins on the Back, so that you will know where to beg working from the Graph when knitting up the Front. Match center st on Graph with center st on garment, and position motif bearing in mind that your Front neckline will be approximately 26 (28,28,28,30) rows lower than Back.

Work as for Back to **, noting to work from Graph, if desired.

Work a further 3 (3,7,7,9) rows st st.

Shape neck. Next row. K21 (22,24,25,25), turn. Cont in st st on these 21 (22,24,25,25) sts, dec one st at neck edge in alt rows until 15 (16,18,18,18) sts rem. Work a further 13 (15,15,13,15) rows st st.

Shape shoulder. Cont in st st, cast off 5 (5,6,6,6) sts at beg of next row and foll alt row.

Work one row.

Cast off rem 5 (6,6,6,6) sts.

With right side facing, sl next 11 (13,13,13,15) sts on a stitch-holder and leave.

Join yarn to rem 21 (22,24,25,25) sts and work to correspond with side just completed.

Sleeves

Using MC and No.3 needles, cast on 34 (38,38,38,42) sts.

Work 10 (12,14,14,16) rows rib as for Back, inc 6 (6,8,8,8) sts evenly across last row...40 (44,46,46,50) sts.

Change to No.6 needles.

Knit 4 rows garter st.

Cont in st st, inc one st at each end of next and foll 6th (6th,6th,6th,8th) rows until there are 52 (58,62,64,66) sts.

Cont straight in st st until work measures 8 (9,9,10,11)″ from beg, or ½ (½,1,1,1)″ less than desired length to allow for loose fit, ending with a purl row.

Shape top. Cont in st st, cast off 3 sts at beg of next 2 rows, then dec one st at each end of next and foll alt rows until 38 (44,48,46,46) sts rem, then dec one st at each end of every row until 12 (14,14,16,16) sts rem.

Cast off.

Neckband

Join right shoulder seam. With right side facing, using MC and No.3 needles, knit up 86 (94,94,98,102) sts evenly around neck, incl sts from holders. Knit 3 rows garter st. Work 16 (16,18,20,22) rows rib as for Back. Cast off loosely in rib.

TO MAKE UP

With a slightly damp cloth and warm iron, press lightly. Using back-stitch, join left shoulder, Neckband, side and Sleeve seams. Sew in Sleeves. Fold rib section of Neckband in half to wrong side and slip-stitch in position. Press seams.

Projects by Coats Patons
Photography by Georgia Moxham

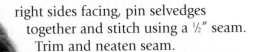

Simple Summer Dress

Here's an easy way to make a dress using a knit top as a bodice — nothing could be quicker!

MATERIALS

Purchased T-shirt or singlet; length of fabric for skirt.

Note. To calculate fabric quantity required for skirt, measure the length needed and add 8". Buy one length of 45"-wide fabric.

METHOD

Measure down from armhole to find waistline (as a guide: approximately 5" for girl aged 5). Use pins to mark the waistline around the T-shirt.

Cut a 20" length of fabric (or length desired for skirt plus 2" for seam and hem allowance) across the width of the fabric. With right sides facing, pin selvedges together and stitch using a ½" seam. Trim and neaten seam.

Stitch two rows of gathering at skirt top, ¼" and ½" from raw edge. Pull up bobbin threads to gather, and pin skirt to marked waist of T-shirt. Adjust gathers to fit; stitch. Cut away excess T-shirt fabric, and neaten the seam. Adjust the skirt length, neaten the edge and stitch a 2" hem.

Sleeve trim

Cut a 1"-wide strip across the width of fabric. Turn in both long edges to the center of strip and press to form a strip ½"-wide.

To form the sleeve band, pin and stitch strip to sleeves 1" from sleeve edge.

Neckbow

Cut a 16" x 1" strip of fabric. Fold, right sides facing and long edges together, stitch long edges with a ¼" seam; trim, turn through and press. Knot ends of strip; tie tiny bow and stitch to neck edge.

Project by Christine Moss
Photography by Ross Coffey

Scrunchies, Holder and Box

Bright and fun to wear, but easy to misplace, scrunchies can be easily found on this holder, and the matching box can store treasured items.

SCRUNCHIES

MATERIALS

For each scrunchie: one 32″ x 6″ rectangle of fabric; thread; 10″ length of ¼″-wide elastic.

METHOD

Fold fabric with right sides facing and long edges together. Stitch long edge, leaving approximately 2″ unstitched at each end. Trim seam, turn through and, with right sides facing, stitch short ends together. Insert elastic through opening on long edge; stitch ends of elastic together. Stitch opening closed.

SCRUNCHIE HOLDER AND BOX

MATERIALS

Paper towel holder; sealer; acrylic paint in wine color and gold; brush; small sea sponge; paper towel; papier-mâché box; ribbon; craft glue.

METHOD
Scrunchie holder

Paint towel holder with one coat of sealer and two coats of wine color paint, allowing drying time between each coat. Dampen sponge in water, wring out excess. Dip sponge into gold paint and dab excess onto paper towel. Dab towel holder, creating a speckled effect.

Box

Paint and sponge box as for holder, allow to dry. Glue ribbon around lid. Tie a ribbon bow and glue on one side over ribbon trim.

Project by Christine Moss
Photography by Andrew Elton

Charm Bracelets

Little girls, and bigger ones, too, will be delighted with these pretty charm bracelets. Nothing could be easier than making the bracelets, so plan on creating more than one — they'll cost only a couple of dollars each.

MATERIALS

For each bracelet: small pliers; 8" length of chain; 7 small jump rings; ring-clasp; 1 large jump ring; 6 brass charms.

METHOD

Using small pliers, attach a small jump ring to one end of the length of chain and attach clasp to the jump ring. Fix the large jump ring to the other end of chain. Fix a jump ring to each charm and attach jump rings to chain, positioning charms equal distances apart.

Project by Judy Newman
Photography by Andrew Elton

Fancy Dress for Kids

A little fantasy is something that no child can resist — so try these easy-to-make dress-up ideas.

SUPERBOY

This costume is designed to fit a six-year-old. Make the cape larger for an older child. Instructions are included for cape and belt.

out. Remove paper and press motif to back of cape. Zigzag stitch around edge of motif.

Belt: From heavy interfacing, cut a belt 3″ wide, and long enough to fit child, with an overlap. Cover interfacing with fabric.

Using the broder thread and zigzag stitch, sew close to the edges of the belt to form a trim. Turn in ends of belt and sew Velcro on each end for closure. Make two loops, each 1″ x 8″, from main fabric. Sew zigzag borders as for belt. Fold each loop in half, then sew to inside of belt on each side.

Appliqué a smaller lightning bolt to the center front of the belt as for the cape.

MATERIALS

40″ of 45″-wide rayon taffeta; 4″ x 16″ of contrast fabric for trims; 4″ of 36″-wide heavyweight interfacing; 4″ x 16″ of double-sided, press-on web; matching thread; 8″ length of Velcro; broder cotton in contrast color to trim belt.

METHOD

Cape: Cut a rectangle from taffeta measuring 35″ x 40″ for the cape. Hem all four sides. Stitch a square of Velcro at both corners of one short side for neckline closure.

If desired, copy the lightning bolt motif ❖ onto the double-sided web (some other motif may be substituted). Cut out and press one side of web to contrast fabric and cut

SUPERGIRL

To fit a girl aged eight.
Instructions are included for the
skirt, cape and belt.

MATERIALS

40″ of 45″-wide rayon
taffeta; 40″ of 45″-wide
contrast fabric for skirt and
motif; 8″ x 36″ of firm
interfacing; 4″ length of
whalebone; 8″ strip of
Velcro; matching thread; broder
cotton; 8″ of double-sided press-on
web.

METHOD

Cape: Cut a rectangle, 35″ x 45″, for
cape. Make the cape as for Superboy,
applying a star motif ❖ rather than the lightning bolt.
Skirt: Enlarge pattern ❖ for skirt to correct
size on paper and cut out from contrast
fabric. Cut waistband, 27″ x 3″, from the
same fabric.

Place right sides of skirt pieces together.
Pin, sew and neaten the four seams, leaving
one seam open to dot, for placket. Gather
waistline. Pin and sew waistband to skirt,
easing gathers. Sew Velcro at waist for
closure.

Turn up a small hem.
Belt: Enlarge pattern for belt on paper and
cut out from same fabric as cape. Use
same pattern to cut out interfacing.

Pin and tack material over interfacing.
Using zigzag stitch, sew broder cotton ¼″
in from edge of belt, as for Superboy.

Press double-sided web onto a piece of
fabric large enough for the star. Cut out star,
peel off backing paper from web and press in
position at center front of belt. Zigzag stitch
around edge of star. Turn in ends of belt to
fit, and sew on Velcro.

Stitch whalebone inside center front of
belt to stiffen.

Projects by Betty Smith
Photography by Justine Kerrigan

Gorgeous Gifts

Terracotta Pot Candles

During summer, when we all love to entertain outdoors, these terracotta pot candles will make a special display. Easily made, they will be a welcome gift.

MATERIALS

Candle wax; double boiler (or Candle Magic Boil Bags); terracotta pots; Blu-Tack; wick (we used Candle Magic stiffened wick which is precoated with wax to make it stand straight).

Note. Do not leave melted wax unattended.

METHOD

Melt wax over a low heat in a double boiler (or use Candle Magic Boil Bags). Block the hole in the pot using Blu-Tack. Prepare wick by cutting to approximate length needed. If using uncoated wick, dip it in wax then allow to dry straight. Pour wax into pot, filling up to 1″ from the top to allow for topping up. Allow wax to cool a little and, before it sets, push stiffened wick into the candle center. As wax hardens, it will shrink, so top up the pot with more melted wax.

Project by Kylie Slater
Photography by Cath Muscat

Stylish Make-up Purse and Glasses Case

Tapestry fabric makes a perfect choice for this stylish and super-practical set.

MATERIALS

8″ of 55″-wide tapestry fabric; thread; 6″ zip; two purchased tassels.

FINISHED SIZE

Make-up Purse: 6″ x 5″.
Glasses Case: 7″ x 3″.

METHOD
Purse

Cut two 7″ x 6″ rectangles in fabric. Using ½″ seam allowance, pin one side of zip to one long edge of fabric piece; stitch. Repeat using other fabric piece. Topstitch each side of zip on right side of fabric. Open zip and place fabric pieces right sides together. Pin side and bottom seams; stitch. Trim corners, neaten seams and turn right side out. Using a double thread, stitch tassel to eye of zip pull.

METHOD
Glasses Case

Cut 9″ x 7″ rectangle in tapestry fabric. Fold rectangle in half, right sides facing and 9″ edges together. Using ½″ seam allowance, stitch bottom and side seam. Neaten seams. Turn a 1″ hem at open top edge and slip-stitch hem; turn right side out.
Stitch tassel to center top of case for decoration.

Project by Christine Moss
Photography by Andrew Elton

Découpage Floral Tray

This lovely tray features colorful spring blooms on a rich green background trimmed with gold.

MATERIALS

1" foam brush; sealer (eg, Liquitex Gloss Medium and Varnish); découpage wrapping papers of a suitable design; Liquitex Artist's acrylic paints in Hooker's Green, Iridescent White, Iridescent Gold and Iridescent Copper; palette; sea sponge; 22" x 16" timber tray; curved cuticle or iris scissors; Clag paste; PVA glue; 4" rubber roller; Wettex; No.00 brush; Treasure Gold — Renaissance or Classic; workable fixative; varnish, Wattyl Estapol or Jo Sonja Polyurethane Varnish, water based; tack cloth; No.600 and 1200 wet and dry sandpapers or Vecro Block and 320 paper and Micromesh Kit.

METHOD

Using foam brush, seal wrapping paper, brushing sealer on in one direction on one side of paper, allow to dry, seal in opposite direction on other side. Allow to dry completely.

Put equal quantities of paint and sealer on palette. Using sponge, pick up sealer and paint separately. Using a dabbing action, sponge the surface of tray. Do not premix as paints become muddy. Depending on the size of the holes in the sponge, various textures will appear. To allow the colors to be viewed separately, do not overwork the surface. Allow to dry.

Using cuticle scissors, cut out images, beginning with interior background, in a clockwise direction. (The reverse applies for left-handed workers.) Cut away the background areas from within images by piercing with scissor point, then bring scissors through from reverse side of paper. Cut with the points of the scissors angled at 45 degrees to achieve a bevelled edge (so white cut edges do not show). Cut the outside edge of images with a continuous movement anti-clockwise. The paper must always be sealed before cutting to prevent curling.

Arrange your composition on the tray. Now, prepare to glue in place with a mixture of Clag and PVA glue (mixed in the proportion of 3 to 1), smearing tray surface with fingertips to distribute glue evenly.

Place image on glue, massage with a small amount of glue on top of picture, radiating fingers out from the center of the image. When bonding is evident between paper and tray, lightly roll the surface (with rubber roller) radiating from center of each image to eliminate air bubbles and distribute glue. Glue each image separately. Allow glue to dry, then clean excess glue from surface with Wettex and clear water.

If white edges are evident on images, use No.00 brush and paint from palette to touch up edges lightly. Paint edges with Iridescent Copper. Using finger-tip, apply a hint of Treasure Gold to outside edge of tray. Spray complete surface with workable fixative. When dry, in about 5 minutes, apply a sparing coat of sealer.

VARNISH

Using your favored brand, varnish regularly following manufacturer's instructions (Jo Sonja varnish will remain clear whereas Wattyl Estapol will mellow to an ivory tone). Lightly wipe surface with a tack cloth before each subsequent varnish application. When a good depth of varnish protects the composition, lightly sand using wet 600 sandpaper or use the 320 dry technique following manufacturer's instructions. The tray will require constant sanding and re-varnishing to achieve a flat surface.

Finish by sanding with 1200, or polish with each cushioned abrasive in the Micromesh Kit.

Project by Nerida Singleton
Photography by Ross Coffey

Bejewelled Pots and Platter

Terracotta pots and an extra large pot saucer have never looked so good!

MATERIALS

Terracotta pots and saucers; sealer; brush; Matisse acrylic paint in Metallic Gold, Aqua Green and Magenta; chalk; quick-dry craft glue; fake gemstones in various sizes.

METHOD

Coat the terracotta pieces with sealer inside and out. Allow to dry thoroughly and then paint with two or three coats of paint, allowing drying time between coats. When dry, use chalk to mark even positions for gems around pot rims and saucer edge and glue in place.

Project by Judy Newman
Photography by Cath Muscat

Travellers' Aid

Whether in a masculine check or a feminine floral with colored tassels, very little is simpler to make than a shoe bag. Yet it's the ideal gift for those who travel often or those who like to take care of their wardrobe.

Shoe bag with tassels

MATERIALS

12″ x 36″ fabric; 12″ x 36″ co-ordinated lining; 60″ fine cord; bought tassels; thread.

METHOD

Cut two fabric pieces and two linings 12″ x 15″. Curve ends for bottom of bag. With right sides together, sew fabric seam starting 2″ from top. Repeat for lining but leave a 2″ opening in bottom of bag. With right sides of fabric and lining together, sew top edge seam and down each side, leaving a 1″ opening each side 2″ down from top seam. Turn out through lining opening, sew opening closed, press bag, sew two casing lines 1″ apart, aligned with 1″ openings. Insert a cord each way, tie ends. Attach tassels over tied ends.

Checked shoe bag

MATERIALS

Fabric 30″ wide x 20″ deep (or to fit shoe); 3 wooden buttons; thread.

METHOD

With right sides together, fold 30″ width in half and sew seam across 15″ and up 20″. Turn and make a 2″ finished hem. Sew 3 button-holes and sew on 3 buttons to close the top

Project by Betty Smith
Photography by Andrew Elton

Clever Tea-cosy

A patchwork border decorates this pretty tea-cosy.

MATERIALS

Two 5" x 45"-wide lengths of contrasting fabrics; thread; 12" x 45"-wide cotton fabric, for lining; 12" x 45"-wide main fabric; 12" x 36"-wide wadding; 8" x ¼"-wide elastic.

FINISHED SIZE

Tea-cosy will fit a medium-size teapot.

METHOD

Step 1. From each contrast fabric, cut one 45" x 2" strip. Join strip together and then recut across the width into 2" pieces.

Step 2. Stitch each piece together, alternating colours.

From this piece cut two strips, each 13" long. Cut two 13" x 12" pieces of lining fabric. Cut four 13" x 5" pieces of main fabric.

Step 3. Stitch two pieces of main fabric to either side of patchwork strip. These form the outer rectangles of the cover. Place one lining fabric piece and one outer rectangle, right sides together. Stitch sides and one long edge (this will be the top). Turn right side out, press and mark lines 2" and 3" from the top; stitch along these lines to form casing. Unpick side seams between casing lines. Repeat for other side of tea-cosy.

Cut four 12" x 6" pieces of wadding. Insert two pieces into each tea-cosy segment, pushing wadding up to casing line. Turn ¼" seam allowance on bottom edge of each segment to the inside and machine stitch along bottom edge. Stitch again 1" higher to form casing; unpick side seams between casing lines.

Insert the elastic length through bottom casings of both tea-cosy segments; stitch elastic ends securely.

Cut a 40" x 1"-wide strip from one of the contrast fabrics. Fold in half lengthwise, wrong sides together, and stitch along raw edges, turn right side out and knot ends. Thread this tie through top casing of both pieces and tie in a bow.

Project by Denise Lawler
Photography by Cath Muscat

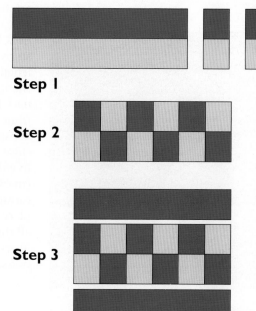

Step 1

Step 2

Step 3

Sunflower Set

Add a little sunshine to a kitchen with this cheery set of pot holder-cum-tablemat and apron.

Pot Holder or Table Mat

MATERIALS

12″ square of felt; 12″ of 45″-wide yellow cotton fabric; scrap of yellow checked fabric; scrap of fusible webbing; soft lead pencil; thread.

METHOD

Make actual-size pattern ❖. Sandwich felt square between wrong sides of two 12″ squares of cotton fabric, baste. Lightly mark sunflower pattern using pencil. Satin stitch by machine (close zigzag) along lines marked, stitching lower petals first, then top petals.

Fuse webbing to wrong side of checked fabric. Cut a 3″-diameter circle, remove paper backing and fuse to center of the sunflowers. Satin stitch around the center circle. Carefully trim away fabric outside satin stitched petals.

Apron

MATERIALS

60″ of 45″-wide fabric; fusible webbing; 6″ square of yellow fabric; scrap of checked yellow fabric; soft lead pencil; thread.
Note. 1″ seam allowance is included.

METHOD

Make pattern ❖ for apron and cut out. Appliqué sunflower to bib front by tracing pattern ❖ and using actual size. Fuse webbing to square of plain yellow fabric and cut out sunflower shape. Mark petal lines lightly using pencil. Fuse webbing to wrong side of checked fabric. Cut center circle, remove paper backing and fuse to center of sunflower. Remove the paper backing from sunflower and fuse to the center of the apron, at top.

Satin stitch by machine (close zigzag) over the petals, working underneath petals first then those on top. Finally satin stitch around the center.

Cut a 25″ x 10″ rectangle for apron pocket. With right side of pocket facing wrong side of bottom edge of apron, stitch together along bottom edge. Trim seam; neaten top edge of pocket and stitch under a 1″ hem.

With right side of pocket to wrong side of apron, stitch seams at each side of pocket piece. Trim seams and turn pocket to apron front. Divide pocket into three sections and machine stitch.

Clip seam allowance on apron where top of pocket meets apron and zigzag the raw edge; turn seam allowance to wrong side. Topstitch from bottom edge to armhole. Stitch a 1″ hem along top edge of bib front.

Cut a 2″-wide bias strip approx. 16″ long; fold bias in half with wrong sides together and pin to armhole with all raw edges aligned. Machine stitch, trim and turn in raw edges on ends. Turn folded edge to wrong side and slipstitch fold to machine stitching. Repeat for other armhole.

Cut one 28″ x 2″ strip for neck loop and two 40″ x 2″ strips for waist ties. Fold in half lengthways with right sides facing, stitch, trim and turn through. Pin neck loop to either side of bib front and slipstitch in place. Topstitch through all thicknesses close to top edge of bib. Pin ties to either side of apron waist (marked on pattern with X) and, turning in raw ends, slipstitch in place. Machine stitch through all thicknesses to reinforce. Tuck in remaining raw ends of ties and oversew.

Project by Christine Moss
Photography by Andrew Elton

❖ *indicates pattern on pattern pages*

Towels With Hearts

Wrapped with a fragrant soap, these pretty towels make perfect standby gifts.

MATERIALS

Fusible webbing scrap; scraps of cotton fabric for appliqué; hand towel; matching thread.

METHOD

Trace our heart pattern ❖. Apply fusible webbing to wrong side of fabric scrap and cut out heart shape. Peel away backing paper and fuse heart to a corner of the hand towel. Machine stitch around heart using a narrow satin stitch (close zigzag).

Project by Christine Moss
Photography by Andrew Elton
❖ indicates pattern on pattern pages

Knitted String Bag

This bag can hold an enormous amount of shopping. It's made from just one simple square of knitting with sturdy handles and edging crocheted in place.

MATERIALS

Three balls of 8 ply Cotton thread (2oz); one pair No.13 knitting needles; No.D/3 crochet hook; tapestry needle for darning ends.

FINISHED SIZE

Length: 14".
Note. Design consists of one main piece.

TENSION

12sts and 13 rows to 4" over stocking st, using No.13 needles.

SPECIAL ABBREVIATIONS

Dec: draw up a lp in each of next 2sc, yoh and draw through all 3 lps on hook.
Dec2: draw up a lp in each of next 3sc, yoh and draw through all 4 lps on hook.

Bag

On completion, the bag measures 24" in width.

Using No.13 needles, cast on 72sts.

Work in purl fabric (reverse stocking st): 1 row purl (right side), 1 row knit (wrong side), until work measures 24" from beg, ending with a purl row.
Cast off.

Top edging

With right side of work facing and using crochet hook, join yarn with a sl st to first cast on st.

1st row. 1ch, 1sc in same place as sl st, miss 1 st, *1sc in next st, miss 1 st; rep from * to last st, 1sc in last st...37sc.

2nd row. 1ch, 1sc in first sc, (Dec) 18 times...19sc.

3rd row. 1ch, working through front lp of each sc only — work (1sc, 1ch) in first sc, 1dc in each sc to end, turn, 1ch, working through back lp of sc row — work 1dc in each sc to end.

4th row. 1ch, 1sc in each dc to end, working through front and back row of dc tog. Fasten off.

Work same edging along cast-off edge.

Side edging and handles

With right side of work facing, working across side edge of bag, ** work 2sc across end of top edging, 1sc into each of next 15 row ends, (Dec2) 16 times along next 48 rows, 1sc into each of next 15 row ends, 2sc across end of top edging, make 45ch, ** with right side still facing but working along other side of bag; rep from ** to ** once, sl st in first sc at beg.

Next row. 1ch, 1sc in same place as sl st, 1sc in each st to end, sl st in first sc at beg...190sc.

Rep 3rd and 4th rows of Top edging. Fasten off.

Project by Cleckheaton
Photography by Andrew Elton

Kitchen Chalkboard

Available in craft stores, this pine chalkboard needed only a quick coat of paint and some decorative sponge printing to become an appealing and useful gift.

MATERIALS
Pine chalkboard; Matisse paints in Straw and Antique Green; foam brush; kitchen sponge; palette.

METHOD
Paint frame of chalkboard with Straw, allow to dry. Trace our actual-size square and heart ❖ and cut out shapes in kitchen sponge. Dampen sponge with water, wring out. Dip square sponge into Antique Green paint, dab onto palette to remove excess paint. Starting from the center of each side of the frame and working towards the corners, print around frame edge. Print heart shape at the top of the frame.

Project by Christine Moss
Photography by Andrew Elton

❖ *indicates pattern on pattern pages*

Towel Trims

Add a personal touch to a towel, hand-towel or washer.

MEASUREMENTS
Knitted Edging width is approximately 2″. Crocheted Edging width is approximately 3″.

MATERIALS
4-ply Cotton (2oz): one ball will make approximately 8′ of Knitted Edging or 6′ of Crocheted Edging. One pair No.3 knitting needles or No.3 crochet hook.

SPECIAL ABBREVIATIONS
Cluster: (yoh, draw up a loop in next sp, yoh and draw through first 2 loops on hook) 3 times in same sp, yoh and draw through all 4 loops on hook; **Shell:** (2dc, 2ch, 2dc) in next 2 ch sp.

Knitted Edging
Using needles, cast on 8 sts.

1st row. Sl 1, K2, yfwd, K2tog,(yfwd) twice, K2tog, K1...9sts.

2nd row. K3, P1, K2, yfwd, K2tog, K1.

3rd row. Sl 1, K2, yfwd, K2tog, K1, (yfwd) twice, K2tog, K1...10sts.

4th row. K3, P1, K3, yfwd, K2tog, K1.

5th row. Sl 1, K2, yfwd, K2tog, K2, (yfwd) twice, K2tog, K1...11sts.

6th row. K3, Pl, K4, yfwd, K2tog, K1.

7th row. Sl 1, K2, yfwd, K2tog, K6.

8th row. Cast off 3 sts, K4 (so there are 5 sts on right-hand needle), yfwd, K2tog, K1...8 sts.

Last 8 rows form patt.

Cont in patt until work measures required length, ending with an 8th row.

Cast off.

Sew Edging to towel.

Crocheted Edging
Using hook, make 13ch loosely.

1st row. (wrong side). Miss 5ch, 1dc in next ch, miss 2ch, 2dc in next ch, 2ch, 2dc in next ch (to form Shell), 1ch, miss 2ch, 1dc in last ch.

2nd row. 5ch, 1dc in 1ch sp, 1ch, Shell in next 2ch sp, 1ch, 1dc in next 1ch sp, turn.

Rep 2nd row twice more.

5th row. 5ch, 1dc in 1ch sp, 1ch, Shell in next 2ch sp, 1ch, 1dc in next 1ch sp, 3ch, in next 5ch loop along edge work (Cluster, 3ch) 4 times, 1sc in next 5ch loop, turn.

6th row. 1ch, (1sc, 1hdc, 1dc, 1hdc, 1sc) in each of next five 3ch sps, 3ch, 1dc in next 1ch sp, 1ch, Shell in next 2ch sp, 1ch, 1dc in next 1ch sp, turn.

7th row. As 2nd row.

Rows 2 to 7 incl form patt.

Cont in patt until work measures required length, ending with a 6th row. Fasten off.

Sew Edging to towel.

Project by Betty Smith
Photography by Andrew Elton

Painted Soap

MATERIALS

Soap; brushes — No.001 Liner, Nos. 4 and 6 Square Shaders; FolkArt Acrylic paints in the following colors — Tapioca, Tartan Green, Rose Garden, Coffee Bean, Schoolbus Yellow, Licorice; stylus; black graphite paper; palette; water-based varnish.

METHOD

Transfer pattern ❖ onto soap using graphite paper and stylus. For sharper outline, lightly engrave pattern using stylus.

Roses

Corner load three quarters of the No.6 brush with Rose Garden and quarter with Tapioca. Pat brush on paper to remove excess paint. Form each petal as a ruffled crescent ensuring an even flow of color through all petals. Mix a little Rose Garden with Licorice and, with line brush, apply a fine outline.

Paint a center spot with Tapioca. With stylus, apply dots of Coffee Bean around outside edge of flower center. With Schoolbus Yellow and liner brush, paint stamens

in fine strokes from center outwards.
Add a

scattering of Schoolbus Yellow dots at random on outside of lines.

Leaves

Paint stems with liner brush and Tartan Green. With No.4 brush and Tartan Green, tip quarter of brush in Tapioca. Paint leaves following their shape and forming serrated edges by painting small crescents.

Allow 24 hours to dry before applying two coats of varnish.

Project by Sally Anne Sparke

Recipe Album and Matching Tea Towels

Covered in colorful madras checked fabric, a self-adhesive photo album becomes an attractive hold-all for collected recipes.

MATERIALS
Recipe Album

Self-adhesive photograph album; fabric to cover; fine cardboard; 7" x 2" Aida band; DMC Art 117 embroidery thread; craft glue.

METHOD

Cover album with fabric and glue in position. Cut two cardboard pieces slightly smaller than cover and glue inside the back and front to hide the turned-in fabric. Embroider 'Recipes' ❖ in cross-stitch onto Aida band using two threads of stranded cotton; turn in ends and stitch to covers.

MATERIALS
Tea Towel

Plain colored tea towels (or simple check); 8" co-ordinating fabric.

METHOD

Cut strip of fabric 4" wide and long enough to cover end of towel with turn-under allowance at each end. Fold strip ends under and, with right sides together, stitch strip to towel 1" in from towel end. Press strip under 1" along unstitched length and fold strip over towel end to bind and border other side of towel. Sew strip in position, stitching ends as well.

Project by Betty Smith
Photography by Andrew Elton
❖ indicates pattern on pattern pages

Découpage Box

If the man in your life loves music, here's the perfect present!

MATERIALS

Sandpaper; timber book box (ours measures 9″ x 7″ x 2″); sealer; acrylic paint in black and metallic gold; old pieces of sheet music; photograph; foam brush; glue, mixed from 3 parts Clag to 1 part PVA; kitchen sponge; matt and gloss varnish; tack cloth; wet and dry sandpaper in 280, 400 and 600; No.0000 steel wool.

METHOD

Sand box lightly. Mix some sealer with paint, paint box front, back and inside with black. Paint 'pages' of box with gold. Coat front and back of sheet music and photograph with sealer; allow to dry. Tear the sheet music into pieces.

Apply glue to the inside front cover of box and to the back of photo and some music pieces. Working with one piece at a time, coat each with glue and massage from the center to remove air bubbles. Work from inside lid to top of lid. When bonding is evident, clean excess glue from surface with damp sponge. When the work is dry, repeat the découpage procedure for the back cover and spine.

Varnish frequently with gloss varnish following manufacturer's directions and wiping with a tack cloth before each application. Do not apply varnish in wet or humid weather. When a good depth of varnish has been built up (approximately 20 to 30 coats), wet-sand vigorously with 280 paper, progressing to 400 (which should be used more lightly). Finish with a light sand, using 600 paper.

To achieve a matt finish, apply 3 to 4 coats of matt varnish. When dry, lightly sand with 600 paper. Dry and remove scratches with steel wool. Polish with beeswax if desired.

Project by Joy Ash
Photography by Andrew Elton

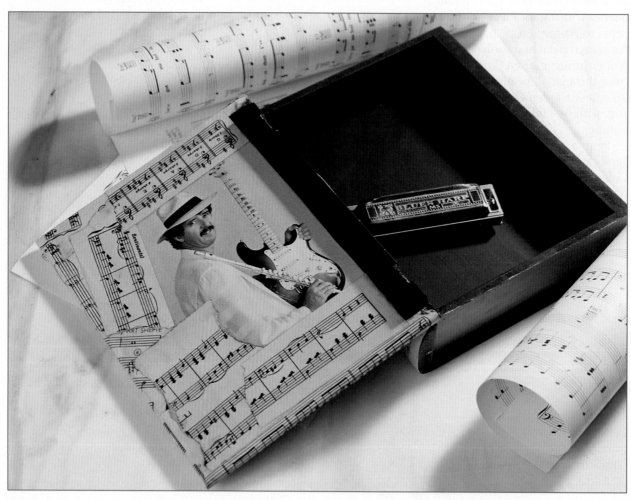

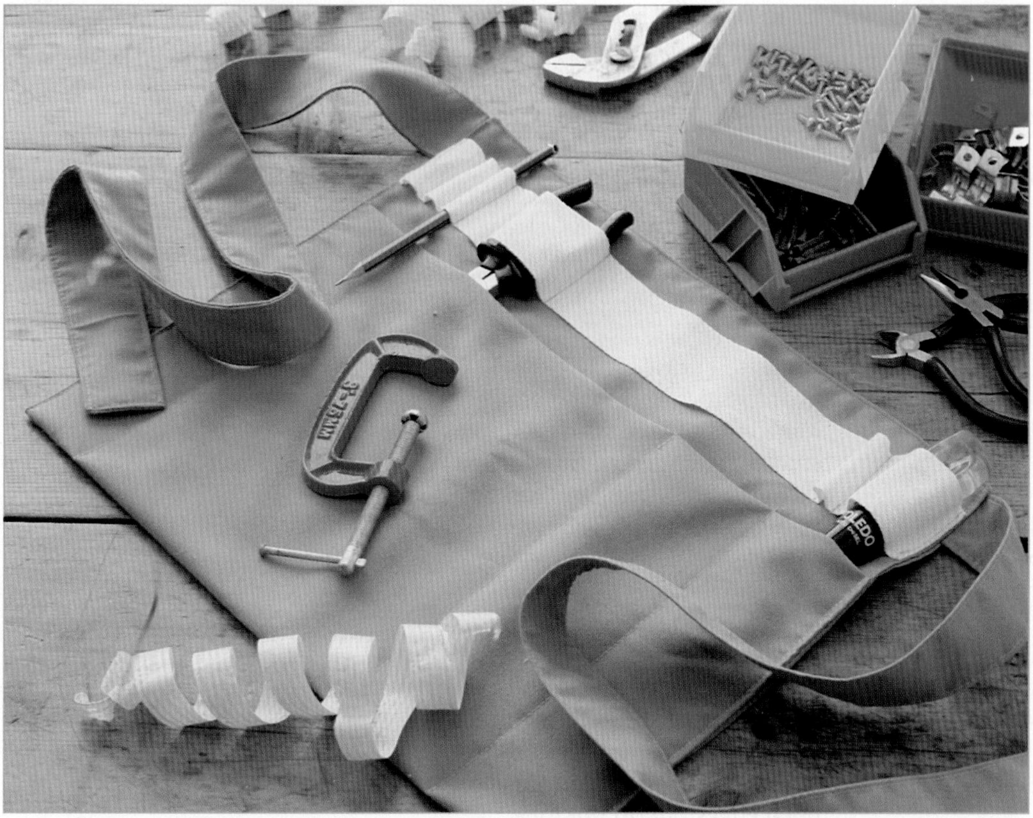

divisions as desired. We have stitched one 2″-wide pocket on one side and two 3″-wide pockets on the other side, leaving a large pocket in the center of the apron.

Pin and stitch tape across apron top to form loops above pockets, and stitch divisions to hold pencils, screwdrivers and so on.

Project by Christine Moss
Photography by Andrew Elton

Practical Work Apron

A great one for the handyman in your life...

MATERIALS

28″ of 60″-wide heavy cotton fabric; thread; 25″ of 2″-wide cotton tape.

FINISHED SIZE

16″ x 14″.

METHOD

Use 1″ seam allowance. Cut a 50″ x 17″ rectangle in fabric. Fold rectangle in half with right sides facing and 17″ edges together. Stitch all around, leaving small opening at top side corners to insert waist ties and a 8″ opening to turn through (see diagram). Trim seams, neaten, turn through and press.

Cut two 36″ x 5″ strips for waist ties. With right sides facing, fold each strip lengthwise and stitch across one end and along long raw edge. Trim seams, turn through and press.

Topstitch along edges. Insert ties at openings on each side of apron. Pin in position, tucking in seam allowance on apron. Topstitch all around apron, reinforcing stitching at ties.

Turn up lower folded edge of rectangle to form a 9″-deep pocket, stitch in place at sides. Pin and stitch pocket

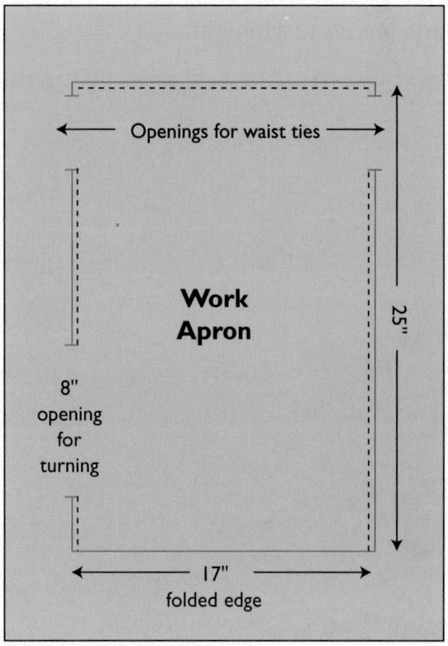

Victorian Sewing Case

Past perfect...a Victorian sewing case for the needle-worker's chairside, office drawer or travel kit.

SIZE
8″ long x 4″ high.

MATERIALS
12″ of 45″-wide fabric (ours is chintz); medium-weight cardboard; stranded embroidery thread and ribbon in co-ordinating color; sewing thread; paper or tracing paper; pencil; sewing needle; darning needle.

METHOD
Trace pattern ❖ onto paper or tracing paper and cut out. Using paper pattern, cut out three cardboard pieces. Adding ½″ to all sides for seam allowance, cut out six pieces from fabric.

Placing right sides together of two fabric pieces, machine or handstitch one side seam. Repeat for other fabric pieces. Press seams and turn each section to right side. Push cardboard inside each fabric section and, turning in seam allowance, slip-stitch other side seams to encase cardboard. Sides of the case are joined with two rows of whipping stitch in stranded embroidery thread.

Work the first row of whipping stitch leaning in one direction, then stitch the second row back the other way, placing the needle back into the same holes but leaning in the other direction so that V-shaped stitches are formed. Join edges to form case at all sides but one. Sew whipping stitch over open edges but do not join. Stitch ribbon at center of open side to close case and trim as desired.

Project by Betty Smith
Photography by Andre Martin

❖ *indicates pattern on pattern pages*

Seaside Key Holder and Box

A great gift for friends with a holiday house, this practical key holder and box are very easy to make.

MATERIALS
Craftwood key holder and box; all-purpose craft glue; gold Folk Art spray paint.

METHOD
Key Holder
Glue any beach treasures you have, such as starfish and shells, onto the key holder, allow glue to dry. Spray paint with metallic gold, applying several coats and allowing drying time between each coat.

METHOD
Box
Glue starfish to lid. Spray gold, applying several coats and allowing drying time between each.

Project by Judy Newman
Photography by Cath Muscat

Treasure Boxes with Crochet Lace Trim

Who can resist these attractive little treasure boxes? Use them to store special items, or to give as beautifully personal gifts.

MATERIALS

Sheet of 10-ply cardboard; sheet of quality wrapping paper; sheet of colored cardboard to match paper; spray adhesive; DMC size 10 crochet cotton in co-ordinating color; No.10 steel crochet hook; hole punch; tapestry needle; oddments of lace, ribbon or other trims
Note: Any medium-to-fine cotton and crochet hooks up to No.2 would be suitable.

METHOD

Spray adhesive on one side of 10-ply cardboard and apply colored cardboard, keeping edges even and surface smooth.

Turn cardboard upside down so that white side is facing. Spray cardboard with adhesive and smoothly apply wrapping paper.

Trace pattern pieces, ❖ in size 1 or 2, onto wrapping paper side of cardboard (one base, one top and eight sides), avoiding any creases. Cut out pieces.

Mark holes on each piece, as indicated on pattern. Make holes with hole punch.

With right side facing, using size 10 crochet cotton and No.10 crochet hook, and starting at bottom righthand edge, work 4 single crochet (sc) in each hole and 7sc at each corner around each piece, leaving long thread ends at beginning and end of work.

Crochet edging around all pieces. Using tapestry needle and long threads at beginnings and ends, stitch edgings of each section together, beginning with the base, then the sides. Stitch top section at one side only, to form a hinge.

Trim box with lace as pictured, or as desired.

Project by Sylvia Panciera.
Photography by Andre Martin.
❖ *indicates pattern on pattern pages*

Great
GARDENERS'
Goods

Matching Gloves and Kneeling Pad

Add a pretty cotton cuff to plain garden gloves and save weary knees too.

Gloves

MATERIALS
10" x 45"-wide fabric; thread.

METHOD
Stretch out the band of your gloves and measure the width. Cut a fabric piece twice this width plus 1" and 10" in depth. Fold fabric in half with right sides facing and 10" edges together; stitch a 1" seam along 10" edge and neaten. Stitch a 2" hem on one edge (this will become the cuff top) and neaten remaining edge. Place neatened edge of cuff and glove band right sides together, positioning cuff seam at palm side of glove. Stretch glove band to fit cuff, pin together at each side. Keeping band stretched, stitch to cuff using a small zigzag stitch. Turn right side out.

Kneeling Pad

MATERIALS
20" x 14" fabric for top; 20" x 14" waterproof or plastic-coated fabric for bottom; thread; 18" x 12" piece of 2"-thick foam.

FINISHED SIZE
18" x 12".

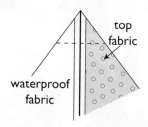

METHOD
Place fabric pieces right sides facing and stitch a 1" seam around, leaving one short side open. From inside, open out each corner point and bring adjacent seams together; stitch across folded corner at a right angle to the seam, 1" down from the corner point. (This will take out excess fabric at corner, creating a wall in the kneeling pad, see diagram.) Turn right side out and insert foam, stitch opening closed.

Project by Judy Newman
Photography by Andrew Elton

Rose Swag

Trimmed with roses and dried flowers, this swag makes a pretty feature over a doorway or window.

MATERIALS

Bunch dried misty blue (fairy statice); varnished 26″ twig swag; hot glue gun and glue sticks; 1″ gold-edged, cream, wired ribbon; bunch dried dollar blue gum; 12 large, 12 small cream roses (wood, paper or dried).

METHOD

Trim stems of misty blue and arrange on the swag with stems at the center; using hot glue gun, glue in place. Add extra stems of misty blue so you have layers from the center to each end. Fold ribbon into loops and glue to center of swag. Place 3 stems of gum on each side of swag and glue under bow. Arrange 6 large roses at each end of swag. Scatter the 12 small roses evenly over the swag; glue in place.

Project by C & S Imports
Photography by Valerie Martin

Herb Hangers

Attractive hangers for herbs allow you to enjoy the fragrance and keep them within handy reach.

MATERIALS

For each hanger you need two 7″ squares of fabric; thread.

METHOD

Place squares right sides together, stitch along two adjoining sides using ¼″ seam allowance. Trim corner, open out and bring seams together, creating a triangle. Stitch along long edge (see diagram) leaving an opening. Press seams.

Turn right side out, stitch opening closed. Slip one half of triangle inside the other, to make a lined cone. At top corner, work a buttonhole for hanging. Fill with dried herbs.

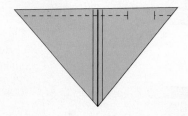

Project by Judy Newman
Photography by Andrew Elton

Gardener's Set

Anyone who loves gardening will be thrilled to receive this gorgeous set including kneeling mat, apron and cushion.

Cushion

MATERIALS

20″ of 45″-wide cotton drill; assorted scraps of fabric for appliqué; fusible webbing; thread; 16″ square cushion insert.

FINISHED SIZE

16″ square.
Note. ½″ seam allowance is included.

METHOD

Cut one 17″ square of fabric for cushion front. Press webbing to back of fabric pieces for flower appliques. Using a photocopier set at 200 per cent, enlarge flower shapes, leaves and stems and cut in fabrics as desired. Remove paper backing and position pieces on cushion front. Iron in position.

Using narrow machine satin stitch (close zigzag), stitch around each shape using machining threads.

Cut two 17″ x 13″ rectangles for cushion backs. Stitch a 2″ hem on one long edge of each back piece. Place backs and front, with right sides facing, overlapping hemmed edges of backs so back fits front. Stitch around cushion, trim and neaten seams and turn through. Fill with insert.

Apron

MATERIALS

60″ of 45″-wide cotton drill; scraps of different cotton fabrics for applique flowers; fusible webbing; matching threads.

90

apron waist (marked on pattern with X) and turning in raw ends, slipstitch in place. Machine stitch through all thicknesses to reinforce. Tuck in remaining raw ends of ties and oversew.

Kneeling mat

MATERIALS

16″ of 45″-wide cotton drill; assorted scraps of fabric for appliqué; fusible webbing; 18″ x 12″ rectangle of 2″-thick foam.

FINISHED SIZE

Approximately 18″ x 12″.
Note. 1″ seam allowance is included.

METHOD

Cut two 20″ x 14″ rectangles in cotton drill. Appliqué flowers on one piece as for cushion.

With right sides facing, stitch around rectangles, leaving a 12″ opening in one side. Trim seams and turn through; insert foam and slipstitch opening closed.

Project by Christine Moss
Photography by Andrew Elton

Note. 1″ seam allowance is included.

METHOD

Make pattern for apron following diagram and cut out in drill fabric. Appliqué flowers to bib front as for cushion. Cut a 25″ x 10″ rectangle for apron pocket. With right side of pocket facing wrong side of bottom edge of apron, stitch together along bottom edge. Trim seam; neaten top edge of pocket and stitch under a 1″ hem.

With right side of pocket to wrong side of apron, stitch seams at each side of pocket piece. Trim seams and turn pocket to apron front. Divide pocket into three sections and machine stitch.

Clip seam allowance on apron where top of pocket meets apron and zigzag the raw edge; turn seam allowance to wrong side. Topstitch from bottom edge to armhole. Stitch a 1″ hem along top edge of bib front.

Cut a 2″-wide bias strip approximately 16″ long; fold bias in half with wrong sides together and pin to armhole with all raw edges aligned. Machine stitch, trim and turn in raw edges on ends. Turn folded edge to wrong side and slipstitch fold to machine stitching. Repeat for the other armhole.

Cut one 28″ x 2″ strip for neck loop and two 40″ x 2″ strips for waist ties. Fold in half lengthways with right sides facing, stitch, trim and turn through. Pin neck loop to either side of bib front and slipstitch in place. Topstitch through all thicknesses close to top edge of bib. Pin ties to either side of

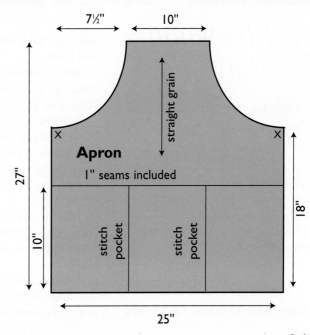

diagram labels:
7½″ 10″
straight grain
X X
Apron
1″ seams included
27″
stitch pocket
stitch pocket
10″
18″
25″

Firewood Carrier

Five, six, pick up sticks — or logs, or whatever it is you use on your fire.

MATERIALS
48" of 55"-wide hessian
20" of contrast fabric; two
1"-wide dowels, each 26" long;
thread.

METHOD
From contrast fabric, cut 6"-wide strips to make binding for sides and ends.

Fold hessian in half, lengthwise, and press fold flat (so that hessian is used double). ❖

Turn in 1" on each side of binding strips, place evenly over long edges of hessian, then sew in place using a zigzag or a fancy embroidery stitch for extra strength.

Mark the center of each end and, using a plate as a template, draw and cut a semicircle around mark.

From contrast fabric, and using the same plate as a guide, mark out four curved binding pieces, each 2" wide. Add an extra 1" for seam allowances on inner and outer curves, then cut out.

With right sides together, sew two bindings together around inner curve, and clip. Repeat to make a second binding, then pin bindings evenly over the curves. Turn under and baste seam allowance on outer curves, then sew in place using a zigzag or fancy embroidery stitch.

Cut four bindings to make dowel casings for the ends of the carrier, allowing an extra 1" seam allowance at each end. Turn under seam allowance at both ends of each binding strip, then stitch flat the ends which will sit to the center of the carrier.

Turn under 1" on the long sides of each binding strip. Pin the strips in their correct positions on the ends, encasing the hessian between, then, allowing space for the dowels, topstitch in place using a zigzag or fancy embroidery stitch. Slide dowels into place and stitch end opening closed.

Project by Betty Smith
Photography by Scott Cameron
❖ indicates pattern on pattern pages

Garden Stakes

These whimsical painted stakes add color to your garden bed.

MATERIALS

¾"-thick timber; ½"-diameter dowel; acrylic folk art paint; matte varnish; paint brushes; PVA wood glue; twig for perch on birdhouse.

METHOD

Trace patterns. ❖ Using a jigsaw, cut out shapes from pine timber. Drill a ½"-diameter hole in the base of each shape to fit dowel, cut to length desired. Paint shapes as desired, using acrylic paint. When dry, coat with matte varnish. Fix dowel into drilled hole using PVA glue. For birdhouse shape, drill a hole to fit twig below the doorway as marked on pattern. Glue twig 'perch' into hole.

Project by Judy Newman
Photography by Andrew Elton
❖ indicates pattern on pattern pages

Gardener's Hold-all

Add a kneeling cushion and a tool bag and this weeding mat becomes a gardening hold-all. What a rustic way to keep all that gardening paraphernalia together.

MATERIALS

72" of 55"-wide hessian; 60" of patterned fabric; two 1"-wide dowels, each 26" long; thread.

METHOD

Make as for the firewood carrier, sewing all but the dowel casings in place. ❖

For kneeling cushion, cut one rectangle of hessian and one of patterned fabric, each 27" x 14", and two strips, each 3" x 5", for cushion hangers. Fold hanger strips in half across the width, with right sides together, and sew seams. Turn right side out and pin in position on right side along one long edge of a cushion piece, 3" in from edges.

With right sides together, sew cushion pieces together, keeping hangers inside and leaving a small opening. Turn right side out, fill cushion and handstitch opening closed.

To make tool bag, cut two pieces of patterned fabric, each 29" x 18" (fabric is used double for added strength), and for bag hangers cut two strips each 3" x 5".

Make hangers as for cushion, stitching in same position along one long edge of a bag piece. With right sides together, sew bag pieces together along short ends, keeping hangers inside. Turn right side out, fold rectangle in half, then sew the side seams.

Pin free ends of hangers for both tool bag and cushion to one end of mat, on either side of curved opening. Position end bindings as for wood carrier.

Project by Betty Smith Photography by Scott Cameron

Pressing Flowers

Make some of our delicious projects using flowers from your own garden, or those of friends. Here is a simple method for pressing.

Step 1. Select flowers — many from your garden are suitable for pressing. Pansies, yellow jonquils, lavender, roses, baby's breath, bougainvillea and fuchsias are some that press well, as do most ferns and herbs.

Step 2. Prepare flowers for pressing by trimming stems and, if flowers are too solid, cut them in half or separate the petals. As well as your plant material, you'll need a craft knife, cutting mat, scissors, tweezers and flower press.

Step 3. Lay flowers on one half of flower press with enough space between to stop them touching when flattened. We used a microwave-safe flower press, the Microfleur, which retains flower color extremely well and produces pressed flowers in minutes. Alternatively, use a traditional press of blotting paper sand-wiched between cardboard with timber covers, held in place with wing nuts. Or press flowers between layers of blotting paper in a heavy telephone book.

Step 4. If using the Microfleur, place a small bowl of water in the microwave with the press and cook on HIGH for 30-45 seconds. If needed, microwave for further 10-second periods until petals are papery and dry. If using a traditional press, leave in a warm, dry place for several weeks.

Warning: There is a wonderful range of plant material available to collect and enjoy, but please remember never to pick protected or rare plants. Collection in national parks and nature reserves is not permitted.

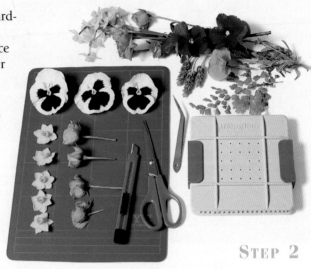

STEP 2

STEP 3

STEP 1

STEP 4

Key Holder with Pressed Flowers

As well as bringing the garden indoors, we've brought a little bit of the fence, too! Our rustic key holder is made by cutting out a heart shape from an old fence paling, using a jigsaw. Coat the

timber heart with two coats of sealer, then use the sealer to attach an arrangement of pressed flowers. Follow with at least three more coats of sealer. Screw in two cup hooks at the front, and a hanger at the back and it's complete. If you don't have a jigsaw, wooden shapes are available, precut, from most craft stores.

Say It In Flowers

Spell out a name or initials in foliage to make a picture. We've fashioned each letter using stems of passionfruit vine, then we've glued nandina leaves next to it. You also could create letters by using individual flowers or petals.

To make your own picture, cut paper to fit your chosen frame and arrange pressed material to spell out the name. Make a border of flowers and greenery (ours includes fuchsia, seaside daisy, yellow jonquils, ivy leaves, ferns and grass seeds) along the bottom. When you're happy with the arrangement, use dots of PVA craft glue to secure it. Cover picture with plastic wrap, put a heavy book on top, leave overnight to dry. Fit it into frame.

Pressed In Paper

Pressed blossoms are ironed into waxed paper to make this pretty paper which can be used to cover books or to wrap a special gift. It's easy to make — just cover your ironing board with muslin and place a sheet of waxed paper, wax side up, on the muslin. Arrange pressed flowers on paper and cover with a second sheet of waxed paper, wax side down. Place another piece of muslin on the top and, with a hot dry iron, press the muslin 'sandwich'. Allow to cool before checking paper. Very flat blooms and leaves work best.

Projects by Jennie Beecroft
and Judy Newman
Photography by Cath Muscat

95

Herb Pictures

Pressed, dried herbs make simple decorative pictures for your home. We used lavender and rosemary. Just glue the dried herbs onto paper, label with a felt pen, and fit the picture into a plain pine frame.

Project by Judy Newman
Photography by Andrew Elton

Pressed Flower Picture

To make this colorful picture we chose blooms which keep their color well and are easy to press because they are so flat.

MATERIALS

10″ x 8″ backing paper (we used handmade acid-free cotton and algae paper, not recycled. Other acid-free papers from art supply stores are suit-able); forceps; freshly pressed flowers, leaves and stems — cream and yellow tones; wattle, bossiaea, achillea, pansies, buttercups, jonquils, Queen Anne's Lace. Pink tones: cineraria, boronia, tea-tree flowers, peach blossoms, cherry blossom, ixia. Foliage: buttercup stems, ivy leaves, nasturtium leaves, rose leaves; rubber-based glue; cocktail stick; 8″ of ¼″-wide yellow ribbon; 10″ x 8″ wooden frame, painted as desired.

FINISHED SIZE

10″ x 8″.

Note. The background paper should be acid-free so color is not leached from the flowers.

METHOD

Place the background paper in the frame. Work your picture with the paper in the frame so you can see the progression of the total design. Use forceps to handle the pressed flowers. Start your design by positioning the flowers on the outside of the bunch then place the stalks at the bottom of the bunch. Fill in the bunch with the smaller flowers and leaves, working from the outside edge to the center.

To give the three-dimensional effect of the large center flowers being on the outside of the rounded bunch, overlap some of the smaller flowers behind them by sliding them partially underneath the petals. Fill gaps with small flowers and leaves. When satisfied with the design, glue flowers in place. Again starting from the outside and working inwards, partially lift each flower with the forceps and, using a cocktail stick, apply some glue to the paper.

When all flowers are glued in place, remove unwanted specks of plant material or glue using forceps. Tie a ribbon bow and glue over the stems at the base of the bunch.

Frame your picture with glass and seal with tape to keep out insects.

Display your picture away from direct sunlight. Clean the glass with a damp cloth — do not spray with glass cleaner — then wipe, as the moisture can seep behind the glass.

Project by Brigitte Eckhardt
Photography by Andrew Elton

Drying Flowers

For maximum color retention, blooms should be freshly picked; however, colors may still change during the drying process.

HANG DRYING

Tie flowers in a bunch using a rubber band. Hang upside down in a warm, dark, dry place. This is the most inexpensive and easiest method and gives good results for roses, strawflowers, lavender, catmint and hydrangeas.

MICROWAVE DRYING

Thick flowers such as pansies, roses and chrysanthemums dry well in the microwave. Place a single layer of flowers between layers of paper kitchen towel and microwave on HIGH for 3 minutes. Check the result; if further drying is needed, replace the paper towels. Be prepared to use trial and error as the thickness and moisture content of flowers will vary.

WATER DRYING

Use this method for hydrangeas, Queen Anne's lace and baby's breath. Place flowers in a container with a little water. Allow to stand in a warm place out of direct sunlight until water evaporates and the blooms dry.

Warning: There is a wonderful range of plant material available to collect and enjoy, but please remember never to pick protected or rare plants. Collection in national parks and nature reserves is not permitted.

Dried Flower Basket

Our rustic basket is exquisitely decorated.

MATERIALS

Dried flowers: 9 large hydrangea heads, 16 rose heads and leaves, pink and white gomphrena or baby strawflowers, pink and white daisy, pink pepper-corns, statice, catmint, lavender, nigella (love-in-the-mist); hot glue gun and glue sticks; 12″-diameter basket; hairspray or flower preserving spray.

METHOD

Cut the hydrangea heads from the stems and glue them around the top of the basket using hot glue. Ensure the top edge of the basket is covered.

Attach roses by placing them in an informal zigzag pattern around the basket. Glue roses in place with rose leaves around them.

Place small bunches of gomphrena or strawflowers between the roses. Continue filling the spaces between roses with bunches of daisy, statice and nigella until the floral border is quite full. Push in pieces of catmint and lavender around the edge of the basket to give a wispy effect. Finally add some pink peppercorns. Spray flowers with hairspray or flower preserving spray.

Avoid placing your basket in direct sunlight as colors will fade.

Project by Elisabeth Lowe
Photography by Andrew Elton

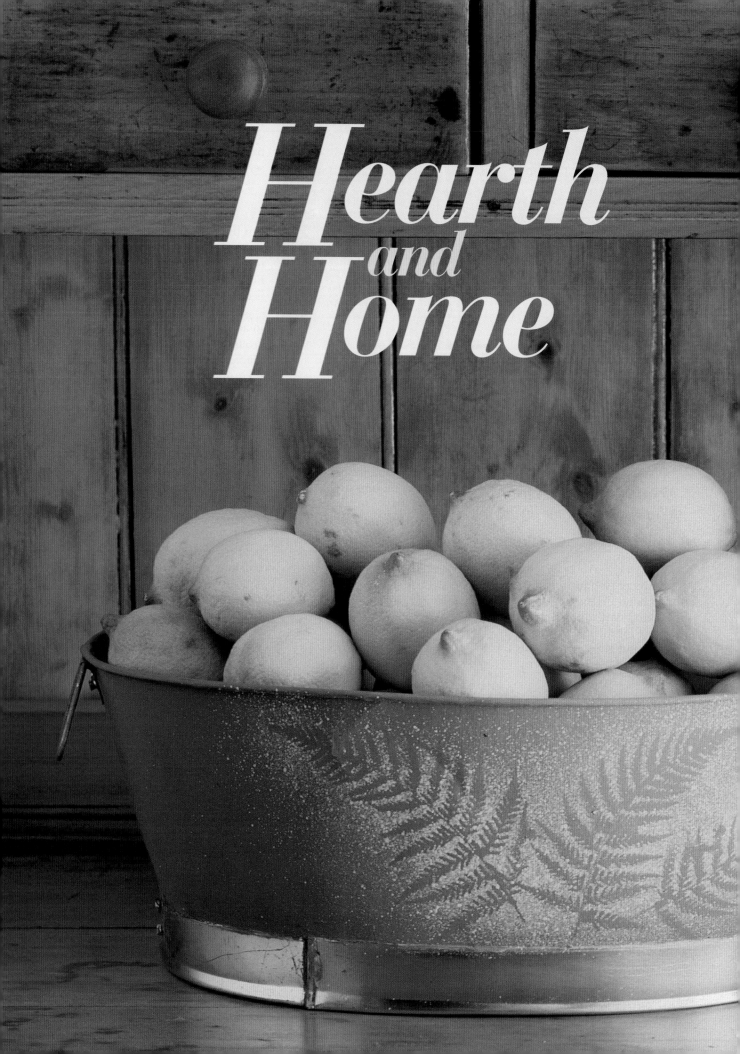

Hearth
and
Home

Simple Cushions

Wonderfully comfortable, these are always great decorator items which enhance any room.

SIZE

20″ square, approximately.

MATERIALS

(to make one cushion). 24″ x 48″ fabric; a 16″ square cushion insert; 4″ strip of Velcro; thread.

METHOD

From fabric, cut one top, 20″ x 20″, and two backs, 20″ x 12″ and 20″ x 14″.

Press under and along one 20″ edge of back piece. overlap the smaller hemmed back piece over the larger piece and tack through all layers.

With right sides together, pin and sew seam. Turn right side out, press and then remove tacking. Mark a line, 1½″ in from outside edges. Carefully topstitch along line.

Sew Velcro at back opening, then fill cushion cover.

Project by Betty Smith

Fabulous Frame

Decorate a plain timber frame using paint and impasto medium with our cute fish design to make it into something really special.

MATERIALS

Stencil film; craft knife; frame; stencil brush; paint brush; Matisse Impasto medium; Matisse acrylic paint in Cadmium Red Medium, Yellow Light, Metallic Gold.

METHOD

Trace fish design onto stencil film and cut out using a craft knife. Mark positions for fish shapes on top and bottom edges of frame, placing one fish in the center and positioning others at equal distances from it. Place stencil on frame and apply a thick layer of Impasto medium through cut-out area of stencil using a stencil brush. Dab Impasto lightly to give a rough texture then lift stencil straight off. Allow to dry for several hours.

Mix equal parts Cadmium Red Medium and Yellow Light to make orange paint. Apply two coats of orange to frame, allowing drying time between coats.

Dip a dry brush into a little Metallic Gold, brush lightly over the entire frame, reworking the fish area so the shapes are clearly defined in gold; allow to dry. Dip brush end in Metallic Gold and use it to add gold dots for bubbles above each fish; allow to dry.

Fabulous Frame

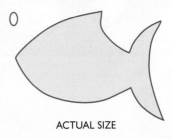

0

ACTUAL SIZE

Project by Judy Newman
Photography by Andrew Elton

Fish Printed Cushion

Look out for colorful lengths of fabric — or even cheap sarongs — to make into cushion covers and then overprint using our simple fish motif, or any other motif you desire.

MATERIALS

Kitchen sponge; 20″ of 45″-wide fabric for each cushion; white acrylic paint, such as Matisse flow medium; fabric fixative; paper towel; three 1″ buttons for each cushion; 6yds medium piping cord (optional), for trim for each cushion; PVA glue (optional), for trim; cushion insert; thread.

FINISHED SIZE

18″ square.

METHOD

Step 1. Draw pattern for fish shape. Cut out pattern and draw fish onto sponge. Cut out fish shape. Cut out one 20″ square of fabric for cushion front.

Step 2. Mix equal parts acrylic paint and fabric fixative. Press sponge onto paint and remove excess on paper towel. Place carefully onto fabric in position desired. Avoid twisting the sponge as this will cause smudging. Lift sponge straight off fabric. Repeat for other prints. When paint is dry, iron from the wrong side or fix paint according to manufacturer's instructions.

Step 3. Cut two 20″ x 14″ pieces for cushion back. Along one long side of each piece, turn under a 1″ hem then turn again. Stitch hem. Overlap hemmed edges of backs (2″) to make a 20″ square, tack together at overlapped edges. Stitch three buttons, evenly spaced, in center of one hemmed edge and stitch buttonholes on the other to correspond. Place back and front right sides together, stitch around cushion.

Nautical trim (optional)

Place made-up cushion cover flat on table. Lay piping cord around it, making a loop at each corner and three loops on each edge. Use a dot of PVA glue to fix loops in place, pin cord around cushion. Slipstitch cord in place. To neaten cord ends, overlap them, trim and wind thread around each end to secure it before stitching ends together.

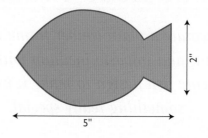

Project by Judy Newman
Photography by Valerie Martin

STEP 1

STEP 2

Country Chest and Frame

Your favorite country motifs are glued onto a raw timber frame and chest before a simple but stunning paint technique is applied.

MATERIALS

Timber shapes, such as pigs, apples, teddies and stars; PVA glue; raw timber chest of drawers; frame; Matisse acrylic paints in Permanent Green Light and Yellow Light; brush; sponge or absorbent cloth.

METHOD

Glue the timber cut-out shapes onto drawers in positions that appeal to you. Paint chest with Yellow Light, allow to dry. Then paint with water-thinned Permanent Green Light and, with a damp sponge, wipe off excess green paint. Decorate the frame in the same way.

Project by Judy Newman
Photography by Cath Muscat

Make It Easy Tableware

Use fresh blue and white print to make a pretty breadbasket liner and napkin holder. Both are simple to make from lined fabric squares — this is the easiest of sewing projects!

MATERIALS

For napkin holder: Four 9″ squares of co-ordinating fabric; thread; 1″ button.
For bread cloth: Two 15″ squares of co-ordinating fabric (or size to fit basket).

FINISHED SIZE

Napkin holder: 8″ square.
Bread cloth: 14″ square.

METHOD
Napkin holder

Place 2 fabric squares right sides together, stitch around using a 1″ seam and leaving an opening on one side. Trim corners and turn right side out, stitch opening closed. Repeat for remaining two fabric squares. Place two lined squares together and top-stitch them together along two edges, ¼″ from edge. Work a 1″ buttonhole in the unattached corner of one fabric square. Stitch button to center of the same square. Turn back corner with buttonhole and fasten button.

Bread cloth

Place fabric pieces right sides together, stitch around using a ½″ seam. Leave an opening on one side. Trim corners and turn right side out, stitch opening closed. Press and top-stitch ¼″ from edge.

Project by Judy Newman
Photography by Andrew Elton

Sunny Drawers and Vase

Handy timber storage drawers and a vase are given a celestial theme with sun motifs glued over a vivid blue, painted finish.

MATERIALS

Matisse acrylic paint in Cerulean Blue and Metallic Gold; drawer set; brush; sun motif wrapping paper; small sharp scissors; sealer; glue stick; clear varnish; terracotta container.

METHOD
Drawers

Thin Cerulean Blue paint with water and apply one coat to drawers (paint should be thin enough to allow wood grain to show through). Allow to dry. Using a dry brush, apply a little Metallic Gold paint to edges of drawers.

Using small sharp scissors, cut out sun motifs. Coat each side of motifs with sealer, allow to dry. Apply glue to cut-out motifs, glue in place on each drawer, allow to dry. Coat drawers with sealer; allow to dry. Coat with varnish. *Optional:* for a découpage finish, apply additional coats of varnish as desired, sanding after every third coat to remove bumps. Check fit of drawers as you proceed — too much varnish may cause them to jam.

Vase

Paint terracotta container with one coat of sealer (inside and out) and two coats of Cerulean Blue (outside only), allowing drying time between coats. Using a dry brush, apply a little Metallic Gold paint to give a touch of gold. Paint top edge of vase with gold. Apply motifs as for drawers. Seal, then varnish as desired.

Project by Judy Newman
Photography by Andrew Elton

107

Kitchen Set

Practical pieces like this hand towel, oven mitt and pot holder to match, liven any kitchen, and you can even paint the peg rack to match.

¼" seams used throughout.

MATERIALS

10" of 55"-wide heavy checked cotton fabric; thread; 10" of 36"-wide lightweight wadding (we used Pellon); thread; 1" of ½"-wide bias tape; 10" of 36"-wide muslin; 4-knob plain wooden peg rack; sealer; acrylic paint in blue; brush.

FINISHED SIZE

Pot holder: 8" square.
Mitt: Finished height: 12".

METHOD

Pot holder

Cut two 8" squares in checked fabric and one in wadding. Place fabric squares wrong sides together with wadding sand-wiched

between. Following straight lines of checks, tack and machine-stitch squares to quilt the layers together. Trim corners so that they are rounded. Pin bias tape around edge, extending tape into a loop hanger at one corner; stitch in place.

Oven mitt

Enlarge mitt shape. ❖ Cut two shapes in checked fabric, two in muslin and two in wadding. Tack and quilt one checked fabric, one wadding and one muslin shape together in same way as for pot holder. Repeat with remaining shapes. With muslin facing, pin two mitt shapes together and machine baste around edge. Trim excess fabric away and pin bias tape around edge; stitch. Pin and stitch tape in same way around opening and make hanger in same way as for pot holder.

Peg rack

Paint with one coat of sealer then two coats of blue paint, allowing drying time between coats.

Handtowel

MATERIALS

Handtowel 18″ x 14″ (or trim one end to desired size); 1 ball Soft Knitting and Crochet Cotton 4-ply; No.1 crochet hook; 1 button.

TENSION

Approximately 11dc to 2″.

SPECIAL ABBREVIATIONS

'Single petal': 4ch, leaving last lp of each tr on hook, work 2tr in first ch of 4ch, yoh, draw yarn through all 3 lps on hook.
'2 petals': leaving last lps on hook, 3tr in next 3 ch sp, miss next 3ch sp, 3tr in foll 3ch sp, yoh and draw through all 7 lps on hook.
'3tr group': leaving last lps on hook, work 3tr, yoh and draw through all 4 lps on hook.

METHOD

Place colored marker in center of top of towel. With right side facing,
1st row. (1sc, 1ch) 36 times to center marker, (1sc, 1ch) 36 times to end, 1sc at end, turn... (73sc).

2nd row. 3ch (to form first dc) 1dc in each 1ch sp, 1dc in end sc...(74dc).

3rd row. 1ch, 1sc in 2nd dc, *3ch, miss 1dc, 1sc in next dc, rep from * to end, turn...(35 3ch spaces).

4th row. 4ch, (2tr, 2ch, 2tr) in first 3ch sp, *work 'single petal', miss 3ch sp, work '2 petals', over next 3 sps. Rep from * 7 times, ending with 'single petal', miss 3ch sp, (2tr, 2ch, 2tr) in next sp, 1 tr in last sc, turn.

5th row. 4ch, (2tr, 2ch, 2tr) in 2ch sp of previous shell, *3ch, into sp between 2 petals below work (3tr, 3ch, 3tr). Rep from * 7 times, 3ch, shell into 2ch sp of shell below, 1tr in top of 4 turning ch, turn. (8 flowers completed.)

6th row. 4ch, shell on shell, * work 'single petal', miss 3ch sp, work '2 petals' into tops of first and second flowers of row below. Rep from * 3 more times, 'single petal', shell on shell, 4ch turn. (First row of four flowers worked.)

7th row. Work as 5th row, repeating 3 times instead of 7...(4 flowers completed.)

8th to 11th rows. Work as rows 5 and 6, having 2 flowers and then 1 flower only.

12th row. 3ch, (2dc, 2ch, 2dc) shell in shell below, 1ch, rep same shell between 2 petals below, 1ch, shell in end shell, 1dc in turning ch, turn.

13th row. As 12th row, omitting 1ch between shells.

14th row. 3ch, dc shell in first shell, 1sc in next shell, shell in last shell, 1dc in top of turning ch, turn.

15th row. 3ch, shell in each of next 2 shells, 1dc in top of turning ch, turn.

Rep last row 12 times.

28th row. 3ch, 2dc in 2ch sp, 4ch, 2dc in next 2ch sp, 1dc in top of turning ch. Fasten off. (4ch forms buttonhole.)

Rejoin yarn at beginning of 1st row and work 1 row sc around outside edge of crochet. Fasten off neatly. Attach button in center of 14th row.

Projects by Christine Moss and Agnes Lennox
Photography by Andrew Elton
❖ indicates pattern on pattern pages

Bathroom Set

Pretty and practical...not only will our gorgeous three-piece set give a bathroom a new lease of life, but the cotton wool and cotton bud holders will travel easily anywhere.

MATERIALS

Purchased basket (ours was 11" x 10");
36" of 45"-wide cotton fabric; 36" of 36"-wide thin wadding (we used Pellon); 10" of 36"-wide cotton fabric (for lining cotton bud and ball holder); thread; 160" of ¼"-wide ribbon; one packet of ½"-wide cotton bias tape.

Note. ¼" seams are used throughout.

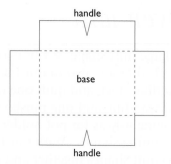

Lined Basket

FINISHED SIZE OF LINING
20" x 18".

METHOD
Lay basket on top of large sheet of newspaper and mark base shape on paper. Measure out from base shape for each side of basket for approximately 6" (or to fit sides) plus 2" over the top edge of basket (depending on depth and size of basket); draw a pattern like ours shown here. Allow for any handles by marking a deep V-shape, cut out a pattern in newspaper and test it for fit inside basket. Make any necessary adjustments. Cut two pattern pieces in fabric and one in wadding. Place fabric pieces right sides facing, and lay wadding on top. Stitch around, leaving an opening to turn through. Trim and clip seams, turn right side out. Topstitch around edge. Cut 10" lengths of ribbon and stitch them to each corner of liner. Fit liner into basket and tie decorative bows on outside edge of basket.

Cotton Bud Holder

FINISHED SIZE
5" long x 3" diameter.

METHOD
Cut two 4"-diameter circles and one 5" x 10" rectangle in fabric and the same in lining and wadding. Place each fabric piece wrong sides facing with corresponding lining piece, sandwiching wadding between, tack. Machine stitch ¼" in from circle edges to mark seam line.

Machine stitch in a line 1" in from each long edge of rectangle to hold fabric layers together. Fold bias tape over raw edge of each short side of rectangle; stitch in place. Neaten raw edges of rectangle and circles. Pin one long edge of rectangle around edge of one circle, right sides together; stitch in place. Repeat with other long edge and remaining circle; turn right side out. Stitch ribbon bows at each end of opening.

Cotton Ball Holder

FINISHED SIZE
8" long x 3" diameter.

METHOD
Cut one 9" x 10" rectangle and two 4"-diameter circles, and the same in lining and wadding. Make as for cotton bud holder.

Project by Christine Moss
Photography by Andrew Elton

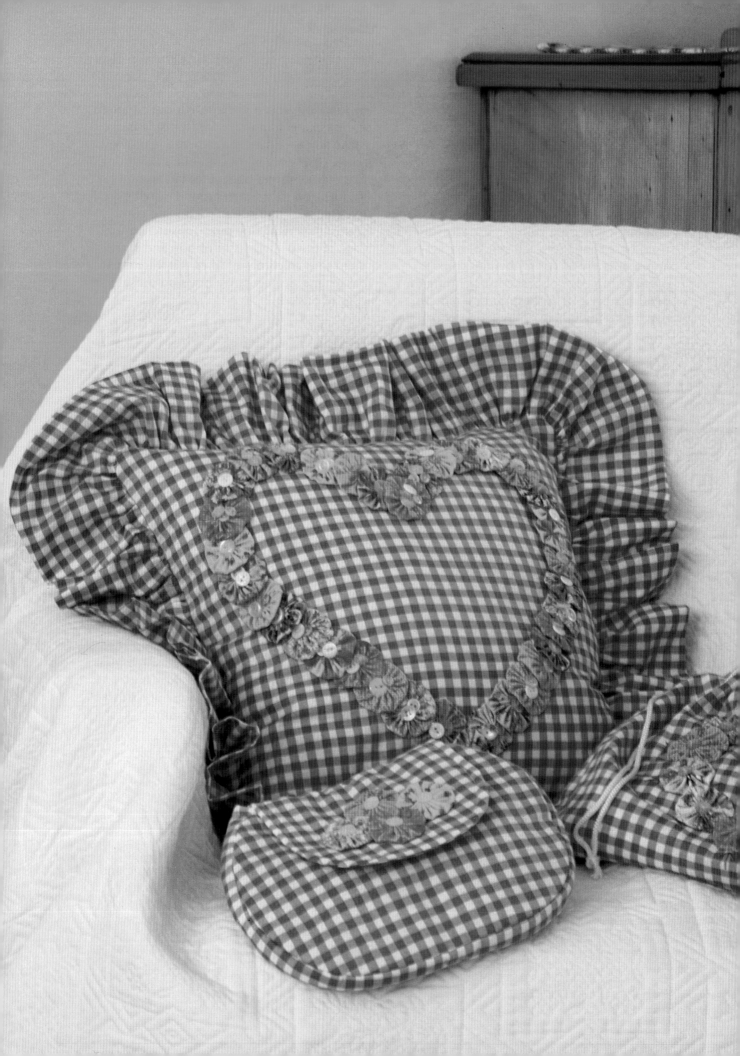

Checked Bedroom Set

The gathered circles of fabric featured here are known by patchworkers as yo-yos. This three-piece set features pink . yo-yos on a ruffled cushion cover, lingerie bag and make-up bag.

TO MAKE YO-YOS

Use a compass to draw 4″ and 3 ½″ diameter circles on cardboard; cut out circles. Draw around circle onto fabric and cut out. Finger-press a ¼″ hem to the wrong side of fabric. Using a matching sewing thread and starting with a knot, tack hem in place. When circle is tacked, pull thread tight to gather circle edge to the center. Pass your needle through the center to the back and secure thread with a knot.

Cushion Cover

MATERIALS

44″ x 45″-wide checked fabric; thread; paper; three large buttons; 36 fabric yo-yos made with 4″-diameter circles (see instructions, above); small buttons for yo-yo centers.

FINISHED SIZE

16″ square plus ruffle.
Note. ½″ seam allowance is included.

METHOD

Cut one 17″ square of checked fabric for cushion front. Cut two 17″ x 12″ pieces for cushion back. Cut three 45″ (fabric width) x 8″ strips for ruffle. Make a paper heart pattern by folding paper in half, mark 7″ along the

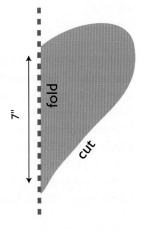

fold and cut out half heart measuring 7″ from point to point. Take cushion front and, using heart pattern, draw heart shape in center of front. Pin yo-yos around heart shape. Tack in place from wrong side. Stitch two or three buttons onto the center of yo-yos. On cushion back pieces, press under a doubled 1″-wide hem on one 17″ edge of each piece, stitch. Join narrow edges of ruffle strips to make a circle. Fold in half lengthwise, wrong sides together, press. To gather ruffle, have a contrast thread handy. Zigzag along the raw edge of ruffle while feeding contrast thread under the center of the zigzag stitch. When edge is stitched, pull up the contrast thread to form gathers. Divide ruffle into four, place on right side of cushion front, raw edge to raw edge, and pin, positioning more gathers at each corner. Stitch around all sides. Overlap hemmed edges of back pieces and place right sides together with cushion front, enclosing ruffle. Stitch around all sides, turn right side out. Stitch buttons on hemmed edge of one back piece and work buttonholes on other to correspond.

Make-up Bag

MATERIALS
10″ x 45″-wide checked fabric; 10″ x 45″-wide piece of lining; 10″ x 36″-wide thin wadding; thread; four fabric yo-yos made with 3½″-diameter circles; four small buttons; Velcro adhesive dots.

FINISHED SIZE
10″ x 8″.

METHOD
Enlarge patterns ❖ for bag pieces. Pattern includes ¼″ seam allowance. Cut one back, one front, one flap and one 26″ x 2″ strip from checked fabric, lining and wadding. Place wadding next to wrong side of main fabric pieces before making bag. With right sides together, stitch the strip around the curved edge of bag front, trim excess on fabric strip. Place back piece right sides

together with strip and stitch. Make up lining in the same way, but leave an opening in one seam at base for turning through. Stitch yo-yos and buttons to right side of flap.

Place flap and lining right sides together and stitch around curved edge, leaving the top, straight side open. Turn right side out and topstitch around curve. Pin flap onto top edge of bag back, right sides together. Slip lining into fabric bag, right sides together. Stitch around top edge and turn bag through opening left in the lining. Stitch opening closed. Topstitch around edge of bag. Stick Velcro dots on inside of flap and front of bag to fasten.

Lingerie Bag

MATERIALS
20″ x 45″-wide fabric; 6 fabric yo-yos made with 3½″-diameter circle and 6 with 4″-diameter circle; 12 small buttons; green embroidery thread; 80″ narrow cord.

FINISHED SIZE
16″ x 15″.

METHOD
Cut two 20″ x 16″ rectangles of checked fabric for front and back of bag. Draw a 5″-diameter circle on right side of front, positioned about 4″ from the bottom edge. Pin yo-yos around circle and tack in place from the wrong side. Stitch buttons in the center of yo-yos, securing them. Using the embroidery thread, make leaves in simple straight stitch. Place back and front right sides together. Stitch sides and base of bag, leaving a ¾″ opening in each side seam 7″ from top edge of cord. Stitch a 4″ hem on top edge. Machine a row of stitching around bag, above the side openings, 2″ from top edge to form a casing. Cut cord into two 40″ lengths. Insert one in one side opening, knot ends together; repeat with remaining cord from other side.

Projects by Louise Bugeni
Photography by Cath Muscat
❖ indicates pattern on pattern pages

Mirror and Tissue Box Cover

Butterfly motifs flit across our timber-framed mirror and tissue box cover in co-ordinating moss green and mauve.

MATERIALS

Wooden mirror and tissue box; brush; sealer; Jo Sonja acrylic paint in Azure, Warm White, Yellow Light, Red Earth, Oakmoss; stencil film; craft knife; stencil brush; paper towel; Jo Sonja Glass and Tile medium.

METHOD

Mirror

Remove mirror from frame. Paint frame with one coat of sealer and two coats of Azure, allowing drying time between each coat. Trace butterfly design onto stencil film, tracing separate stencils for wings and body. Cut out stencils using a craft knife. Mix equal parts Warm White with Azure to make mauve paint, dip stencil brush in paint and dab on paper towel to remove excess. Position stencil on frame as desired. Stencil wings with mauve paint by dabbing brush lightly through cut-out area. Add a touch of Yellow Light and Warm White for highlights on inside edges of wings. When dry, stencil bodies with Red Earth.

Mix small quantities of paints with equal parts Glass and Tile Medium and stencil mirror glass in the same way. When dry, fit mirror back into frame.

Tissue Box Cover

Paint with one coat of sealer and two coats of Oakmoss.

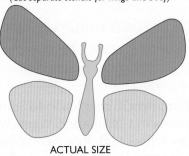

Mirror and Tissue Box Cover Stencil
(Cut separate stencils for wings and body)

ACTUAL SIZE

Position butterflies as desired. Stencil butterfly wings using Azure, then add Yellow Light highlights. When dry, stencil bodies using Red Earth.

Project by Judy Newman
Photography by Andrew Elton

Sunflower Kitchenware

Stencil or stitch sunflower motifs on kitchenware, table linen or walls.

MATERIALS

Stencil film; pencil; craft knife; Jo Sonja's acrylic paints in Ultramarine, Warm White, Cadmium Yellow Mid, Raw Sienna; brush, for base coating; stencil brush; wooden tray; paper towel.

METHOD

Enlarge pattern for large sunflower ❖. Draw small and large patterns onto stencil film using pencil. Cut out using craft knife.

Base coat the tray with a mixture of equal parts Ultramarine and Warm White. Allow to dry before applying a second coat.

When the base coat is dry, position the large stencil in the center tray. Dip a dry stencil brush into a tiny amount of Cadmium Yellow Mid paint and dab on paper towel to remove excess. Using an up and down tapping motion, apply paint through stencil, starting at edges and working towards the center of the cut-out area. Continue in this manner until enough paint is applied.

Apply a little Raw Sienna to the outside of the sunflower center, over the yellow; allow to dry.

Stencil small sunflowers on either side of the large one in the same way.

To embroider napkins

Transfer a small sunflower pattern onto fabric using a lead pencil. For embroidery, use DMC Perle 5 thread, working centers in gold (783) in a chain-stitch spiral, starting from the center. Stitch petals in yellow (743), working in long-and-short stitch.

Project by Judy Newman
Photography by Ross Coffey
❖ *indicates pattern on pattern pages*

Paper-cut Shelf Liner

Paper cutting is a craft which has been practised for centuries and has appeared in cultures from China, to Mexico and Eastern Europe. This pretty shelf liner is an easy introduction to this fascinating technique. All you need to start is paper, scissors and a pencil.

MATERIALS

White paper (A3 size is useful); pencil; ruler; tracing paper; manicure scissors with sharp point; craft knife (optional).

METHOD

Cut paper as wide as shelf depth plus 3″, and as long as desired. If you need a length longer than the paper, cut out the design first and then join sections, matching pattern.

Mark 2″ intervals along the length of the paper and fold into pleats, creasing sharply with a ruler. Trace design ❖ and transfer lightly in pencil onto both folded edges, positioning broken lines on folds on one end of the paper.

Using scissors, start from center of design and cut carefully along the lines. To cut out sections not on a fold, pierce the center of the section and cut to the design lines, or use a craft knife, working with paper placed flat on a protected surface. When cutting is complete, open out paper and position on the shelf.

Project by Judy Newman
Photography by Andrew Elton
❖ indicates pattern on pattern pages

117

Transformed Chair

An old chair was given a fresh new look with this combed paint pattern. It's surprisingly easy to do. We painted a Matisse Straw background paint over a base coat of white.

Note: Wear thin latex gloves when you are painting. Practise first on a spare piece of board — sample board.

MATERIALS

Paint for the base and the top coats; brush; scumble medium; piece of soft plastic for comb; craft knife.

STEP 1

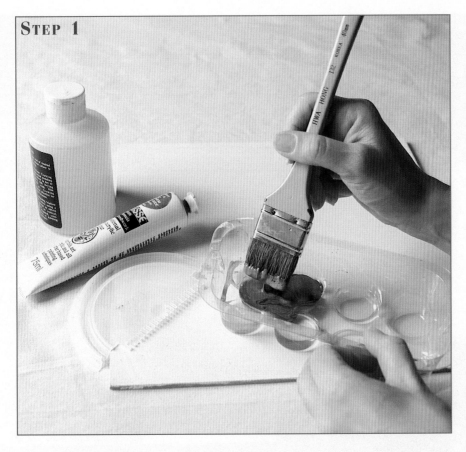

Step 1. Make the combing tool by cutting nicks out of one edge of a piece of soft plastic.

Apply base coat to chair (it will show through the combed pattern, so it needs to contrast with the top coat). Mix glaze for top coat by combining 1 part water, 1 part paint and 3 parts scumble medium.

(The scumble medium lengthens the drying time of the paint, enabling it to be worked and even reworked. It also gives the glaze a texture which holds the combed pattern without running.)

STEP 2

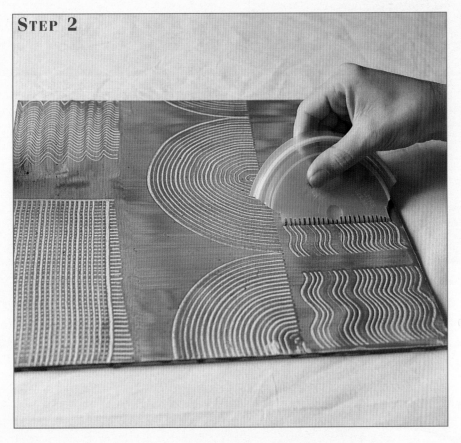

Step 2. Apply top coat glaze, comb it in the desired pattern. Make patterns by using wavy strokes, scallops or a crosshatch.

*Project by
Judy Newman
Photography by
Valerie Martin*

119

Rag-Rolled Frames

This delicate wash of color and hint of a textured pattern comes about when a cloth is rolled over wet, thinned paint. Gel is added to the paint to make it workable, and the effect is fabulous. Our frames were painted with background paints in Straw (Yellow) and Ritz Blue over a base coat of White. Rag Rolling suits large areas which have a smooth surface, such as walls, wide picture or window frames and some pieces of furniture.

Note: Wear thin latex gloves when you are painting. Practise first on a spare piece of board — sample board.

MATERIALS

Paint for base coat and top coat; scumble medium; brush; cotton interlock cloth (such as T-shirt fabric).

Step 1. Apply base coat — we chose a white background to give a light base under top coat. For top coat, mix 1 part paint, 1 part water and 3 parts scumble medium to form what is known as a scumble glaze. Brush scumble glaze evenly over the base coat.

Step 2. Twist and roll a piece of cotton interlock into a sausage shape. Roll it over the wet glaze to form the ragged pattern.

Step 3. The final result from this extremely simple technique is this lovely textured finish. A fairly large surface area will show it off to best effect.

Project by Christine Moss
Photography by Valerie Martin

STEP 1

STEP 2

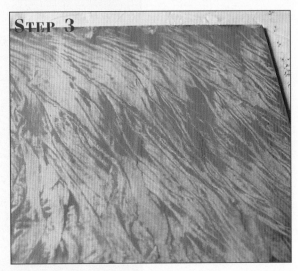

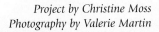

STEP 3

Fern Spattered Tinware

Here's a painted finish which was popular in the past. Chests of drawers and cupboards were decorated simply by holding ferns against them and spattering paint over both. We used Antique Green to base coat the tinware, then spattered over it with Straw. Fern Spattering looks great on furniture — drawer fronts, coffee tables and fire screens — as well as decorative pieces, such as our Spattered Tub and Vase.

STEP 1

STEP 2

Note: Wear thin latex gloves when you are painting. Practise first on a spare piece of board — sample board.

MATERIALS

Paint for base coat and spattering; stiff-bristled brush; ferns; Blu-Tack; nail brush; rubber gloves.

Step 1. Base coat the item. Fix fern in place, securing it flat against the surface using tiny pieces of Blu-Tack.

Step 2. Load paint onto a nailbrush or other stiff-bristled brush. Wearing protective gloves, aim the brush over fern and run your finger over the bristles causing paint to spatter. Work over the fern until enough paint is applied to form a clear outline.

Project by Judy Newman
Photography by Valerie Martin

Fish Stencilled Drawers

STEP 1

STEP 2

STEP 3

Decorate furniture, frames, boxes and walls with stencilling. Use some of the wonderful range of ready-cut stencils available in craft and art stores, or cut your own. We painted the drawers with Matisse Blush background paint then used Napthol Scarlet to Blush to paint over the fish stencil. ❖ Finish by adding a dot of Napthol Scarlet or Yellow Light for the eyes.

Note: Wear thin latex gloves when you are painting. Practise first on a spare piece of board — sample board.

MATERIALS

Paint for base coat and stencilling; brush, for applying base coat; stencil brush; stencil or stencil film and knife; masking tape; paper towel.

Step 1. A stencil brush (available from art and craft stores) is essential for this technique as it applies the paint without any bristles slipping under the stencil edges. If you wish to cut your own stencil, use a commercial stencil film, a sharp craft knife and a cutting mat. Trace the pattern onto stencil film and cut it out carefully.

Step 2. Position the stencil on the item. It can be taped in position by using small pieces of masking tape. Load a small amount of paint (unthinned) onto stencil brush and remove excess by dabbing it on paper towel (it is most important to work with an almost-dry brush). Apply paint through stencil with a soft tapping motion, starting from the edges and working towards the center. Carefully lift off the stencil.

Step 3. When completely dry, add fine details. For our fish design, we used the end of a pencil to dot in the eyes.

Project by Gary Fitz-Roy
Photography by Valerie Martin
❖ *indicates pattern on pattern pages*

Doona Cover and Pillowcase

You can make your own bedlinen, at a fraction of the cost...

SIZE

84″ x 56″ (to fit a single bed)

MATERIALS

93″ x 57″ patterned fabric; 80″ of 90″-wide plain sheeting; nine 1″-wide wooden buttons; matching thread.

Note: 1″ seam allowance throughout.

METHOD

From patterned fabric, cut 86″ x 57″ for front of cover, and two strips, each 4″ x 20″, for pillowcase border.

From plain sheeting, cut 86″ x 57″ for back of cover, and 62″ x 20″ for pillowcase.

Doona Cover

Placing right sides together and leaving one 57″-long side open, pin, sew and neaten front of cover to back. Turn out to right side and press.

Turn in 1″ hems on both open edges, stitch and press. Make six buttonholes, evenly spaced, along patterned hemmed edge. Stitch wooden buttons on along inside edge of plain fabric to correspond.

Pillowcase

Pin, then sew, the right sides of patterned strips over the wrong sides of the plain 20″-long ends of pillowcase. Turn strips to right side and press along seam. Press a ½″ turn-in on opposite edge of each patterned strip. Pin, then sew, to form borders at each end of plain fabric.

Placing right sides together, fold plain fabric in half to form case. Sew side seams and neaten; turn to right side and press. Sew three buttonholes 1″ in from one border edge. Sew buttons to correspond.

Project by Betty Smith
Photography by Andre Martin

Pinboard

Keep postcards, tickets and trivia from recent trips on this easily made pinboard which can be covered in a cheerful cotton fabric.

MATERIALS

24″ x 18″ piece of soft fiberboard (such as Canite); 32″ x 26″ piece of fabric; thumb tacks; decorative upholstery tacks; 8yds of ½″-wide ribbon; screws with round hook to hold cord; 20″ cord for hanger.

FINISHED SIZE

24″ x 18″.

METHOD

Press fabric to remove creases and press under 1″ on all edges to wrong side. Place the board on wrong side of fabric and pull excess fabric to the back of the board. Use thumb tacks to keep fabric in place, neatly folding in excess fabric at each corner. Turn pinboard to right side and cut lengths of ribbon to fit diagonally across the board as desired, allowing enough for ribbon ends to reach the back of the board. Pin ribbon lengths in place using thumb tacks on the back. Push in upholstery tacks where ribbon intersects on the front of the board. Insert screw hooks at each side of the board on the back and tie cord to each hook to make a hanger.

Project by Judy Newman
Photography by Valerie Martin

127

Pleated Paper Lampshade

This is surely the easiest way to cover a lampshade

MATERIALS

Length of strong, fine paper — we used handmade Japanese giftwrap; lampshade frame; glue; hole punch; bodkin; narrow ribbon, needle, thread.

METHOD

Cut the paper into a rectangle twice as long as the measurement around the bottom of your lampshade frame and the height of the frame plus 2″. Mark 1″ intervals along both long edges and fold the paper into sharply creased 1″-wide pleats, concertina fashion. Overlap ends, trimming if necessary so one edge falls inside a pleat; glue ends together. Mark points 1″ from the top edge and use a hole punch to make a hole through the center of each pleat. Using a bodkin, thread a length of narrow ribbon through the holes. Tie ribbon ends in a bow and place the shade on the frame. Using strong thread and a needle, lace the ribbon to the top ring of the frame. Fasten off when complete.

Project by Judy Newman
Photography by Ross Coffey

Cat Draught-Stopper

Our clever cat cheerfully keeps out winter chills. Stitch him in bright tartan or pretty floral fabric.

MATERIALS

20″ of 45″-wide fabric; two 30″ x 3″ pieces of muslin; thread; polyester fiber filling; clean, dry sand.

METHOD

Enlarge and make pattern ❖ continuing the tail to measure 30″ from broken line and tapering to a point; add ½″ seam allowance. Using pattern, cut two pieces of fabric. Place right sides facing, stitch around using small machine-stitches and leaving an opening along the bottom edge of the tail. Clip corners, turn right side out, fill body and tip of tail with fiber.

Stitch muslin pieces, right sides facing and rounding all corners, and leave an opening. Turn right side out and fill with sand; stitch opening closed. Place sand bag inside cat's tail and partly into body. Fill the rest of the tail area with fiber and stitch opening closed.

Note. To make the actual size pattern, photocopy the shape on the pattern pages on a photocopier set at 200%, then photocopy the enlargement again with the machine set at 200%. Extend the tail of the cat until it measures 30″ from the broken line, tapering to a point. Add ½″ seam allowance.

Project by Judy Newman
Photography by Ross Coffey
❖ *indicates pattern on pattern pages*

129

Fête
Favourites

Fabric-Covered pots

MATERIALS

20″ square of each fabric; 5″-high terracotta pots; PVA glue.

METHOD

Cut one 19″-diameter circle of fabric for each pot cover. Center base of pot on wrong side of fabric. Dot glue around outside edge of fabric and inside pot. Gather up fabric and tuck into pot, pressing against inside of pot and gluing to secure. Place pot plant inside decorative holder. Remove before watering.

Project by Christine Moss
Photography by Andrew Elton

Shell Candles

Bed your shells in a dish of sand so they don't topple over when being filled with wax. Cut a small section from the top of a household candle, just high enough to

sit inside the shell, then pour melted wax over it until the shell is almost filled. When using these candles, sit them in a sand dish, or place a little Blu-Tack on the base of the shell to avoid spills of hot wax.

Project by Judy Newman
Photography by Valerie Martin

Float Candles

MATERIALS

Candle wax granules; Boil Bags or old saucepan; shallow candle molds; candlewick.

METHOD

Place wax in Boil Bag and place bag in a saucepan of water over a medium heat, until wax is melted. Alternatively, place wax in old saucepan over a very low heat. Do not leave melting wax unattended. Pour wax into molds and allow to cool slightly. Trim wick to a suitable length and stand in center of candle. Allow to cool; top up with melted wax if cooled wax shrinks in center. Remove candles from mold when set hard.

Project by Judy Newman
Photography by Andrew Elton

Beeswax Candles

MATERIALS

9″ square sheet of beeswax; 9″ length of candlewick.

METHOD

To create a candle with a tapered top, mark a point 1″ or more from one corner of the wax sheet. Using a knife or pizza cutter, trim from this point to the adjacent corner to create an angled edge on one side of the sheet (this will be the candle top). Place wick along one long edge. Firmly press edge of wax onto wick, then roll wax sheet around wick, pressing gently but firmly until entire sheet is rolled. Vary the taper of the candle by trimming a larger piece from the top edge of wax sheet. For a straight top candle, make as above, but without trimming the wax sheet.

To decorate candles, you can mold or cut out a shape, such as a bow, and simply press it in place; or wrap strips of colored wax around candle base.

Project by Judy Newman
Photography by Andrew Elton

Drawstring Bags

Handy drawstring bags have myriad uses, from tiny ones for marbles to giant ones for laundry. Make them in various fabrics (including ultra-cheap muslin, which is great for ham and mushroom bags) so there's one for every use — shoes, library books, gym gear or beach wear. Just take a rectangle of fabric about twice the length of the finished bag, fold it crosswise and stitch side seams. Stitch a casing at top edge, make a button-hole in it, and insert cord or ribbon.

Découpaged Soaps

Yes, you can découpage soap. Not only does it make a pretty gift — it holds together that last sliver when the soap gets thin! Apply 6-8 coats of clear, water-based varnish to soap, just to the spot where the picture will sit. Seal both sides of the picture, using clear sealer. Allow to dry, then stick picture in place, using sealer. Apply several more coats of varnish over picture, allowing drying time between coats.

Storage Jars

Invest in some glass paint and liquid leading to pretty up plain glass containers. Draw simple shapes onto the glass with a chinagraph pencil. Draw over outlines with liquid leading, allow to dry, then color the glass.

Tips: Clean the glass with methylated spirits before painting. Choose jars with flat sides. Follow paint manufacturer's directions as details vary.

Juggling Balls

To make these juggling (or stress) balls, you'll need dried millet seeds, balloons and a funnel. Inflate a balloon to stretch it, release the air, then, with the help of the funnel, fill with about ¾ cup of millet, or until the ball is the size you want. Tie the neck in a knot and trim. Cut the neck off four or five other balloons and stretch them to cover the filled ball, cutting some holes in the last two to show the other colors underneath. These will sell best with a juggling demonstration, so start practising!

All projects on this page by Judy Newman Photography by Cath Muscat

133

Patchwork Jar Covers

MATERIALS

Scraps of assorted fabrics, patterned and plain; lining fabric; thread; ¼"-wide elastic.

Cut lining fabric to match and, with right sides facing, stitch together leaving a small opening. Trim and clip curves, turn right side out and slipstitch opening closed. Topstitch close to edge. Stitch two rows of stitching to form casing about 2" in from circle edge. Make a small slit in lining between casing lines and work a small handmade buttonhole around it. Cut elastic to fit around lid. Thread through casing, stitch ends together.

sides facing. Stitch along edge using ¼" seam allowance, turn shape over and press seam flat. Cut a second shape and stitch to next side of the center piece, working clockwise. Flip shape to right side as before, turning under the raw edge on side which overlaps previous piece and stitching down. Press and continue to work in this way until base fabric is covered. Fill any gaps by overstitching a patch on top. Finish as for strip patchwork jar cover.

FINISHED SIZE
8"-diameter.

Strip patchwork jar cover

Cut eight 2"-wide strips 8"-12" long (this will depend on size of jar top). Join strips, using 1/4" seams, and cut a circle big enough (ours was 8") to allow a 'skirt' to form around jar top.

Crazy patchwork jar cover

Cut an 8" muslin circle for base. Cut a small five-sided geometric shape in a dark fabric and pin to center of muslin circle. Cut a shape (any geometric shape will do) from another fabric scrap and lay one edge of this piece against one edge of the center piece, with right

Checkerboard jar cover

Cut 2" fabric squares (larger if desired); join into strips. Stitch strips together into a piece large enough to cut an 8" circle, or size desired. Finish as for strip patchwork cover.

Project by Christine Moss
Photography by Andrew Elton

Floral Bookmark

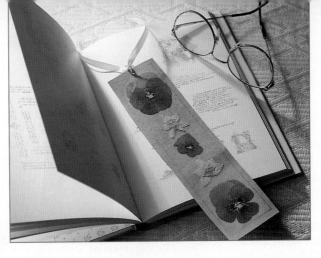

MATERIALS

Heavy paper; gold felt pen; pressed flowers (we used 2 pansies, 1 viola and 2 jonquils); rubber-based glue; clear adhesive vinyl (Contact); 8″ narrow ribbon.

METHOD

Cut a 8″ x 3″ piece of heavy paper then, using a gold felt pen, draw a border ½″ from the outside edge.

Position your pressed flowers and glue them in place using a small amount of rubber-based glue. Cut a piece of clear adhesive vinyl to fit the bookmark and fix it in place over the flowers. Trim the vinyl edges to align with the paper.

Pierce a hole at the top edge and tie a ribbon bow.

Project by Judy Newman
Photography by Andrew Elton

Lace Lavender Ball and Bolster

Lavender Ball

MATERIALS

Scrap of lace fabric; thread; dried lavender; 8″ of ½″-wide lace; tapestry needle; 1 tassel; 10″ of ¼″-wide white ribbon; 10″ of ¼″-wide mauve ribbon, tied into a bow.

FINISHED SIZE

2″ diameter.

METHOD

Cut 5″-diameter circle in lace fabric. Gather around the edge of circle and draw up. Fill with lavender, pull up tightly, stitch ball closed.

Run a gathering thread along one edge of ½″-wide lace, draw up. Oversew raw ends together and stitch on top of ball. Using a tapestry needle, thread the tassel ties and pull through bottom of ball, securing ties at top.

Stitch white ribbon in a loop for hanger to top of ball and stitch the mauve ribbon bow on top.

Lavender Bolster

MATERIALS

7″ x 5″ lace fabric; thread; 12″ of ½″-wide edging lace; 32″ of ¼″-wide white ribbon; 32″ of ¼″-wide mauve ribbon; dried lavender.

FINISHED SIZE

Approximately 8″ long. *Note.* ¼″ seam allowance is included.

METHOD

Using a tiny, narrow zigzag stitch, sew lace edging to the 5″ edges of lace fabric. (If lace puckers while stitching, place paper underneath.) Fold lace, right sides facing, with raw edges together and stitch side seam. Cut ribbons in half and tie one length of each ribbon around one end of the cylinder; fill with lavender. Tie other end with ribbon and tie ribbon ends to bows.

Project by Christine Moss
Photography by Andrew Elton

Bath Crystals

Using water-softening, skin-soothing washing soda, bath crystals are inexpensive and easy to make. Put soda crystals in a plastic bag and crush with a rolling pin. Add a little food coloring, mix well, then add a drop or two of lavender oil. Pack in a Cellophane bag and finish with a pretty ribbon tie.

water. Lift it off, and you'll have captured the swirling colored pattern. Lay sheets individually on the sink to dry. Inks vary slightly, so follow manufacturer's directions. Tie sets of stationery with raffia.

Photograph Frames

Two same-size pieces of corrugated cardboard glued flat sides together are the basis for these frames. Our frames measure 8″ x 4″ — the standard photo size.

Make sure corrugations on the front and back run in opposite directions, as this will strengthen the frame and help it to stand rigid. Before you glue, use a craft knife to cut out a hole for the picture and glue three sides only, so the photo can be inserted. Also, glue on a strip of cardboard (about 5″ x 2″) at the back to make a stand. Vary the sizes of frames and make some to hold two photos. Color some with acrylic paint and leave some natural.

All projects on this page by Judy Newman
Photography by Cath Muscat

Marbled Stationery

Transform inexpensive white paper and envelopes into pretty stationery using marbling inks (from art supply stores). Float the ink on a water bath, swirl the water gently with a paint brush then place paper on top of the

Fridge Magnets

MATERIALS
Wooden clothes pegs; tiny timber shapes; acrylic paints; brush; PVA glue; 1 small magnet for each peg.

METHOD
Paint pegs and timber shapes as desired, allow to dry. Glue one shape to the top of one side of each peg and glue a magnet to the back of the peg.

Project by Judy Newman
Photography by Andrew Elton

Lavender Sacks

MATERIALS
For each bag: 22" x 7" fabric piece; thread; lace motif (optional); 1 cup dried lavender; 20" cord or ribbon.

FINISHED SIZE
8" x 6".

METHOD
Fold fabric in half, with right sides facing and 7" edges together. Stitch sides using ½" seam allowance. Stitch 3" hem on top edge. Turn right side out. Handstitch lace motif on one side of bag, if liked. Fill bag with lavender. Tie with cord or ribbon.

Project by Judy Newman
Photography by Andrew Elton

Herb Bath Sachets

Fill an 8"-diameter circle of muslin with ¼ cup of dried lavender, rosemary or lemon verbena. Gather fabric into a sachet and tie with ribbon, leaving a loop for hanging over the bath tap. These can be used once or twice before discarding.

Project by Judy Newman
Photography by Andrew Elton

Beaut Bangles

Buy raw wooden bangles from craft stores and, using acrylic paint, cover them in the latest fashion colors and add dots or stripes for trim.

Project by Judy Newman
Photography by Cath Muscat

Catnip Mouse

MATERIALS
Scrap of floral fabric; polyester fiber filling; dried catnip or catmint; scrap of pink felt; 10" length of silky cord; bell; grey embroidery thread.

FINISHED SIZE
5" long.
Note. ¼" seam allowance is included.

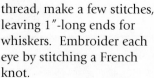

METHOD
Enlarge pattern ❖ then cut out fabric. Place body pieces with right sides facing; stitch around curved edge.

Pin base to body, easing to fit, then stitch, leaving an opening to turn through. Trim seams, clip curves and turn right side out. At tail end, undo a couple of stitches and insert cord end through, handstitch tail securely. Thread the other end of cord through bell and tie a knot to secure.

Fill mouse with dried catnip or catmint and fiber filling, stitch opening closed.

Cut out ears in pink felt and stitch a few gathers along the bottom edge. Stitch ears to mouse. Using 3 strands of embroidery thread, make a few stitches, leaving 1"-long ends for whiskers. Embroider each eye by stitching a French knot.

Project by Christine Moss
Photography by Andrew Elton
❖ *indicates pattern on pattern pages*

Ribbon Streamers

MATERIALS
4" length of cord; 1 brass barrel swivel (from fishing stores); craft glue; 12" length of ½"-diameter dowel; strong thread; 7' length of 1"-wide ribbon.

METHOD
Thread cord through one loop of the brass swivel and glue cord ends over one end of the dowel. Tie thread over cord then wrap cord with thread, glueing ends to secure. Pass one end of ribbon through the other end of the swivel then knot the ribbon. Cut ribbon ends at angle.

Project by Judy Newman
Photography by Andrew Elton

Heart Key Rings

Make these lovely key rings for just a few dollars. Simply attach a heart pendant to a keyring fitting for the quickest project ever!

Project by Judy Newman
Photography by Andrew Elton

long side using running stitch.

Oversew ends together to form a gathered circle.

Make remaining rosettes in the same way and stitch them close together at the top of the headband.

Ponytail and Baby Bows

MATERIALS
Beige (or white) knee-high stockings; thread; 16″ of 2″-wide ribbon

Walnut pin cushions

Cut a 4″ diameter circle and make as for pots; glue ribbon handle inside rim.

Unusual Pin Cushions

MATERIALS
Cotton fabric, fiber filling, rubber band; 4″ narrow ribbon for walnuts; PVA glue; 2″-diameter terracotta pot; walnut shell halves.

METHOD
Pot cushions

Cut a 10″-diameter fabric circle. Take enough polyester fiber to fill pot; place it in center of circle. Pull up the edges of circle and secure with a rubber band. Dab glue inside pot and press fabric ball into pot.

Rosette Headbands

MATERIALS
12″ of 36″-wide cotton fabric; plastic headband; thread.

METHOD
Cut one 15″ x 2″ bias strip (or size to fit headband). With right sides together, join long sides using ¼″ seam allowance; trim and turn right side out. Slip onto headband, turn ends in and stitch to secure.

Cut five 7″ x 2″ strips for gathered circles. For each one, with right sides facing, stitch one end and long sides together. Trim and turn through.

Turn in other end and slipstitch opening closed. Using a double thread, take two tiny stitches to secure and then gather up one

METHOD
Cut off elasticised end of stocking. Overlap edges and stitch together. Cut 12″ of ribbon, fold into a loop and overlap ends; stitch ends to oversewn ends of stocking. Take remaining 4″ piece, fold in half and place over center of ribbon loop to form a bow. Pull up tightly to secure and stitch in place.

For baby bows cut a length of pantyhose to fit baby's head and fold one end over the other to secure. Stitch bow in place.

All projects on this page by Christine Moss Photography by Andrew Elton

139

Nicest Knits & Classic Crochets

Tartan Traveller's Rug

Join the clan and make this terrific rug based on Stewart tartan.

SIZE
Approximately 40" x 60"

MATERIALS
Cleckheaton Country 8-ply (50g/4oz). 14 balls Main Color (MC, we used red); 4 balls 1st Contrast (C1, we used royal blue); 4 balls 2nd Contrast (C2, we used white); 4 balls 3rd Contrast (C3, we used yellow); 7 balls 4th Contrast (C4, we used dark green); and 10 balls 5th Contrast (C5, we used black). One No.5/F crochet hook. Knitter's needle for darning in ends.

Tension
18.5 sts and 9 rows to 4" over patt, using No.5/F hook. Adjust the crochet hook size if necessary.

METHOD
Using MC and hook, make 218ch loosely.

Foundation row. 1dc in 6th ch from hook, *1ch, miss 1ch, 1dc in next ch; rep from * to end...107 spaces.

** **Next row.** Using MC (1sc, 1ch) in first dc, *1 ch, miss 1ch, 1dc in next dc, rep from * to end, working last dc in 4th ch at beg.

Next row. (1sc, 1ch) in first dc, *1ch, miss 1 ch, 1dc in next dc; rep from * to end, working last dc in top of turning ch.

Rep last row in stripes of 6 rows MC, 1 row C1, 2 rows C5, 1 row C3, 1 row C5, 1 row C2, 1 row C5, 3 rows C4, 2 rows MC, 1 row C5, 1 row MC, 1 row C2, 1 row MC, 1 row C5, 2 rows MC, 3 rows C4, 1 row C5, 1 row C2, 1 row C5, 1 row C3, 2 rows C5, 1 row C1.**

Rep from ** to ** twice, then work 8 rows MC.

Fasten off.

WEAVING
Work lengths of ch (the length of the Rug) as folls: 38 in MC, 6 in C1, 9 in C2, 6 in C3, 18 in C4 and 30 in C5.

Thread ch from top to bottom of Rug, beg at side edge and securing at each end in foll order: 5MC, 1C1, 2C5, 1C3, 1C5, 1C2, 1C5, 3C4, 2MC, 1C5, 1MC, 1C2, 1MC, 1C5, 2MC, 3C4, 1C5, 1C2, 1C5, 1C3, 2C5, 1C1; rep twice more ending with 5MC.

EDGING
Using MC, work 1 round crab st evenly around all edges.

Project by Kath Baker
Photography by Stephen Lowe

Lacy Cotton Tunic

This pretty crocheted top is perfect for the spring months.

MEASUREMENTS

To fit size. S (M,L). Fits bust. 30-32(34-36,38-40)". Actual measurements. 45(50,54)". Length. approximately 29" (all sizes). Sleeve length. approximately 16" (all sizes).

MATERIALS

Cotton Soft (50g/2 oz). 14(15,16) balls. One No.4/E crochet hook, or the size needed to give correct tension. Knitter's needle for sewing seams.

TENSION

19.5 sts and 10.5 rows to 4" over dc fabric, using No.4/E hook.

SPECIAL ABBREVIATION

DEC: (yoh, draw up a lp in next st, yoh and draw through first 2 lps on hook) twice, yoh and draw through all 3 lps on hook.

Back and Front

(alike)
Using No.4/E hook, make 133 (147,161) ch.

1st row. Miss 9ch, 1sc in each of next 2ch, *7ch, miss 5ch, 1sc in each of next 2ch; rep from * to last 3ch, 3ch, miss 2ch, 1tr in last ch.

2nd row. 1ch, 1sc in first tr, (1dc, 2ch, 1dc) in each of next 2sc, *1sc in next 7ch lp, (1dc, 2ch, 1dc) in each of next 2sc, rep from * to turning ch lp, miss 3ch, 1sc in next ch of turning ch lp.**

3rd row. 1ch, 1sc in first sc, *(1hdc, 3dc) in next 2ch sp, miss

2dc, (3dc, 1hdc) in next 2ch sp, miss 1dc, 1sc in next sc, rep from * to end.

4th row. 7ch, miss (1sc, 1hdc, 2dc), 1sc in each of next 2dc, *7ch, miss (2dc, 1hdc, 1sc, 1hdc, 2dc), 1sc in each of next 2dc; rep from * to last (2dc, 1hdc, 1sc), 3ch, 1tr in last sc.
Rep 2nd and 3rd rows once.

7th row. 7ch, miss (1sc, 1hdc, 2dc), 1 sc in each of next 2dc, *5ch, miss (2dc, 1hdc, 1sc, 1hdc, 2dc), 1sc in each of next 2dc; rep from * to last (2dc, 1hdc, 1sc), 3ch, 1tr in last sc.

8th row. (1sc, 1ch) in first tr, 2dc in next 3ch sp, 1dc in each of next 2sc, *4dc in next 5ch lp, 1dc in each of next 2sc; rep from * to turning ch lp, 1dc in turning ch lp, 1dc in 4th ch of turning ch lp...109 (121,133) dc, counting (1sc, 1ch) as 1dc.

9th row. (1sc, 1ch) in first dc, 1dc in each dc to end, 1 dc in top of turning ch.

Rep 9th row twice more.

12th row. 1ch, 1sc in first dc, *5ch, miss 3dc, 1sc in next dc, rep from * to end, working last sc in top of turning ch...27 (30,33) lps.

13th row. 5ch, 1sc in first 5ch lp, 13dc in next 5ch lp, *1sc in next 5ch lp, 5ch, 1sc in next 5ch lp, 13dc in next 5ch lp; rep from * to last 5ch lp, 1sc in last 5ch lp, 2ch, 1dc in last sc.

14th row. 1ch, 1sc in first dc, *5ch, miss (1sc, 3dc), 1sc in next dc, miss 2dc, 7dc in next dc, miss 2dc, 1sc in next dc, 5ch, 1sc in next 5ch lp; rep from * to end, working last sc in 3rd ch of turning ch.

15th row. 5ch, 1sc in first 5ch lp, 5ch, miss (1sc, 3dc), 1sc in next dc, *(5ch, 1sc in next 5ch lp) twice, 5ch, miss (1sc, 3dc), 1sc in next dc; rep from * to last 5ch lp, 5ch, 1sc in last 5ch lp, 2ch, 1dc in last sc.

16th row. 3ch, 6dc in first 2ch sp, 1sc in next 5ch lp, 5ch, 1sc in next 5ch lp, *13dc in next 5ch lp, 1sc in next 5ch lp, 5ch, 1sc in next 5ch lp; rep from * to turning ch lp, 6dc in turning ch lp, 1dc in 3rd ch of turning ch.

17th row. 3ch, 3dc in first dc, miss 2dc, 1sc in next dc, 5ch, 1sc in next 5ch lp, 5ch, miss (1sc, 3dc), 1sc in next dc, miss 2dc, *7dc in next dc, miss 2dc, 1sc in next dc, 5ch, 1sc in next 5ch lp, 5ch, miss (1sc, 3dc), 1sc in next dc, miss 2dc, rep from * to turning ch, 4dc in top of turning ch.

18th row. 1ch, 1sc in first dc, *(4ch, 1sc in next 5ch lp) twice, 4ch, miss (1sc, 3dc), 1sc in next dc; rep from * to end, working last sc in top of turning ch.

19th row. (1sc, 1ch) in first sc, *3dc in next 4ch lp, 1dc in next sc; rep from * to end...109 (121,133)dc.

Rep 9th row 3 times.

23rd row. 7ch, miss 2dc, 1sc in each of next 2dc, *7ch, miss 4dc, 1sc in each of next 2dc; rep from * to last 2dc and turning ch, 3ch, miss 2dc, 1tr in top of turning ch...17 (19,21) lps and two half lps.

Rows 2 to 23 incl form patt.

Work a further 39 rows patt, thus ending with an 18th row.

Shape neck. 1st row. (1sc, 1ch) in first sc, (3dc in next 4ch lp, 1dc in next sc) 10 (11,13) times, 1 (3,1) dc in next 4ch lp, turn

Cont on these 42 (48,54) dc.

2nd row. (1sc, 1ch) in first dc, DEC, 1dc in each dc to end, 1dc in top of turning ch.

3rd row. (1sc, 1ch) in first dc, 1dc in each dc to last 2dc and turning ch, DEC, 1dc in top of turning ch.

4th row. As 2nd row...39 (45,51) dc.

5th row. 7ch, miss 2dc, 1sc in each of next 2dc, (7ch, miss 4dc,

1sc in each of next 2dc) 5 (6,7) times, 3ch, miss 4dc, 1tr in top of turning ch.

6th row. 1ch, 1sc in first tr, (1dc, 2ch, 1dc) in each of next 2sc, patt to end.

7th row. Patt to end...6 (7,8) patts.

8th row. Sl st across first 5 sts, 1ch, 1sc in next dc *5ch, miss (2dc, 1hdc, 1sc, 1hdc, 2dc), 1sc in each of next 2dc*; rep from * to * 4 (5,6) times, 3ch, 1tr in last sc.

Fasten off.

With right side facing, miss next five (six, five) 4ch lps at center,

join yarn with a sl st in next 4ch lp, 1ch, work [1sc, 1ch, 0 (2,0) dc] in same 4ch lp as sl st, *1dc in next sc, 3dc in next 4ch lp; rep from * to last sc, 1dc in last sc.

Cont on these 42 (48,54) dc.

2nd row. (1sc, 1ch) in first dc, 1dc in each dc to last 2dc and turning ch, DEC, 1dc in top of turning ch.

3rd row. (1sc, 1ch) in first dc, DEC, 1dc in each dc to end, 1dc in top of turning ch.

4th row. As 2nd row...39 (45,51)dc.

5th row. 7ch, miss 4dc, 1sc in each of next 2dc, (7ch, miss 4dc, 1sc in each of next 2dc) 5(6,7) times, 3ch, miss 2dc, 1tr in top of turning ch.

6th row. 1ch, 1sc in first tr, *(1dc, 2ch, 1dc) in each of next 2sc, 1sc in next 7ch lp*; rep from * to * 5(6,7) times, working last sc in 4th ch of turning ch lp, turn.

7th row. Patt to end...6 (7,8) patts.

8th row. 7ch, miss (1sc, 1hdc, 2dc), *1sc in each of next 2dc, 5ch, miss (2dc, 1hdc, 1sc, 1hdc, 2dc)*; rep from * to * 4 (5,6) times, 1sc in next dc.

Fasten off.

Sleeves

Using No.4/E hook, make 63ch. Work as given for Back and Front to **.

3rd row. 7ch, (1hdc, 3dc) in next 2ch sp, miss 2dc, (3dc, 1hdc) in next 2ch sp, patt to last sc, 3ch, 1tr in last sc.

4th row. 1ch, 1sc in first tr, 7ch, miss (3ch, 1hdc, 2dc), 1sc in each of next 2dc, 7ch, patt to last (2dc, 1hdc and turning ch lp), 7ch, miss (2dc, 1hdc, 3ch), 1sc in next ch of turning ch lp.

5th row. 5ch, 1dc in first sc, 1sc in next 7ch lp, (1dc, 2ch, 1dc) in each of next 2sc, patt to last sc, (1dc, 2ch, 1dc) in last sc.

6th row. 3ch, (3dc, 1hdc) in first 2ch sp, miss 1dc, 1sc in next sc, patt to turning ch lp, (1hdc, 3dc) in turning ch lp, 1dc in 3rd ch of turning ch lp.

7th row. 1ch, 1sc in each of first 2dc, *5ch, miss (2dc, 1hdc, 1sc,

1hdc, 2dc), 1sc in each of next 2dc; rep from * to end, working last sc in top of turning ch.

8th row. (1sc, 1ch, 1dc) in first sc, 1dc in next sc, *4dc in next 5ch lp, 1dc in each of next 2sc; rep from * to end...57dc.

9th row. (1sc, 1ch, 1dc) in first dc, 1dc in each dc to turning ch, 2dc in top of turning ch.

10th row. (1sc, 1ch) in first dc, 1dc in each dc to end, 1dc in top of turning ch.

11th row. As 9th row...61dc.

12th row. 1ch, 1sc in first dc, *5ch, miss 3dc, 1sc in next dc; rep from * to end, working last sc in top of turning ch...15lps.

13th row. 8ch, 1sc in first 5ch lp, 13dc in next 5ch lp, 1sc in next 5ch lp, 5ch, patt to last 5ch lp, 1sc in last 5ch lp, 5ch, 1dc in last sc.

14th row. 5ch, 1sc in first 5ch lp, 5ch miss (1sc, 3dc), 1sc in next dc, miss 2dc, 7dc in next dc, patt to turning ch lp, 5ch, 1sc in turning ch lp, 2ch, 1dc in 3rd ch of turning ch lp.

15th row. 1ch, 1sc in first dc, 5ch, 1sc in next 5ch lp, 5ch, miss (1sc, 3dc), 1sc in next dc, 5ch, patt to turning ch lp, 5ch, 1sc in 3rd ch of turning ch lp.

16th row. (1sc, 1ch) in first sc, 13dc in first 5ch lp, 1sc in next 5ch lp, 5ch, patt to last 5ch lp, 13dc in last 5ch lp, 1dc in last sc.

17th row. 4ch, miss first 4dc, 1sc in next dc, miss 2dc, 7dc in next dc, patt to last 13dc and turning ch, 5ch, miss (1sc, 3dc), 1sc in next dc, miss 2dc, 7dc in next dc, miss 2dc, 1sc in next dc, 1tr in top of turning ch.

18th row. 1ch, 1sc in first tr, 4ch, miss (1sc, 3dc), 1sc in next dc, 4ch, patt to turning ch, 4ch, 1sc in top of turning ch.

19th row. (1sc, 1ch) in first sc, *3dc in next 4ch lp, 1dc in next sc;

rep from * to end...69dc.

Rep rows 9 to 11 incl once...73dc.

23rd row. 7ch, miss 2dc, 1sc in each of next 2dc, *7ch, miss 4dc, 1sc in each of next 2dc; rep from * to last 2dc and turning ch, 3ch, miss 2dc, 1tr in top of turning ch...11lps and two half lps.

Rep rows 2 to 8 incl once more...81dc.

Rep rows 9 to 11 incl once more...85dc.

Rep rows 12 to 18 incl once more, having 21lps after 12th row.

41st row. (1sc, 1ch, 1dc) in first sc, 3dc in next 4ch lp, *1dc in next sc, 3dc in next 4ch lp; rep from * to last sc, 2dc in last sc...95dc.

42nd row. (1sc, 1ch, 1dc) in first sc, 1dc in each dc to turning ch, 2dc in top of turning ch...97dc.

Shape top. 1st row. Sl st across first 6dc, 1sc in each of next 6dc, 1hdc in each of next 6dc, 1dc in each of next 61dc, 1hdc in each of next 6dc, 1sc in each of next 6dc, turn.

2nd row. Sl st across first 18 sts, 1sc in each of next 6dc, 1hdc in each of next 6dc, 1dc in each of next 25dc, 1hdc in each of next 6dc, 1sc in each of next 6dc, sl st across next 18 sts. Fasten off.

TO MAKE UP

Tie markers to sides of Back and Front 10" down from shoulder edge. Using a flat seam, join shoulder edge. Sew in Sleeves evenly between markers, placing center of Sleeves to shoulder seams. Join side and Sleeve seams. With right side facing and using No.4/E hook, work 6 rounds sc evenly around neck, lower edge of body and Sleeves, inc and dec where necessary to keep work flat. Fasten off.

Project by Cleckheaton
Photography by Andre Martin

Tea-time Trimmings

A beaded milk jug cover and a pretty border for cloths are as much a hit today as they were 60 years ago.

Milk Jug Cover

MEASUREMENTS
Approximately 8″ diameter (from point to point).

MATERIALS
One ball white Coats Mercer Crochet Cotton, ticket 20 and small ball Coats Mercer Crochet Cotton, variegated. Twelve china or glass jug cover beads. One No.10 crochet hook. Petal Porcelain or craft glue (optional). Plastic thimble (optional).

SPECIAL ABBREVIATIONS
Bbl: bobble; **GR:** group.

METHOD
Using hook and white cotton, make 10ch, join with sl st to form ring.

1st row. 4ch, 35tr into ring, join with sl st in 4th ch.

2nd row. 5ch, *miss 1tr, 1dc in next tr, 2ch; rep from * to end, join with sl st in 3rd of 5ch.

3rd row. 1 sl st in first sp, 3ch, 4dc in same sp, drop lp from hook, insert hook into back of 3rd ch, draw dropped lp through firmly (Bbl formed), *5ch, 5dc in next sp, drop loop from hook, insert hook into back of 1st dc, draw dropped lp through (another Bbl formed); rep from * ending with 2ch, 1dc into top of first Bbl.

4th row. *6ch, 1sc in next lp; rep from * ending with 3ch, 1dc into

dc of previous row.

5th row. *7ch, 1sc in next lp; rep from * all around, ending with 3ch, 1tr into dc of previous row.

6th row. *7ch, 1sc in next lp, 11tr in next lp, 1sc in next lp; rep from *, omitting 1sc at end of last rep, 1 sl st in tr of previous row.

7th row. 1 sl st to center of next lp, 1sc in same lp, *7ch, 1sc in next tr, (2ch, miss 1tr, 1sc in next tr) 5 times, 7ch, 1sc in next lp; rep from * ending last rep with 3ch, 1tr in first sc.

8th row. 7ch, 1sc in next lp, *7ch, (1Bbl in next 2ch lp, 2ch) 4 times, 1Bbl in next 2ch lp, (7ch, 1sc in next lp) twice; rep from *, omitting (7ch, 1sc) twice at end of last rep, 3ch, 1tr in tr of previous row.

9th and 10th rows. As 8th row, having 1Bbl less on each pineapple and 1 lp more between each row (3Bbls and 5 lps on 10th row).

11th row. *(7ch, 1sc) in next 4 lps, 4ch, 2tr into 2ch lp, 4ch, 2tr in next 2ch lp, 4ch, 1sc in next lp; rep from * to last 2tr, 2ch, 1dc in

the first 7ch lp.

12th row. *(7ch, 1sc) in next 5 lps, 3ch, 1tr in top of each tr of last row leaving last lp of each on needle, yarn over hook, pull through to form GR, 3ch, 1GR in middle 2ch of 4ch lp, 2ch, 1GR in next 2tr, 3ch, 1sc in next lp; rep from * to last GR, 1dc in first 7ch lp.

13th row. *(7ch, 1sc) in next 5 lps, 7ch, 1sc in top of first GR, (5ch, 1sc) in each of next 2GR; rep from * to last 5ch; substitute for this 2ch, 1dc.

14th row. (7ch, 1sc) in each lp, ending 3ch, 1tr in last lp.

15th row. 4ch, 5tr in same lp, 1sc in next lp, *(7ch, 1sc) in next 2 lps, 11tr in next lp, 1sc in next lp; rep from * to last lp, 5tr in last lp, join with sl st to top of 4ch at beg. Break off yarn and fasten off securely.

Join in variegated thread on which 12 beads have been threaded. Join should be at right of any fan.

16th row. *1sc in each of first 6tr, 6ch, slide one bead over ch above 6th tr, 1sc in same tr, 1sc in each of next 5tr, (1sc in sc,

7sc in lp) twice; rep from * to end, join with sl st, fasten off.

Decorative Cup and Saucer (optional)

Saucer

1st row. Join variegated cotton into foundation ring, work (1 sc, 1ch) into every 2nd st. Join with sl st.

2nd row. Sl st into first ch sp, 4ch (as tr), 1tr into same sp, 2tr into each sp to end. Join with sl st.

3rd row. 3ch, *miss next tr, 1sc in next st, 2ch; rep from * to end, sl st to join. Fasten off securely.

Cup

1st row. Join variegated thread in foundation row, work 1sc in every 2nd st, join with sl st.

2nd row. 3ch as first dc, *2dc into next sc, 1dc into next sc; rep from * to end, sl st to join.

3rd row. 3ch as dc, 1dc in each dc; sl st to join.

4th and 5th rows. As 2nd and 3rd rows. Do not break off yarn.

Handle. 8ch, 1 sl st into side of Cup (2nd row) turn, 10sc into lp, sl st into 1st ch. Fasten off securely.

TO FINISH

Coat Cup and Saucer with Petal Porcelain or craft glue to stiffen, and allow to dry using a plastic thimble to hold the Cup to the desired shape.

Cloth Edging

MEASUREMENTS

Edging can be worked to any required width and length, but it may be necessary to work extra ch either side of sc to keep work flat.

MATERIALS

Coats Mercer Crochet Cotton, ticket 20 (quantity will depend on size of cloth). One No. 6 crochet hook, or size needed to give correct tension. Firm cotton fabric to required size.

Tension

20sc to 2" when worked into fabric.

METHOD

Fold a 2" hem along four sides of cloth. Stitch hem neatly in place and press flat.

1st rnd. With right side of cloth facing and working over hemmed edge, insert No.6 hook into any corner, 1ch, work in sc over hem (placing approximately 20sc to each 2") along first side, 2sc in corner, then cont in this manner around cloth to end, finishing with 1sc in same sp as 1ch. Join with a sl st.

2nd rnd. 5ch, miss 2sc, 1dc in next sc, *2ch, miss 2sc, 1dc in next sc; rep from * to end, join with sl st to 3rd of 5ch.

3rd rnd. 3ch, (1dc, 2ch, 2dc) in same sp, 4ch, miss one 2ch sp, (2dc, 2ch, 2dc) in next 2ch sp (called shell), *4ch, miss two 2ch sps, shell in next sp*, rep from * to * to within one sp of next corner, 4ch, miss 1sp, shell in next sp, miss 1sp. Cont from * to * to next corner, turn corner with 1sp between shells and proceed in this manner to within 1sp of end, 4ch, join with sl st to top of 3ch.

4th rnd. Sl st to center of first shell, work shell in center of shell, 2ch, 1sc in 4ch sp, 2ch, *shell in next shell, 2ch, 1sc in 4ch sp, 2ch, rep from * to end, join with sl st.

5th rnd. *Shell in shell, 2ch, 1sc in sc, 2ch; rep from * to end, join with sl st.

6th rnd. Into first shell work *2dc, 5ch, sl st back into 4th of 5ch (picot formed), 1ch, 2dc in same shell, 3ch, 1sc in sc, 3ch; rep from * to end, join with sl st. Fasten off.

Projects by Norma Corney and Roe Borland
Photography by Andre Martin

Timeless Tunic

Light, yet comfortable and roomy, this classic is perfect for those warm, sunny days.

MEASUREMENTS

To fit size: S (M,L). Fits bust. 30-32 (34-36,38-40)". Actual measurement. 42 (47,52)". Length. approximately 28" (all sizes).

MATERIALS

Cotton Soft (50g/2oz). 10(11,12) balls. One No.5/F crochet hook, or the size needed to give correct tension.

Tension

One patt to 2½" in width over Body Patt.

Back

Make 98 (110,122)ch.

1st row. (wrong side). Miss 1ch, 1sc in each ch to end...97 (109,121)sc.

2nd row. 1ch, 1sc in each sc to end.

Rep 2nd row 4 times.

Beg Body Patt. 1st row. (wrong side). 3ch, miss first sc, *1sc in next sc, 3ch, miss 1sc, 1sc in next sc, 2ch, miss 2sc, (2dc,2ch,2dc) in next sc, 2ch, miss 2sc, (1sc in next sc, 3ch, miss 1sc) twice; rep from * to end, working section in brackets at end of last rep once only instead of twice, then work 1sc in next sc, 1ch, 1dc in last sc.

2nd row. 1ch, 1sc in first dc, *3ch, 1sc in next 3ch lp, 2ch, miss next 2ch sp, (2dc,2ch) 3 times in next 2ch sp, miss next 2ch sp, 1sc in next 3ch lp, 3ch, 1sc in next 3ch lp; rep from * to end.

3rd row. *3ch, 1sc in next 3ch lp, 2ch, miss next 2ch sp, (2dc,2ch,2dc) in next 2ch sp, 1ch, (2dc,2ch,2dc) in next 2ch sp, 2ch, miss next 2ch sp, 1sc in next 3ch lp; rep from * to end, 1dc in last sc.

4th row. 1ch, 1sc in first dc, *2ch, miss next 2ch sp, (2dc,2ch,2dc) in next 2ch sp, 2ch, 1sc in next 1ch sp, 2ch, (2dc,2ch,2dc) in next 2ch sp, 2ch, miss next 2ch sp, 1sc in next 3ch lp; rep from * to end.

5th row. 6ch, miss first 2ch sp, *2dc in next 2ch sp, 2ch, 1sc in next 2ch sp, 3ch, 1sc in next 2ch sp, 2ch, 2dc in next 2ch sp, 1ch, miss next two 2ch sps; rep from * to end, missing one 2ch sp instead of two at end of last rep, 1dtr in last sc.

6th row. 4ch, 2dc in first dtr, 1ch, miss next 2ch sp, 7dc in next 3ch lp, 1ch, miss next 2ch sp, *(2dc,2ch,2dc) in next 1ch sp, 1ch, miss next 2ch sp, 7dc in next 3ch lp, 1ch, miss next 2ch sp; rep from * to end, (2dc,1ch,1dc) in top of turning ch.

7th row. 5ch, 2dc in first 1ch sp, *2ch, miss next 1ch sp, (1sc in next dc, 3ch, miss 1dc) 3 times, 1sc in next dc, 2ch, miss next 1ch sp, (2dc,2ch,2dc) in next 2ch sp; rep from * to end, ending last rep with (2dc,2ch,1dc) in turning ch lp instead of (2dc,2ch,2dc) in next 2ch sp.

8th row. 3ch, (1dc,2ch,2dc) in first 2ch sp, *2ch, miss next 2ch sp, (1sc in next 3ch lp, 3ch) twice, 1sc in next 3ch lp, miss next 2ch sp, (2ch, 2dc) 3 times in next 2ch sp; rep from * to end, omitting (2ch, 2dc) 3 times in next 2 ch sp at end of last rep and working (2ch, 2dc) twice into turning ch lp instead.

9th row. 3ch, *(2dc,2ch,2dc) in next 2ch sp, 2ch, miss next 2ch sp, 1sc in next 3ch lp, 3ch, 1sc in next 3ch lp, 2ch, miss next 2ch sp, (2dc,2ch,2dc) in next 2ch sp, 1ch; rep from * to end, omitting 1ch at end of last rep and working 1dc in top of turning ch instead.

10th row. 1ch, 1sc in first dc, *2ch, (2dc,2ch,2dc) in next 2ch sp, 2ch, miss next 2ch sp, 1sc in next 3ch lp, 2ch, miss next 2ch sp, (2dc,2ch,2dc) in next 2ch sp, 2ch, 1sc in next 1ch sp; rep from * to end, working last sc in top of turning ch instead of 1ch sp.

11th row. 4ch, *1sc in next 2ch sp, 2ch,2dc in next 2ch sp, 1ch, miss next two 2ch sps, 2dc in next 2ch sp, 2ch, 1sc in next 2ch sp, 3ch; rep from * to end, omitting 3ch at end of last rep and working 1ch, 1dc in last sc instead.

12th row. 3ch, 1dc in first dc, 2dc in next 1ch sp, *1ch, miss next 2ch sp,

(2dc,2ch,2dc) in next 1ch sp, 1ch, miss next 2ch sp, 7dc in next 3ch lp; rep from * to end, ending last rep with 4dc in turning ch lp instead of 7dc in next 3ch lp.

13th row. (3ch, miss 1dc, 1sc in next dc) twice, *2ch, miss next 1ch sp, (2dc,2ch,2dc) in next 2ch sp, 2ch, miss next 1ch sp, (1sc in next dc, 3ch, miss 1dc) 3 times, 1sc in next dc; rep from * to end, working last section in brackets once instead of 3 times at end of last rep, then working 1sc in next dc, 1ch, 1dc in top of turning ch.

Rows 2 to 13 incl form Body Patt. Work a further 46 rows Body Patt, thus ending with an 11th row.

Beg Yoke Patt. 1st row. (1sc, 1ch) in first dc, miss next 1ch sp, *(2dc,2ch,2dc) in next 2ch sp, (2dc,2ch,2dc) in next 1ch sp, (2dc,2ch,2dc) in next 2ch sp, miss next 3ch lp; rep from * to end, omitting miss 3ch lp at end of last rep and working 1dc in 3rd ch of turning ch...24 (27,30) patt.

2nd row. (1sc,1ch) in first dc, (2dc,2ch,2dc) in each 2ch sp to end, 1dc in top of turning ch.

2nd row forms Yoke Patt.**

Work a further 4 rows Yoke Patt.

Shape neck. 1st row. (1sc, 1ch) in first dc, (2dc,2ch,2dc) in each of next 8 (9,10) 2ch sps, 2dc in next 2ch sp, turn.

2nd row. (1sc,1ch) in first dc, (2dc,2ch,2dc) in each 2ch sp to end, 1dc in top of turning ch.

3rd row. Patt to last 2ch sp, 2dc in last 2ch sp, 1ch, 1dc in top of turning ch.

Shape shoulder. Next row. (1sc,1ch) in first dc, 1ch, 2dc in first ch sp, (2dc,2ch,2dc) in each of next 2 (3,3) 2ch sps, (2hdc,2ch,2hdc) in each of next 3 (3,4) 2ch sps, (2ch,1sc in next 2ch sp) twice.

Fasten off.

With right side facing, miss next 6

(7,8) 2ch sps at center and join yarn with a sl st in next 2ch sp (1sc, 1ch, 1dc) in same place as sl st, (2dc, 2ch, 2dc) in each 2ch sp to end, 1dc in top of turning ch.

2nd row. (1sc,1ch) in first dc, (2dc,2ch,2dc) in each 2ch sp to end, 1dc in top of turning ch.

3rd row. (1sc,1ch) in first dc, 1ch, 2dc in next 2ch sp, (2dc,2ch,2dc) in each 2ch sp to end, 1dc in top of turning ch.

Shape shoulder. Next row. Sl st in each of first 3dc, (1sc in next 2ch sp, 2ch) twice, (2hdc,2ch,2hdc) in each of next 3 (3,4) 2ch sps, (2dc,2ch,2dc) in each of next 2 (3,3) 2ch sps, (2dc,1ch,1dc) in turning ch lp.

Fasten off.

Front

Work as for Back to **.

Shape neck. 1st row. (1sc,1ch) in first dc, (2dc,2ch,2dc) in each of next 9 (10,11) 2ch sps, 2dc in next 2ch sp, turn.

2nd row. (1sc,1ch) in first dc (2dc,2ch,2dc) in each 2ch sp to end, 1dc in top of turning ch.

3rd row. Patt to last 2ch sp, 2dc in last 2ch sp, 1ch, 1dc in top of turning ch.

4th row. (1sc,1ch,1dc) in first ch sp, (2dc,2ch,2dc) in each 2ch sp to end, 1dc in top of turning ch.

5th row. Patt to last 2ch sp, (2dc,2ch,2dc) in last 2ch sp, 1dc in top of turning ch.

6th row. (1sc,1ch) in first dc, 1ch, 2dc in next 2ch sp, (2dc,2ch,2dc) in each 2ch sp to end, 1dc in top of turning ch.

7th row. (1sc,1ch) in first dc, (2dc,2ch,2dc) in each 2ch sp to end, (2dc,1ch,1dc) in turning ch lp, turn.

Shape shoulder. Complete as given for first side of Back. With right side facing, miss next 4(5,6)

2ch sps at center and join yarn with a sl st in next 2ch sp, (1sc,1ch,1dc) in same place as sl st, (2dc,2ch,2dc) in each 2ch sp to end, 1dc in top of turning ch.

2nd row. Patt to last 2ch sp, (2dc,2ch,2dc) in last 2ch sp, 1dc in top of turning ch.

3rd row. (1sc,1ch) in first dc, 1ch, 2dc in next 2ch sp, (2dc,2ch,2dc) in each 2ch sp to end, 1dc in top of turning ch.

4th row. (1sc,1ch) in first dc, (2dc,2ch,2dc) in each 2ch sp to end, 2dc in turning ch lp, turn.

5th row. (1sc,1ch) in first dc, (2dc,2ch,2dc) in each 2ch sp to end, 1dc in top of turning ch.

6th row. Patt to last 2ch sp, 2dc in last 2ch sp, 1ch, 1dc in top of turning ch.

7th row. (1sc, 1ch) in first dc, 1ch, 2dc in next ch sp, (2dc,2ch,2dc) in each 2ch sp to end, 1dc in top of turning ch.

Shape shoulder. Complete as given for second side of Back.

Neckband

Join right shoulder seam. With right side facing, work 6 rows sc evenly around neck, dec where necessary to keep work flat. Fasten off.

Armbands

Join left shoulder and Neckband seam. Tie a marker 9½ (10, 10½)″ down from beg of shoulder shaping on side edges of Back and Front to mark armholes. With right side facing, work 6 rows sc evenly between markers, dec where necessary to keep work flat. Fasten off.

TO MAKE UP
Join side seams.

Project by Cleckheaton
Photography by Scott Cameron

Hooked On Colour!

Crochet motifs in bright, bold colors, then join the squares and create a jacket!

MEASUREMENTS
To fit bust. 30-36". Garment measures. 43". Length to shoulder. 21". Sleeve seam. 17" (when sewn in).

MATERIALS
Patons 8-ply (50g/2 oz). 8 balls Main Color (MC, black); 4 balls 1st Contrast (C1, electric blue); 3 balls 2nd Contrast (C2, rouge); 3 balls 3rd Contrast (C3, gold); 3 balls 4th Contrast (C4, new pink); 3 balls 5th Contrast (C5, bright red); 3 balls 6th Contrast (C6, fleece). One No.4/E crochet hook. Tapestry needle for sewing motifs tog. Seven buttons.

Tension
Each large motif measures 4½" square. Each small motif measures 2" square. This garment has been designed to be worked on a smaller hook than usually recommended, and the Jacket will soften with wear.

SPECIAL ABBREVIATIONS
dc3tog: (yoh, draw up a loop in next sp, yoh and draw through first 2 loops on hook) 3 times, yoh and draw through all 4 loops on hook; **dc4tog:** (yoh, draw up a loop in next sp, yoh and draw through first 2 loops on hook) 4 times, yoh and draw through all 5 loops on hook.

Traditional Square (TS)

Using C2 and hook, make 4ch, join with a sl st to form a ring.

1st rnd. 5ch (counts as 1dc and 2ch), (3dc into ring, 2ch) 3 times, 2dc into ring, sl st in 3rd ch of 5ch.

2nd rnd. Using C2, sl st into first 2ch sp (do not break off C2), using C3, 3ch, (2dc, 2ch, 3dc) all in same ch sp as sl st, *1ch, (3dc, 2ch, 3dc) all in next ch sp; rep from * to end, sl st in 3rd ch at beg of rnd, sl st across 2dc and into next ch sp (do not break off C3).

3rd rnd. Using C2, 3ch, (2dc, 2ch, 3dc) all in same ch sp as sl st, 1ch, 3dc in next ch sp, 1ch, *(3dc, 2ch, 3dc) all in next corner ch sp, 1ch, 3dc in next ch sp, 1ch; rep from * to end, sl st in 3rd ch at beg of rnd, sl st across 2dc and into next ch sp.

4th rnd. Using C3, 3ch, (1dc, 2ch, 2dc) all in same ch sp as sl st, *1dc in each dc and ch to next corner sp, (2dc, 2ch, 2dc) all in corner ch sp, rep from * twice more, 1dc in each dc, ch and sl st to end, sl st in 3rd ch at beg of rnd, sl st across 1dc and into next ch sp...60dc, counting 3ch as 1dc.

Break off C3.

5th rnd. Using C2, work as for 4th rnd (noting there will be extra dc made).

Break off C2.

6th rnd. Using MC, work as for 4th rnd (noting there will be extra dc made).

Fasten off.

Make another 25 TS motifs, changing colors from above as indicated below.

Make 3 motifs more using colors as above.

Make 2 motifs, using C3 in place of C2, and C5 in place of C3.

Make 2 motifs, using C1 in place of C2, and C5 in place of C3.

Make 4 motifs, using C5 in place of C2, and C1 in place of C3.

Make 1 motif, using C1 in place of C2, and C4 in place of C3.

Make 2 motifs, using C4 in place of C2, and C2 in place of C3.

Make 1 motif, using C6 in place of C2, and C5 in place of C3.

Make 3 motifs, using C3 in place of C2, and C1 in place of C3.

Make 2 motifs, using C6 in place of C3.

Make 4 motifs, using C1 in place of C2, and C2 in place of C3.

Make 1 motif, using C6 in place of C2, and C4 in place of C3.

Wheel Motif (WM)

Using C5 and hook, make 6ch, join with a sl st to form a ring.

1st rnd. 5ch (counts as 1dc and 2ch), (1dc into ring, 2ch) 7 times, sl st in 3rd ch of 5ch...8 sps.

2nd rnd. 3ch, work dc3tog into next sp (counts as dc4tog), (5ch, work dc4tog into next sp) 7 times, 5ch, sl st in top of first cluster, then sl st into next ch sp. Do not break off C5).

3rd rnd. Using C3, 3ch, 5dc into same place as sl st, *6dc into next ch sp, 4ch, 6dc into next ch sp; rep from * to last ch sp, 6dc into last ch sp, 4ch, sl st in 3rd ch at beg of rnd.

4th rnd. Using C5, 3ch, *1dc in each dc to corner ch sp, (2dc, 2ch, 2dc) all in corner ch sps; rep from * all around edges, then sl st in 3rd ch at beg of rnd.

5th rnd. Using C5, work as for 4th rnd.

Break off C5.

6th rnd. Using MC, work as for 4th rnd.

Fasten off.

Make another 13 WMs, changing colors from above as indicated below.

Make 3 motifs more using colors as above.

Make 2 motifs, using C6 in place of C5, and C5 in place of C3.

Make 2 motifs, using C4 in place of C5, and C2 in place of C3.

Make 2 motifs, using C2 in place of C5, and C4 in place of C3.

Make 2 motifs, using C3 in place of C5, and C6 in place of C3.

Make 2 motifs, using C1 in place of C5, and C4 in place of C3.

Cornish Motif (CM)

Using C1 and hook, make 6ch, join with a sl st to form a ring.

1st rnd. 3ch, 5dc into ring, picot, *6dc into ring, picot, rep from * twice more, join with a sl st in 3rd ch at beg of rnd. Fasten off.

Join C2 in any picot.

2nd rnd. 3ch, (5dc, picot, 6dc) in same picot, 1ch, *(6dc, picot, 6dc) in next picot, 1ch, rep from * twice more, join with a sl st in 3rd ch at beg of rnd.

Fasten off.

Join C6 in any picot.

3rd rnd. 3ch, 13dc in same picot, 5dc in next 1ch sp, *14dc in next picot, 5dc in next 1ch sp, rep from * twice more, sl st in 3rd ch at beg of rnd.

Break off C6 and join in C1.

4th rnd. 4ch, *1dc in next st, 1hdc in next st, 1sc in each of next 4 sts, 3hdc in next st, 1sc in each of next 4 sts, 1hdc in next st, 1dc in next st, 1tr in next st, 1dc in each of next 4 sts, 1tr in next st; rep from * to end, omitting last tr in last st, sl st in 4th ch at beg of rnd.

5th rnd. 2ch, *1hdc in each st to corner sts, 3hdc in corner sts; rep from * all around edges, sl st in 2nd ch at beg of rnd.

Break off C1 and join in MC.

6th rnd. As 5th rnd.

Fasten off.

Make another 21 CMs, changing colors from above as indicated below.

Make 1 motif more using colors as above.

Make 4 motifs, using C5 in place of C1, C3 in place of C2, and C2 in place of C6.

Make 1 motif, using C6 in place of C1, C3 in place of C2, and C2 in place of C6.

Make 4 motifs, using C6 in place of C1, C5 in place of C2, and C3 in place of C6.

Make 2 motifs, using C6 in place of C1, C3 in place of C2, and C5 in place of C6.

Make 3 motifs, using C3 in place of C2.

Make 4 motifs, using C4 in place of C1, C5 in place of C2, and C1 in place of C6.

Make 2 motifs, using C6 in place of C1, C1 in place of C2, and C4 in place of C6.

Square Treble (ST)

Using C4 and hook, make 4ch, join with a sl st to form a ring.

1st rnd. 5ch (counts as 1dc and 2ch), (3dc into ring, 2ch) 3 times, 2dc into ring, sl st into 3rd ch of 5ch, sl st across 1dc and into corner ch sp. Do not break off C4.

Join in C2.

2nd rnd. 3ch, (1dc, 2ch, 2dc) all in same ch sp as sl st, 1dc in each dc across side of square, *(2dc, 2ch, 2dc) all in corner ch sp, 1dc in each dc across side of square; rep from * to end, sl st in 3rd ch at beg of rnd, sl st across 1dc and into next ch sp.

3rd rnd. As 2nd rnd.

Break off C2.

4th and 5th rnds. Using C4, as 2nd rnd.

Break off C4.

6th rnd. Using MC, as 2nd rnd. Fasten off.

Make another 15 ST motifs, changing colors from above as indicated below.

Make 3 motifs more using colors as above.

Make 2 motifs, using C6 in place of C2.

Make 2 motifs, using C2 in place of C4, and C1 in place of C2.

Make 2 motifs, using C5 in place of C4, and C1 in place of C2.

Make 4 motifs, using C3 in place of C4.

Make 2 motifs, using C3 in place of C4, and C1 in place of C2.

Half Square (HS)

Using C2 and hook, make 4ch, join with sl st to form a ring.

1st rnd. As 1st rnd of Traditional Square.

2nd rnd. Using C4, as 2nd rnd of Traditional Square.

Break off C2 and C4, join in MC.

3rd rnd. 2ch, *1hdc in each dc and ch along sides of motif, (2hdc, 2ch, 2hdc) in each corner ch sp; rep from * all around motif, sl st in 2nd ch at beg of rnd.

Fasten off.

Make another 3 HS motifs, changing colors from above as indicated below.

Make 1 motif, using C5 in place of C2, and C6 in place of C4.

Make 1 motif, using C3 in place of C4.

Make 1 motif, using C1 in place of C2, and C5 in place of C4.

To make up
Using MC, sew motifs tog with a flat-stitch, following charts and placing colors as desired. Sew in Sleeves. Join side and Sleeve seams.

Lower Band

With right side facing, using MC and hook, work 132sc evenly along lower edge of Jacket.

1st row. 1ch, 1sc in each sc to end.

Rep 1st row until lower band measures 1¾", working last row on wrong side.

Fasten off.

Cuffs

With right side facing, using MC and hook, work 1 rnd of sc evenly along cuff edge, noting to miss every 2nd st, so that cuff is beg to gather.

Next rnd. Work 1 rnd of sc, dec down to 50sc.

Work in sc until Cuff measures 2". Fasten off.

Front Bands and Neckband

With right side facing, using MC and hook and beg at lower edge of Right Front, work 1 row sc evenly along Right Front, around neck edge and along Left Front, dec where necessary to keep work flat. Work 3 rows sc evenly around same edges, do not fasten off.

Right Front

Work 4 rows sc evenly along Right Front only, working seven 3ch-buttonholes evenly spaced in first of these rows. Fasten off.

Left Front

With right side facing, join MC at neck of Left Front and work as Right Front, omitting buttonholes. Fasten off. Sew on buttons.

Photography by Scott Cameron

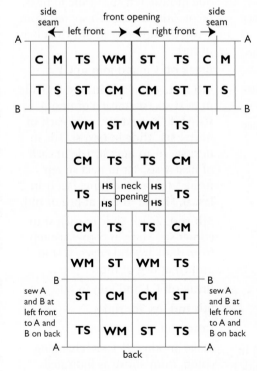

Tartan Rug In Tunisian Crochet

A bright and colorful rug which is so quick and simple, made in a cross between knitting and crochet.

Tunisian crochet is worked with a special hook, rather like a long crochet hook with a knob on one end. It produces a looser stitch than knitting or crochet, but a denser fabric. The fabric is reversible, but is worked with the same side facing throughout.

The first half of the row is worked from right to left, making and storing loops on the hook. The second half is worked back from left to right, drawing through these loops in a cast-off fashion, called 'discard-return'. These two steps are counted as one row.

Before commencing the rug, we suggest you test your tension and become acquainted with the method. To do this, make 17ch loosely and work the foundation row and a further 6 rows in Tunisian Simple patt. This sample should measure 5" x 2", not including the foundation row.

MEASUREMENTS

Approximately 34" x 35", excluding fringe.

MATERIALS

Cleckheaton Country 8-ply (50g/2oz): 3 balls red, 3 balls yellow, 3 balls blue, 3 balls green, 4 balls black and 3 balls white. One No.I/9 Tunisian crochet hook (14" long). Tapestry needle. 3"-wide stiff cardboard for fringe.

Tension

17 sts to 5" and 6 rows to 2". Please check your tension carefully and adjust hook size if necessary.

METHOD

Using hook and red yarn, make 108ch fairly loosely.

Foundation row. Miss first ch from hook, hook into next ch, yoh and draw through (2 sts on hook), *hook into next ch, yoh, and draw through (3 sts on hook). Rep from * to end of ch (108 sts on hook, counting starting loop as first st).

Do not turn.

Discard-return. With same side of work facing, and working from left to right, yoh and draw yarn through end st on hook, *yoh and draw yarn through next 2 loops. Rep from * to end, leaving first st on hook.

**Tunisian Simple patt. Miss first vertical bar formed by previous row, *hook under next vertical bar, yoh and draw yarn through (2 sts on hook). Rep from * to end (108 sts on hook).

Discard-return. Work as given above.**

Cont in patt from ** to ** throughout, working a further 5 rows in red, then one row white, 2 rows black, then one row white.

11th row. Using yellow work over 36 sts, do not break off yarn, join blue and work next 36 sts, join in second ball of yellow and work to end.

Discard-return using yellow until one yellow st remains, pick up blue and discard until one blue st remains, then pick up yellow and discard to end st.

Work a further 5 rows in above colors.

Join black and work 2 rows, join green and work 3 rows, then join black and work a further 2 rows.

24th row. Using blue work over 36 sts, do not break off yarn, join yellow and work next 36 sts, join in second ball of blue and work to end. Discard-return, matching colors as before.

Work a further 5 rows in above colors.

Work one row in white, 2 rows in black, then one row in white.

Rep last 33 rows twice more, then work 6 rows in red (105 patt rows).

Finishing row. Working from right to left, *hook under vertical bar (2 loops on hook), yoh and draw through both loops. Rep from * to end of row, fasten off.

Finish off ends neatly along back of work.

Side edging. With right side of work facing and using green, work in Tunisian Simple along side edge, working into each row end (107 sts).

Dicard-return and break off yarn. Join yellow and work one row, then work one row in green. Complete in green, working finishing row as before. Work other side to match.

Vertical lines are worked in surface crochet, with the yarn at back of work and hook at front. Using white, make a slip loop towards the end of yarn. Beginning at lower edge, place hook between 6th and 7th vertical st. Place yarn and slip st in same position at back of work and draw loop through to right side. Insert hook into corresponding st in row above, yoh and draw thread through from back to front and through slip loop on hook. Cont in this manner, working one ch st for every row and maintaining even tension. Fasten off. Work 5 lines in black, two to correspond with change of color from yellow to blue, then one black line in center of the yellow and blue blocks. Work a further 5 lines in white, evenly spaced.

Fringe. Using three of the colors together, wind around cardboard and cut at one end to make 6"-long strands. Rep with other three colors. Make fringe knots in alternating colors along commencing and finishing edges.

Project by Leonie Campbell
Photography by Andre Martin

Fig 1. Foundation row. First half. Miss first ch from hook, insert hook through top loop only of second ch from hook, yoh and draw through, forming loop on hook (you should now have 2 loops on hook). Cont across row, *insert hook in next top loop, yoh and draw through, rep from * across to end of ch, keeping all loops on hook. You should have the same number of loops on hook as the number of ch with which you started, counting starting loop as first st. Do not turn.

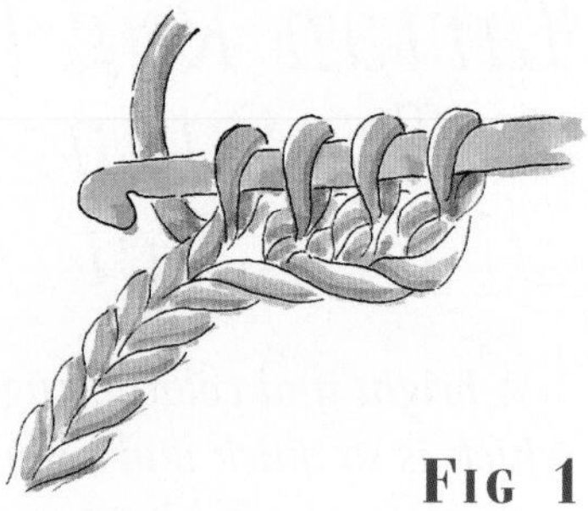

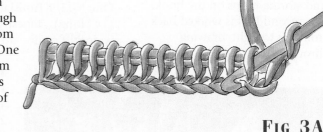

FIG 1

FIG 2

Fig 2. Foundation row. Second half (discard-return). Yoh loosely and draw through first loop, *yoh and draw through 2 loops; rep from * across row. One loop should rem on hook; this is the first stitch of the next row.

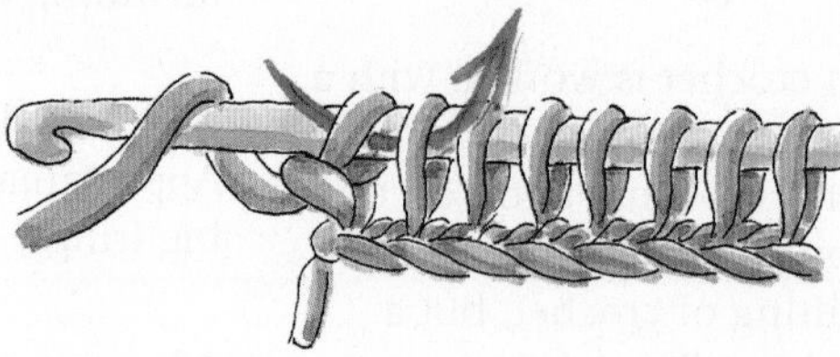

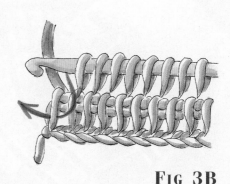

FIG 3A

Figs 3A & 3B. First half of Tunisian Simple row. Insert hook in second vertical bar (fig 3A, beg of row), yoh and draw through forming a new loop on hook. Pull up a loop in same manner in each bar to last bar. There should be same number of loops on hook as the number of starting ch. If you are short a loop, you have probably missed picking up the last bar at the end of the row (fig 3B, end of row).

FIG 3B

Fig 4. Second half of Tunisian Simple row. Work as for second half of foundation row.

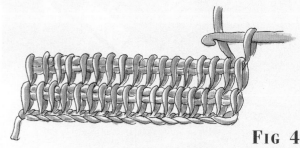

FIG 4

A Pretty Heirloom Cloth

The elegance of lace and the ease of crochet are brought together in this magnificent tablecloth.

MEASUREMENTS

Finished tablecloth measures approximately 90" x 122" (43 motifs wide and 59 motifs long). Each motif measures 2" square; border measures 2" across.

MATERIALS

Approximately 34 balls DMC Size 10 Crochet Cotton (Art 149); one No.7 crochet hook.

1st Motif

Make 8ch and join with sl st to form a ring.

1st rnd. 3ch (to stand as 1dc), 23dc into center of ring. Join with sl st to top of 3ch (24dc).

2nd rnd. 4ch, (1dc, 1ch) into each of next 23dc, join with sl st into 3rd of 4ch.

3rd rnd. Sl st into first 1ch sp, 4ch (to stand as 1tr), 1tr in same ch sp, 2tr in each of next four 1ch sps, *13ch, miss (1dc, 1ch, 1dc), 2tr in each of next five 1ch sps**, rep from * to ** twice, 13ch, join with sl st to top of 4ch.

Fasten off, cut thread and finish off neatly.

2nd Motif

Work rnds 1 and 2 as for 1st motif.

3rd rnd. Work as for 1st motif to **, then rep from * to ** once. Make 6ch, join to 1st motif with sl st into 7th of 13ch of 1st motif, 6ch, miss (1dc, 1ch, 1dc), 2tr in each of next 2 sps, 1tr in next sp, join to 1st motif with sl st between 5th and 6th tr of 1st motif, 1tr in same 1ch sp as before, 2tr in each of next 2 sps,

6ch, join as before to 7th of 13ch, 6ch, join with sl st to top of 4ch. Fasten off and finish off neatly.

Cont working further motifs, joining to corresponding edge of preceding motif, or into the ch already joining several motifs where necessary.

Border

1st rnd. Attach yarn with sl st into 7th of the 13ch corner loop. *10ch, (1tr, 2ch, 1tr) between 5th and 6th tr, 10ch, sl st into join of two 13ch loops, rep from * to end of rnd, join with sl st.

2nd rnd. *10ch, (2tr, 2ch, 2tr) in 2ch sp, 10ch, 1sc in sl st, rep from * to end, join with sl st.

3rd rnd. *10ch, (3tr, 2ch, 3tr) in 2ch sp, 10ch, 1sc in sc, rep from * to end. Join with sl st.

4th rnd. As rnd 3, but working (4tr, 2ch, 4tr) in each 2ch sp.

5th rnd. *12ch, (5tr, 2ch, 5tr) in 2ch sp, 12ch, 1sc in sc, rep from * to end, finish with sl st, fasten off.

Project and photography by DMC

Embroidered Vest

This is a simple pattern we have decorated with embroidery, but it can be made plain as well for comfort and warmth.

MEASUREMENTS

To fit size S, (M,L). Fits bust. 30-32 (34-36,38-40)". Actual measurement. 42 (46,50)". Length (excluding peaks). 22 (22½, 23)".

MATERIALS

Cleckheaton Country 8-ply (50g/2oz). 10 (11,12) balls Main Color (MC —black) and 2 (2,2) ball Contrast Color (CC —cream). One pair No.6 knitting needles. One No.5/F crochet hook. Tapestry needle for sewing seams and embroidery. Four buttons.

Tension

22 sts and 30 rows to 4" over st st, using No.6 needles.

Back

Using No.6 needles and MC, cast on 117 (129,139) sts.

Work in st st until Back measures 12" from beg, ending with a purl row.

Shape armholes. Cont in st st for rem, cast off 10 (12,13) sts at beg of next 2 rows...97 (105,113) sts. Dec one st at each end of every row until 79 (83,87) sts rem.

Work 59 rows.

Shape shoulders. Cast off 9 (9,10) sts at beg of next 4 rows, then 9(10,9) sts at beg of foll 2 rows. Cast off rem 25(27,29) sts.

Left Front

Using No.6 needles and MC, cast on 3 sts.

**Working in st st, cast on 2 sts at beg of next 10 rows, then 3 sts at beg of foll 2 rows...29 sts.

Cast on 29 (35,40) sts at beg of next row, work to end of row...58 (64,69) sts.**

Cont in st st (beg with a purl row) until work measures same as Back to armholes, excluding peaks and

ending with a purl row.
Shape armhole. Cast off 10 (12,13) sts at beg of next row...48 (52,56) sts.

Work one row.

Shape front slope. Dec one st at armhole edge in every row 9 (11,13) times, at the same time dec one st at end (front edge) of next and foll 4th rows 3 (5,7) times in all, then in foll 6th rows 9 (8,7) times...27 (28,29) sts.

Work 6 rows.

Shape shoulder. Cast off 9(9,10) sts at beg of next row and foll alt row.
Work one row.
Cast off rem 9(10,9) sts.

Right Front

Using No.6 needles and MC, cast on 3 sts.

Work one row st st.

Work as given from ** to ** of Left Front, noting to beg with a purl row.

Cont in st st until work measures same as Back to armholes, exclud-

ing peaks and ending with a purl row.

Work one row.

Shape armhole. Cast off 10 (12,13) sts at beg of next row...48 (52,56) sts.

Shape front slope. Dec one st at armhole edge in every row 9 (11,13) times, at the same time dec one st at beg (front edge) of next and foll 4th rows 3 (5,7) times in all, then in foll 6th rows 9 (8,7) times...27 (28,29) sts.

Work 6 rows.

Shape shoulder. Work as for Left Front shoulder.

Edging

Join shoulder and side seams. Using No.5/F crochet hook and MC, work 2 rnds sc, then 1 rnd crab st evenly along lower edges, peaks, Fronts and neck edges, inc and dec where necessary to keep work flat and working four 2ch-button loops evenly along Right Front edge in 2nd rnd of sc.

Fasten off.

Armhole Edging

Work as for other Edging, omitting button loops.

TO MAKE UP

Using CC, work embroidery from diagram around lower and front edges of Fronts using picture as a guide. Sew on buttons.

Project by Cleckheaton

ACTUAL SIZE

reverse the design for right front

■ satin stitch
■ lazy daisy stitch

work stem in stem stitch

Fisherman's Rib Sweater

This pattern can be followed to make either a round-necked sweater or a polo neck for extra warmth.

MEASUREMENTS

To fit size. S (M,L). Fits bust. 30-32 (34-36,38-40)". Actual measurement. 47 (51,55)". Length. 27½(28,28½)". Sleeve length. 17" (all sizes).

MATERIALS

Cleckheaton Machine Wash 8-ply (50g/2oz). Round Neck or Polo Collar. 21 (22,23) balls; or Cleckheaton Country 8-ply (50g/2oz). Round Neck or Polo Collar. 20 (21,22) balls. One pair each No. 3 and No. 6 knitting needles. One set of No.3 and No.6 knitting needles for Polo Collar. One cable needle. Four stitch-holders. Tapestry needle for sewing seams.

Tension

22 sts and 44 rows to 4" over fisherman's rib patt, using No.6 needles.

SPECIAL ABBREVIATIONS

K1B: knit one st below: knit into center of next st one row below, sl both sts off needle tog. **CB:** sl next 2 sts on cable needle and leave at back of work, K2, then K2 from cable needle. **CF:** sl next 2 sts on a cable needle and leave at front of work, K2, then K2 from cable needle.

Back

Using No.3 needles, cast on 115 (125,137) sts.

1st row. K2, *P1, K1; rep from * to last st, K1.

2nd row. K1, *P1, K1; rep from * to end.

Rep 1st and 2nd rows 13 times, then 1st row once (29 rows rib in all) inc 16 sts evenly across last row...131 (141,153) sts.

Change to No.6 needles.

Beg patt. 1st row. (wrong side). Knit.

2nd row. P1, *K1B, P1; rep from * to end.

Rep 1st and 2nd rows for fisherman's rib patt.

Cont in fisherman's rib patt until work measures 18" from beg, ending with a knit row.

Shape raglan armholes. Keeping patt correct, cast off 2 sts at beg of next 2 rows...127 (137,149) sts.

Beg raglan patt. 1st row. P1, K4, P1, K2tog, patt to last 8 sts, K2tog tbl, P1, K4, P1.

2nd row. K1, P4, K1, patt to last 6 sts, K1, P4, K1.

3rd row. P1, CB, P1, patt to last 6 sts, P1, CF, P1.

4th row. As 2nd row.

Rep last 4 rows 6 (4,1)time/s...113 (127,145)sts.**

Keeping cables correct in foll 4th rows from previous cable, dec one st at each end of next and foll alt rows (as in first row) until 33 (35,37) sts rem. Break off yarn. Leave sts on a stitch-holder (thus ending with a right side row).

Front

Work as for Back to **.

Keeping cables correct in foll 4th rows from previous cable, dec one st (as before) at each end of next and foll alt rows until 73 (77,81) sts rem.

Shape neck. Next row. (wrong side). Patt 31 (32,34), turn.

***Cont on these 31 (32,34) sts and dec one st at neck edge in

3rd row. As 1st row.

4th row. Inc in first st, K1B, (P1, K1B) 14 (14,15) times, P1, K8, P1, (K1B, P1) 14 (14,15) times, K1B, inc in last st.

5th row. K32 (32,34), P8, K32 (32,34)...72 (72,76) sts.

6th row. K1B, (P1, K1B) 15 (15,16) times, P1, CF, CB, P1, (K1B, P1) 15 (15,16) times, K1B.

7th row. As 5th row.

8th row. K1B, (P1, K1B) 15 (15,16) times, P1, K8, P1, (K1B, P1) 15 (15,16) times, K1B.

Rows 5 to 8 incl form patt. Keeping patt correct and working extra sts made into fisherman's rib, inc one st at each end of 6th (4th,4th) and foll 10th (8th,8th) rows until there are 98 (92,106) sts.

Sizes M and L only. Then inc one st at each end of foll 10th rows until there are (102,108) sts.

All sizes. Cont straight in patt until work measures 17" from beg, working last row on wrong side.

Shape raglan. Keeping patt correct, cast off 2 sts at beg of next 2 rows...94 (98,104) sts.

Beg raglan patt. Keeping center cable patt correct (as before) work rows 1 to 4 incl of Back raglan patt 12 (12,11) times...70 (74,82) sts.

Keeping center and side cables correct throughout, dec one st (as before) at each end of next and foll alt rows until 14 sts rem.

Next row. K3, P2, (P2tog) twice, P2, K3.

Next row. P1, K1B, P1, K6, P1, K1B, P1.

Next row. K3, P1, (P2tog) twice, P1, K3.

Next row. P1, K1B, P1, K4, P1, K1B, P1.

Break off yarn. Leave rem 10 sts on a stitch-holder (thus ending with a right side row).

Neckband

Join raglan seams, noting that tops of Sleeves form part of neck-line. With right side facing, using set of No.3 needles and beg at left back raglan seam, knit across 10 sts from left Sleeve stitch-holder, knit up 29 (30,31) sts evenly along left side of neck, knit across 11,13,13) sts from Front stitch-holder, knit up 29 (30,31) sts evenly along right side of neck, knit across 10 sts from right Sleeve stitch-holder then knit across 33 (35,37) sts from Back neck stitch-holder...122 (128,132) sts.**

1st rnd. *K1, P1; rep from * to end.

Rep 1st rnd 11 times, (12 rnds rib in all).

Cast off loosely in rib.

Polo Collar

Work as for Neckband to **.

1st rnd. Purl.

2nd rnd. *K1B, P1; rep from * to end.

Rep 1st and 2nd rnds 6 times (14 rnds rib in all).

Change to set of No.6 needles.

Cont in fisherman's rib, beg with a 2nd rnd, until work measures 8½" from beg, ending with a 2nd rnd.

Cast off very loosely in patt.

TO MAKE UP
Join side and sleeve seams. Fold Polo Collar to right side.

Project by Cleckheaton

next and foll alt row, then in foll 4th rows 4 (4,5) times, at the same time dec one st (as before) at armhole edge in next and alt rows 20 (21,22) times in all...5 sts.

Next row. P3tog, P2tog, turn, K2tog.

Fasten off.***

With wrong side facing, sl next 11 (13,13) sts on a stitch-holder and leave. Join yarn to rem 31(32,34) sts and patt to end.

Rep from *** to ***.

Sleeves

Using No.3 needles, cast on 53 (55,57) sts.

Work 28 rows rib as for lower band of Back.

29th row. Rib 2 (6,4), inc in next st, *rib 2, inc in next st; rep from * to last 2 (6,4) sts, rib 2 (6,4)...70 (70,74) sts.

Change to No.6 needles.

Beg patt. 1st row. (wrong side). K31 (31,33), P8, K31 (31,33).

2nd row. (P1, K1B) 15 (15,16) times, P1, CF, CB, P1, (K1B, P1) 15 (15,16) times.

Twin Chic

There's nothing old-fashioned about this up-to-the-minute twin set: the long-line cardigan is teamed with a cool singlet top.

MEASUREMENTS

Fits bust: 30(32-34,36-38,40-42)". Singlet: garment measures 40(44,48,52)"; length 24(25,25½,26)". Cardigan: garment measures 43(47,51,55)"; length (approx) 29½(30,30½,31)"; Sleeve fits 17" (all sizes). These garments are designed to be a generous fit.

MATERIALS

Patons Cotton 8-ply (50g/2oz): 6 (7,7,8) balls for singlet and 12 (12,13,14) balls for Cardigan. OR Patons 8-ply (50g/2oz): 8 (8,9,9) balls for Singlet and 14 (15,16,17) balls for Cardigan. One pair each No.3 and No.6 knitting needles. Matching sewing thread for facings. Five butttons for Cardigan. Tapestry needle for sewing seams.

Tension

22 sts and 29 rows to 4" over st st, using No.6 needles.

SINGLET
Back and Front

(alike)
Using No.3 needles, cast on 113 (125,135,147) sts.

1st row. Knit.

2nd row. K1, purl to last st, K1.

Rep 1st and 2nd rows 5 times, then 1st row once.

14th row. Knit (ridge).

Change to No.6 needles.

Rep 1st and 2nd rows 20 times. Cast off one st at beg of next 2 rows (top of side slits)...111 (123,133,145) sts.

Cont in st st until work measures 18½" from ridge, ending with a purl row.

Shape armholes. Cast off 7 (9,11,13) sts at beg of next 2 rows...97 (105,111,119) sts.

Shape neck. Next row. K4, K2tog, K30 (34,36,40), cast off next 25 (25,27,27) sts, K30 (34,36,40), sl1, K1, psso, K4.

Cont on last 35 (39,41,45) sts.

Next row. K1, purl to last st, K1.

Next row. K4, K2tog, knit to last 6 sts, sl1, K1, psso, K4.

Rep last 2 rows 1 (1,1,2) time/s...31 (35,37,39) sts.

Dec one st at neck edge (as before) in foll 4th rows 2 (3,4,4) times, at the same time, dec one st at armhole edge (as before) in alt rows 5 (7,8,8) times...24 (25,25,27) sts.

Work one row.

Dec one st at neck edge only (as before) in foll 4th rows from previous dec until 18 (19,20,22) sts rem.

Work 3 rows.

Cast off.

With wrong side facing, join yarn to rem 35 (39,41,45) sts and work to correspond with side just completed, reversing shapings.

TO MAKE UP

With a slightly damp cloth and warm iron, press lightly. Using backstitch and yarn, join shoulder and side seams above slits. Fold lower edges to right side at ridge, sew ends, turn to wrong side and slipstitch in position. Fold 2 sts at edges of side slits, around armholes and neck edge to wrong side and slipstitch in position with sewing thread. Press seams.

CARDIGAN
Back

Using No.3 needles, cast on 121 (133,143,155) sts.

1st row. Knit.

2nd row. K1, purl to last st, K1.

Rep 1st and 2nd rows 5 times, then 1st row once.

14th row. Knit (ridge).

Change to No.6 needles.

Rep 1st and 2nd rows 20 times.

Cast off one st at beg of next 2 rows (top of side slits)...119

(131,141,153) sts.

Work 106 rows st st.

Tie a colored thread at each end of last row to mark beg of armholes, as there is not armhole shaping.

Work 54 (58,60,62) rows st st.

Shape back neck. Next row. K42 (47,51,56) sts, cast off next 35 (37,39,41) sts, knit to end.

Cont on last 42 (47,51,56) sts.

1st row. Purl to last 6 sts, P2tog, P3, K1.

2nd row. K4, K2tog, knit to end.

Rep 1st and 2nd rows twice, then 1st row once...35 (40,44,49) sts.

Work one row.

Shape shoulder. Cast off 9 (10,11,12) sts at beg of next row and foll alt rows 3 times in all.

Work one row.

Cast off rem 8 (10,11,13) sts.

With wrong side facing, join yarn to rem 42 (47,51,56) sts and work to correspond with side just completed, reversing shapings and working 'P2togtbl' in place of 'P2tog', and 'sl1, K1, psso' in place of 'K2tog'.

Right Front

Using No.3 needles, cast on 61 (67,72,78) sts.

1st row. Knit.

2nd row. K1, purl to last st, K1.

Rep 1st and 2nd rows 5 times, then 1st row once.

14th row. Knit (ridge).

Change to No.6 needles. Rep 1st and 2nd rows 20 times, then 1st row once.

Cast off one st at beg of next row...60 (66,71,77) sts.

Keeping knit st at beg of next row correct, work 28 rows st st.

Next row. K4, cast off 2 sts, knit to end.

Next row. Purl to last 4 sts, turn, cast on 2 sts, turn, P3, K1...buttonhole.

Keeping knit st correct at front edge in purl rows, work 16 rows st st.

Rep last 18 rows 3 times, then buttonhole rows once...5 buttonholes.

Work 4 rows.

Tie a colored thread at beg of last row to mark position of armhole.

Shape front slope. Next row. K4, K2tog, knit to end.

Next row. Purl to last st, K1.

Rep last 2 rows 17 (17,18,19) times...42 (48,52,57) sts.

Dec one st (as before) at front edge in next and foll 4th rows until 35 (40,44,49) sts rem.

Work 2 rows.

Shape shoulder. Cast off 9 (10,11,12) sts at beg of next row and foll alt rows 3 times in all.

Work one row.

Cast off rem 8 (10,11,13) sts.

Left Front

Work to correspond with Right Front, omitting buttonholes and working 'sl1, K1, psso' in place of 'K2tog' at front slope shaping, and reversing all shapings.

Sleeves

Using No.3 needles, cast on 57 (61,65,69) sts.

Work 13 rows st st.

14th row. Knit (ridge).

Change to No.6 needles.

Work in st st, inc one st at each end of 15th and foll 6th rows until there are 87 (91,95,99) sts, then in foll 4th rows until there are 97 (101,105,109) sts.

Work a further 5 rows st st.

Cast off loosely.

TO MAKE UP

With a slightly damp cloth and warm iron, press lightly. Using backstitch, join shoulder and Sleeve seams, and side seams above slits to colored threads.

Fold lower hem on Fronts and Back to right side at ridge, sew ends, turn to wrong side then slip-stitch in position. Sew in Sleeves. Fold hem of Sleeves to wrong side at ridge and slip-stitch in position. Fold 2 sts at edges of side openings and along Front edges and around Back neck to wrong side and slipstitch in position with sewing thread. Sew on buttons. Press seams.

Project by Coats Patons
Photography by Ashley Mackevicius

Classic Cables For Cosy Comfort

Here are the tops in winter fashion — his 'n' her hand-knits with Aran style.

MEASUREMENTS

To fit. Lady (Lady, Lady, Man, Man, Man). Fits bust/chest: 32(34,36,38,40,42)″. Garment measures. approximately 40(42,44,46,48,50)″. Length: approximately 24(24,25,26½,27,27)″. Sleeve length: 17(17,17,19,19,19)″.

MATERIALS

Cleckheaton Country 12-ply Wool (50g/2oz). 20(22,22,27,28,30) balls. One pair each No.7 and No.9 knitting needles. One cable needle. Tapestry needle for sewing seams and 5(5,5,6,6,6) buttons.

Tension

17 sts and 23 rows to 4″ over st st using No.9 needles, and 16.5 sts and 27 rows to 4″ over double moss st (side patt) using No.9 needles.

SPECIAL ABBREVIATIONS

C6B: sl next 3 sts on cable needle and hold at back of work, K3, then K3 from cable needle. **C6F:** sl next 3 sts on cable needle and hold at front of work, K3, then K3 from cable needle. **T5L:** sl next 3 sts on cable needle and hold at front of work, P2, then K3 from cable needle. **T5R:** sl next 2 sts on cable needle and hold at back of work, K3, then P2 from cable needle.

Cable Panel Patt

See Back, Fronts and Sleeves for placement of these 26 sts.

1st row. K6, (P4, K6) twice.

2nd and alt rows. Knit all knit sts and purl all purl sts as they appear.

3rd row. C6B, (P4, C6B) twice.

5th row. As 1st row.

7th row. As 3rd row.

9th row. K3, T5L, P2, K6, P2, T5R, K3.

11th row. (T5L) twice, K6, (T5R) twice.

13th row. P2, T5L, (C6F) twice, T5R, P2.

15th row. P4, (C6B) 3 times, P4.

17th row. P2, T5R, (C6F) twice, T5L, P2.

19th row. (T5R) twice, K6, (T5L) twice.

21st row. K3, T5R, P2, K6, P2, T5L, K3.

23rd row. As 3rd row.

25th row. As 1st row.

27th row. As 3rd row.

28th row. As 2nd row.

Last 28 rows form Cable Panel Patt.

Back

Using No.7 needles, cast on 106(114,118,126,134,138) sts.

1st row. K2, *P2, K2; rep from * to end.

2nd row. P2, *K2, P2; rep from * to end.

Rep last 2 rows 6 times more, then 1st row once.

16th row. (wrong side). Rib 5 (12,6,12,18,16), *inc one st in next st, rib 4(5,6,8,13,14); rep from * to last 1(6,0,6,4,2) st/s, rib 1(6,0,6,4,2)...126 (130,134,138,142,146) sts.

Change to No.9 needles.

1st row. K2 (0,2,0,2,0), (P2, K2) 2 (3,3,4,4,5) times, *P2, K6, P2, work 1st row of Cable Panel Patt across next 26 sts, P2, K6, P2*, (K2,P2) 3 times, K2, rep from * to * once, (K2, P2) 2 (3,3,4,4,5) times, K2 (0,2,0,2,0).

2nd and alt rows. Knit all knit sts and purl all purl sts as they appear.

3rd row. P2 (0,2,0,2,0), (K2, P2), 2 (3,3,4,4,5) times, *P2, C6B, P2, work 3rd row of Cable Panel Patt across next 26 sts, P2, C6B, P2*, (P2,K2) 3 times, P2, rep from* to * once more, (P2, K2) 2(3,3,4,4,5) times, P2 (0.2.0.2.0).

4th row. As 2nd row.

Last 4 rows form patt for sts at sides and between Cable Panel Patts.

Keeping Cable Panel Patt sts correct, cont in patt until row 28 has been completed. Last 28 rows form patt for all sts. Cont in patt until work measures 16(16,16,17,17,17)″ from beg, ending with a wrong-side row.

Shape armholes. Keeping patt correct, cast off 10 (12,14,12,14,16) sts at beg of next 2 rows...106 (106,106,114,114,114) sts.

Work 46 (46,50,54,56,56) rows.

Shape shoulders. Keeping patt correct, cast off 13 (13,13,14,14,14) sts at beg of next 4 rows, then 12 (12,12,13,13,13) sts at beg of foll 2 rows.

Cast off rem 30 (30,30,32,32,32) sts.

Left Front

Using No.7 needles, cast on 50 (54,58,62,66,66) sts.

Work 15 rows rib as for Back.

16th row. (wrong side). Rib 2 (4,8,8,13,10), *inc one st in next st, rib 3 (4,5,8,12,8); rep from * to last 0 (2,0,2,0,1,2) st/s, rib 0

(0,2,0,1,2)...62 (64,66,68,70,72) sts.

Change to No.9 needles.**

1st row. K2 (0,2,0,2,0), (P2, K2) 2 (3,3,4,4,5) times, P2, K6, P2, work 1st row of Cable Panel Patt across next 26 sts, P2, K6, (P2, K2) twice.

2nd and alt rows. Knit all knit sts and purl all purl sts as they appear.

3rd row. P2 (0,2,0,2,0), (K2, P2), 2 (3,3,4,4,5) times, P2, C6B, P2, work 3rd row of Cable Panel Patt across next 26 sts, P2, C6B, P4, K2, P2.

4th row. As 2nd row.

Last 4 rows form patt for sts at sides of Cable Panel Patt. Keeping

Cable Panel Patt sts correct, cont in patt until work measures same as Back to armholes, working same number of rows.

Shape armhole and Front slope. Keeping patt correct, cast off 10 (12,14,12,14,16) sts, patt to last 2 sts, work 2tog...51 (51,51,55,55,55) sts.

Keeping patt correct, dec one st at end of foll alt rows until 47 (47,49,53,53,53) sts rem, then in foll 4th rows until 38 (38,38,41,41,41) sts rem.

Work 3 (3,3,3,5,5) rows patt.

Shape shoulder. Keeping patt correct, cast off 13 (13,13,14,14,14) sts at beg of next row and foll alt row.

Work one row.

Cast off rem 12 (12,12,13,13,13) sts.

Right Front

Work as for Left Front to **.

1st row. (K2, P2) twice, K6, P2, work 1st row of Cable Panel Patt across next 26 sts, P2, K6, P2, (K2, P2) 2 (3,3,4,4,5) times, K2 (0,2,0,2,0).

2nd and alt rows. Knit all knit sts and purl all purl sts as they appear.

3rd row. P2, K2, P4, C6B, P2, work 3rd row of Cable Panel Patt across next 26 sts, P2, C6B, P2, (P2, K2) 2 (3,3,4,4,5) times, P2 (0,2,0,2,0).

4th row. As 2nd row.

Last 4 rows form patt for sts at sides of Cable Panel Patt. Keeping Cable Panel Patt correct, cont in patt and complete to correspond with Left Front, reversing shapings.

Sleeves

Using No.7 needles, cast on 38 (38,38,42,46,46) sts. Work 15

rows rib as for Back.

16th row. (wrong side). Rib 7 (7,5,7,10,10), inc one st in each st to last 7 (7,5,7,10,10) sts, rib 7(7,5,7,10,10)...62 (62,66,70,72,72)sts.

Change to No.9 needles.

1st row. K0 (0,2,0,1,1), (P2, K2) 2 (2,2,3,3,3) times, P2, K6, P2, work 1st row of Cable Panel Patt across next 26 sts, P2, K6, P2, (K2, P2) 2 (2,2,3,3,3) times, K0 (0,2,0,1,1).

2nd and alt rows. Knit all knit sts and purl all purl sts as they appear.

3rd row. P0 (0,2,0,1,1), (K2, P2) 2 (2,2,3,3,3) times, P2, C6B, P2, work 3rd row of Cable Panel Patt across next 26 sts, P2, C6B, P2 (P2, K2) 2 (2,2,3,3,3) times, P0 (0,2,0,1,1).

4th row. As 2nd row.

Last 4 rows form patt for sts at sides of Cable Panel Patt. Keeping Cable Panel Patt correct, cont in patt (noting to work extra sts into double moss st), inc one st at each end of next and foll 6th rows until there are 82 (82,86,88,98,98) sts, then in foll 8th row/s until there are 86 (86,90,96,100,100) sts.

Cont straight in patt until work measures 17 (17,17,19,19,19)" from beg, ending with a wrong-side row. Tie a colored thread at each end of last row to mark end of Sleeve seam.

Work a further 16 (20,22,18,22,26) rows patt.

Shape top. Keeping patt correct, cast off 9 (9,9,10,10,10) sts at beg of next 8 rows. Cast off rem 14 (14,18,16,20,20) sts.

Left Front Band

(If making for a lady, omit buttonholes.)

Join shoulder seams. With right side facing, using No. 7

needles, knit up 14 (14,14,16,16,16) sts evenly across half of Back neck, 43 (43,43,50,50,50) sts evenly along Left Front slope shaping, then 69 (69,69,76,76,76) sts evenly along rem of Left Front edge...126 (126,126,142,142,142) sts.

Work 3 rows rib as for Back, beg with a 2nd row.

4th row. Rib to last 74 sts, *yrn, P2tog, rib 12; rep from * to last 4 sts, yrn, P2tog, rib 2...6 buttonholes.

Work 3 rows rib.

Cast off loosely in rib.

Right Front Band

(If making for a man, omit buttonholes.)

With right side facing, using No.7 needles, knit up 69 (69,69,76,76,76) sts evenly along Right Front edge to beg of Front slope shaping, 43 (43,43,50,50,50) sts evenly along Front slope shaping, then 14 (14,14,16,16,16) sts evenly across other half of Back neck...126 (126,126,142,142,142) sts.

Work 3 rows rib as for Back, beg with a 2nd row.

4th row. Rib 2, P2tog, yrn, (rib 14, P2tog, yrn) 4 times, rib to end...5 buttonholes.

Work 3 rows rib.

Cast off loosely in rib.

TO MAKE UP

Join side and Sleeve seams to colored threads. Sew in Sleeves, placing center of Sleeves to shoulder seams and rows above colored threads to sts cast-off on Back and Fronts at armholes. Join ends of Front Bands at center Back neck. Sew on buttons.

Project by Coats Patons
Photography by Georgia Moxham

His 'N' Her Jumper

Aran-style jumper knitted in warm and quick 8-ply.

MEASUREMENTS

To fit. Lady (Lady,Lady,Man,Man). Fits bust/chest: 30 (32-34, 36-38, 38-40,42-44)". Garment measures: 42(46,50,52,56)". Length. 26½(27,27½,28,28½)". Sleeve fits: 17 (17, 17, 19, 19)", or length desired.

MATERIALS

Patons 8-ply (50g/2oz): 14(15, 17, 18, 19) balls. One pair each No.7 and No.3 knitting needles. One cable needle. Four stitch-holders. Shoulder pads for Lady (optional).

Tension

21 sts to 4" in width over st st, using No.7 needles. To achieve the desired effect, this garment is worked on larger needles at a looser tension than usually recommended.

SPECIAL ABBREVIATIONS

C6: sl next 3 sts on cable needle and hold at front of work, K3, then K3 from cable needle. **C4:** sl next 2 sts on cable needle and hold at front of work, K2, then K2 from cable needle. **C3R:** sl next st on cable needle and hold at back of work, K2, then P1 from cable needle. **C3LK:** sl next 2 sts on cable needle and hold at front of work, K1, then K2 from cable needle. **C3LP:** sl next 2 sts on cable needle and hold at front of work, P1, then K2 from cable needle.

Back

Using No.3 needles, cast on 106 (118,130,134,146) sts.

1st row. K2, *P2, K2; rep from * to end.

2nd row. P2, *K2, P2; rep from * to end.

Rep last 2 rows 8 times more, then 1st row once.

20th row. Rib 3 (4,6,4,7), *inc one st in next st, rib 2 (2,3,3,3), inc one st in next st, rib 2 (3,3,3,4); rep from * to last 1 (2,4,2,4) st/s, rib 1 (2,4,2,4)...140 (150,160,166,176) sts.

Change to No.7 needles.

Beg patt. 1st row. P14 (19,24,27,32), K2, *P2, (K1, P1) 3 times, K1, P2*, K6, P3, K6, rep from * to * once, K2, P13, C4, P13, K2, rep from * to * once, K6, P3, K6, rep from * to * once, K2, P14 (19,24,27,32).

2nd and alt rows. Knit all knit sts and purl all purl sts as they appear.

3rd row. P14 (19,24,27,32), K2, *(P1, K1) 5 times, P1*, K6, P3, K6, rep from * to * once, K2, P12, C3R, C3LK, P12, K2, rep from * to * once, K6, P3, K6, rep from * to * once, K2, P14 (19,24,27,32).

5th row. P14 (19,24,27,32), K2, *P2, *(K1, P1) 3 times, K1, P2*, C6, P3, C6, rep from * to * once, K2, P11, C3R, K1, P1, C3LK, P11, K2, rep from * to * once, C6, P3, C6, rep from * to * once, K2, P14 (19,24,27,32).

7th row. P14 (19,24,27,32), K2, *(P1, K1) 5 times, P1*, K6, P3, K6, rep from * to * once, K2, P10, C3R, (K1, P1) twice, C3LK, P10, K2, rep from * to * once, K6, P3, K6, rep from * to * once, K2, P14 (19,24,27,32).

8th row. As 2nd row.

Last 8 rows form patt for 55 (60,65,68,73) sts at each side edge.

9th row. Patt 55 (60,65,68,73), P9, C3R, (K1, P1) 3 times, C3LK, P9, patt 55(60,65,68,73).

10th and alt rows. As 2nd row.

11th row. Patt 55 (60,65,68,73), P8, C3R, (K1, P1) 4 times, C3LK, P8, patt 55 (60,65,68,73).

13th row. Patt 55 (60,65,68,73), P7, C3R, (K1, P1) 5 times, C3LK, P7, patt 55 (60,65,68,73).

15th row. Patt 55 (60,65,68,73), P6, C3R, (K1, P1) 6 times, C3LK, P6, patt 55 (60,65,68,73).

17th row. Patt 55 (60,65,68,73), P6, K3, (P1, K1) 6 times, Pl, K2, P6, patt 55 (60,65,68,73).

19th row. Patt 55 (60,65,68,73), P6, C3LP, (K1, P1) 6 times, C3R, P6, patt 55 (60,65,68,73).

21st row. Patt 55 (60,65,68,73), P7, C3LP, (K1, P1) 5 times, C3R, P7, patt 55 (60,65,68,73).

23rd row. Patt 55 (60,65,68,73), P8, C3LP, (K1, P1) 4 times, C3R, P8, patt 55 (60,65,68,73).

25th row. Patt 55 (60,65,68,73), P9, C3LP, (K1, P1) 3 times, C3R, P9, patt 55 (60,65,68,73).

27th row. Patt 55 (60,65,68,73), P10, C3LP, (K1, P1) twice, C3R, P10, patt 55 (60,65,68,73).

29th row. Patt 55 (60,65,68,73),

P11, C3LP, K1, P1, C3R, P11, patt 55 (60,65,68,73).

31st row. Patt 55 (60,65,68,73), P12, C3LP, C3R, P12, patt 55 (60,65,68,73).

32nd row. As 2nd row.

Last 32 rows form patt. Cont in patt until work measures 15″ from beg, ending with a wrong-side row.

Shape raglan armholes. Keeping patt correct, cast off 4 sts at beg of next 2 rows.

3rd row. K1, sl1, K1, psso, patt to last 3 sts, K2tog, K1.

4th row. P2, Patt to last 2 sts, P2.**

Rep 3rd and 4th rows until 76 (86,100,102,116) sts rem, ending with a 3rd row.

Next row. (wrong side). P1,

P2tog, patt to last 3 sts, P2tog tbl, P1.

Cont dec in this manner in every row until 46 (48,50,52,54) sts rem. Leave rem sts on a stitch-holder.

Front

Work as for Back to **.

Rep 3rd and 4th rows until 90 (98,106,110,120) sts rem, ending with a 4th row.

Shape neck. Next row. (right side). K1, sl1, K1, psso, patt 31 (35,39,41,46), turn.

Cont in patt on these 33 (37,41,43,48) sts, dec one st (at armhole edge as before) at each end of alt row/s until 21 (27,37,37,46) sts rem.

Next row. Patt to last 3 sts, P2tog tbl, P1.

Next row. K1, sl1, K1, psso, patt to last 2 sts, work 2tog.

Rep last 2 rows until 9 (9,7,7,7) sts rem.

Dec one st (as before) at armhole edge only in every row until 2 sts rem.

Next row. K2tog.

Fasten off.

With right side facing, sl next 22 sts on a stitch-holder and leave. Join yarn to rem 34 (38,42,44,49) sts and work to correspond with side just completed, reversing shapings.

Sleeves

Using No.3 needles, cast on 50 (50,54,58,58) sts.

Work 36 rows rib as for Back (1st row is right side of Cuff).

37th row. Rib 0 (0,2,4,2), *inc one st in next st, rib 1; rep from * to last 0 (0,2,4,2) sts, rib 0 (0,2,4,2)...75 (75,79,83,85) sts.

Change to No.7 needles.

Beg patt. 1st row. P17 (17,19,21,22), K2, *P2, (K1, P1) 3 times, K1, P2*, K6, P3, K6, rep from * to * once, K2, P17 (17,19,21,22).

2nd and alt rows. Knit all knit sts and purl all purl sts as they appear.

3rd row. P17 (17,19,21,22), K2, *(P1, K1) 5 times, P1*, K6, P3, K6, rep from * to * once, K2, P17 (17,19,21,22).

5th row. Inc one st in first st, P16 (16,18,20,21), K2, *P2, (K1, P1) 3 times, K1, P2*, C6, P3, C6, rep from * to * once, K2, P16 (16,18,20,21), inc one st in last st.

7th row. P18 (18,20,22,23), K2, *(P1, K1) 5 times, P1*, K6, P3, K6, rep from * to * once, K2, P18 (18,20,22,23).

8th row. As 2nd row.

Last 8 rows form patt, noting inc. Keeping patt correct and working extra sts into rev st st, inc one st at each end of next and foll 4th rows until there are 105 (99,101,117,117) sts, then in alt rows until there are 109 (115,121,125,129) sts. Cont straight in patt until work measures 13 (13,13,15,15)″ (or 4″ less than desired length to allow for loose fit and deep armhole) from center row of rib cuff, ending with a wrong-side row.

Shape raglan. Keeping patt correct, cast off 4 sts at beg of next 2 rows.

3rd row. K1, sl1, K1, psso, patt to last 3 sts, K2tog, K1.

4th row. P1, P2tog, patt to last 3 sts, P2tog tbl, P1.

5th row. As 3rd row.

6th row. P2, patt to last 2 sts, P2.

Rep rows 3 to 6 incl 2 (3,5,5,6) times...83 (83,77,81,79) sts.

Rep 5th and 6th rows until 25 sts rem, ending with a 6th row. Leave rem sts on a stitch-holder.

Neckband

Using backstitch, join raglan seams, leaving left back raglan open and noting that tops of Sleeves form part of neckline. With right side facing, using No.3 needles and beg at left back raglan, knit across Sleeve sts dec 3 sts across top of each cable, knit up 26 (27,28,31,32) sts evenly along left side of neck, knit across sts from Front stitch-holder dec 2 sts evenly across, knit up 26 (27,28,31,32) sts evenly along right side of neck, knit across Sleeve sts dec 3 sts across top of each cable, then knit across Back sts dec 6 sts evenly across...150 (154,158,166,170) sts.

Work 4 rows st st, beg with a purl row.

5th row. (wrong side). P5 (7,9,1,3), P2tog, *P4, P2tog; rep from * to last 5 (7,9,1,3) sts, P5 (7,9,1,3)...126 (130,134,138,142) sts.

Work 12 (12,12,24,24) rows rib as for Back.

For Lady. Next row. K2, *K2tog, K2; rep from * to end...95 (98,101) sts. Knit 2 rows garter st. Cast off.

For Man. Cast off loosely in rib.

TO MAKE UP

With a slightly damp cloth and warm iron, press lightly, taking care not to flatten patt. Using backstitch, join left back raglan, Neckband, side and Sleeve seams, reversing seam for three quarters of rib for Cuffs. Fold rib section of Man's Neckband in half to wrong side and slipstitch in position. Press seams. Fold Cuffs in half to right side. Insert shoulder pads for Lady if desired.

Project by Coats Patons
Photography by Georgia Moxham

Shore Favourites

Cool, casual cotton handknits

ON THE WATERFRONT

MEASUREMENTS

Fits bust 30(32-34,36-38, 40-42)".
Garment measures: 34(38,42,46)".
Length: 21½ (22,22½,23)".
Sleeve seam: 11" all sizes.

MATERIALS

Patons Cotton 8-ply (50g/2oz): 8(8,9,9)balls. One pair No. 6 knitting needles. One No. 4/E crochet hook. Round elastic.

Tension

22 sts to 4" in width over st st, using No.6 needles.

SPECIAL ABBREVIATION

Picot: 3ch, sl st back into first of these ch.

Back

Using needles, cast on 95(107,117,129) sts. Work in st st until Back measures 13" from beg, ending with a purl row.

Shape armholes. Cont in st st, cast off 5(7,9,10) sts at beg of next 2 rows, then dec one st at each end of next and foll alt rows until 75(79,83,89) sts rem.** Work 35 rows st st.

Shape neck. Next row. K27(29,31,34), cast off 21 sts, knit to end. Cont in st st on last 27(29,31,34) sts, dec one st at neck edge in every row until 13(15,17,20) sts rem.

Shape shoulder. Cast off 7(8,9,10) sts at beg of next row.

Work one row.
Cast off rem 6(7,8,10) sts. With wrong side facing, join yarn to rem 27(29,31,34) sts and work to correspond with side just completed.

Front

Work as for Back to **.

Work 3 rows st st.

Shape neck. Next row. K27(29,31,34),cast off 21 sts, knit to end.

Cont in st st on last 27(29,31,34) sts, dec one st at neck edge in alt rows until 19(21,23,26)sts rem, then in foll 4th rows until 13(15,17,20)sts rem. Work 6 rows st st.

Shape shoulder. Cast off 7(8,9,10) sts at beg of next row. Work one row. Cast off rem 6(7,8,10) sts. With wrong side facing, join yarn to rem 27(29,31,34) sts and work to correspond with side just completed, reversing shapings.

Sleeves

Using needles, cast on 59(63,69,73) sts. Work in st st, inc one st at each end of 9th and foll 8th(8th,6th,6th) rows until there are 73(71,87,85) sts, then in foll 6th(6th,4th,4th)row/s until there are 75(81,89,97)sts.

Cont straight in st st until work measures 11″ from beg, ending with a purl row.

Shape top. Cont in st st, cast off 3(4,5,5) sts at beg of next 2 rows, then dec one st at each end of next and foll alt rows until 39(43,51,63) sts rem, then in every row until 21 sts rem. Cast off.

TO MAKE UP

With a dry cloth and cool iron, press lightly. Using backstitch, join shoulder, side and Sleeve seams. Sew in Sleeves. With right side facing, using hook, work one rnd sc evenly around lower edge, taking care not to stretch work and having a number of sc divisible by 3.

2nd rnd. *1sc in each of next 2sc, picot, 1sc in next sc; rep from * to end, sl st in first sc. Fasten off. Work same edging around neck (placing elastic around neck and catching in elastic by working first rnd over elastic) and Sleeve edges. Press seams and edgings.

WHITE SANDS

MEASUREMENTS

Fits bust: 30(32-34,36-38, 40-42)″.
Garment measures: 36 (40,44,48)″ .
Length: 21½(22,22½,23)″.
Sleeve seam: 6½″ all sizes.

MATERIALS

Patons Cotton 8-ply (50g/2oz): 7(8,8,9) balls. One pair each No.3 and No.6 knitting needles. One cable needle. Two stitch-holders.

TENSION

22 sts to 4″ in width over st st, using No.6 needles.

SPECIAL ABBREVIATION

C5: sl next 3 sts on cable needle and leave at front of work, K2, then K3 from cable needle.

Back

Using No.3 needles, cast on 85 (93,103,113) sts.

1st row. K2, *P1, K1; rep from * to last st, K1.

2nd row. K1, *P1, K1; rep from * to end.

3rd row. K2, (P1, K1) 1 (3,2,1) time/s, P1, *K5, (P1, K1) 4 times, P1; rep from * to last 10 (14,12,10) sts, K5, (P1, K1) 2 (4,3,2) times, K1.

4th row. Knit all knit sts and purl all purl sts as they appear.

5th row. K2, (P1, K1) 1 (3,2,1) time/s, P1, *C5, (P1, K1) 4 times, P1; rep from * to last 10 (14,12,10) sts, C5, (P1, K1) 2 (4,3,2) times, K1.

6th row. As 4th row.

Rep rows 3 to 6 incl twice, then 3rd row once.

16th row. Patt 4 (8,3,3), *inc in next st, patt 4 (3,4,4); rep from * to last 1 (5,0,0) st/s, patt 1 (5,0,0)...101 (113,123,135) sts.

Change to No.6 needles.

Work in st st until Back measures 13″ from beg, ending with a purl row.

Shape armholes. Cont in st st, cast off 4 (7,7,9) sts at beg of next 2 rows, then dec one st at each end of next and foll alt rows until 83 (87,93,99) sts rem.**

Work 49 rows st st without any shaping.

Shape neck. Next row. K28 (30,33,36), turn.

Cont in st st on these 28 (30,33,36) sts, dec one st at neck edge in next 3 rows...25 (27,30,33) sts.

Shape shoulder. Cast off 7 (8,9,10) sts at beg of next and foll alt row, at the same time, dec one st at neck edge in next 4 rows.

Cast off rem 7 (7,8,9) sts.

With right side facing, sl next 27 sts on a stitch-holder and leave. Join yarn to rem 28 (30,33,36) sts and work to correspond with side just completed, reversing shapings.

Front

Work as for Back to **.

Work 21 rows st st without any shaping.

Shape neck. Next row. K31, (33,36,39), turn.

Cont in st st on these 31 (33, 36, 39) sts, dec one st at neck edge in alt rows until 25 (27,30,33) sts rem, then dec one st at neck edge in foll 4th rows until 21 (23, 26, 29) sts rem.

Work 3 rows st st.

Shape shoulder. Cont in st st, cast off 7 (8,9,10) sts at beg of next and foll alt row.

Work one row.

Cast off rem 7 (7,8, 9) sts.

With right side facing, sl next 21 sts on a stitch-holder and leave. Join yarn to rem 31 (33,36,39) sts and work to correspond with side just completed, reversing shapings.

Sleeves

Using No.3 needles, cast on 57 (61,65,71) sts.

Work 11 rows in band patt as for Back.

12th row. Patt 4 (0,0,2), *inc in next st, patt 1 st; rep from * to last st, K1...83 (91,97,105) sts.

Change to No.6 needles.

Work in st st until Sleeve measures 6 ½″ from beg, ending with a purl row.

Shape top. Cont in st st, cast off 3 (4,4,5) sts at beg of next 2 rows, then dec one st at each end of next and foll alt rows until 37 (45,53,61) sts rem, then in every row until 33 sts rem.

Next row. (P3tog) 11 times.

Cast off.

Neckband

Using backstitch, join right shoulder seam. With right side facing, using No.3 needles, knit up 29 sts evenly along left side of neck, knit across sts from Front stitch-holder, knit up 29 sts evenly along right side of neck, then knit up 43 sts evenly around Back neck, incl sts from stitch-holder...122 sts.

1st and alt rows. K2, (P1, K1) 25 times. *P5, (K1, P1) 4 times, K1;

rep from * to end.

2nd row. K2, *(P1, K1) 3 times, P1, C5, P1, K1; rep from *4 times, rib to end.

4th row. K2, *(P1, K1) 3 times, P1, K5, P1, K1; rep from *4 times, rib to end.

Rep 1st and 2nd rows once more.

7th and 8th rows. K2, *P1, K1; rep from * to end.

Cast off loosely in rib.

TO MAKE UP

With a slightly damp cloth and warm iron, press lightly. Using backstitch, join left shoulder, Neckband, side and Sleeve seams. Sew in Sleeves. Press seams.

Projects by Coats Patons
Photography by Stephen Lowe

170

King Of The Knit Parade

This pattern has been included because it is a favorite — and it is fun!

MEASUREMENTS

Approximate width at bust/chest: 52". Approximate length (not including waist band): 25". Approximate Sleeve length (not including wrist band): 17". This is a loose-fitting garment.

MATERIALS

8-ply yarn (50g/2oz): Main Color (MC) 8 balls (black); 1st contrast (C1) 6 balls (blue); 2nd Contrast (C2) 5 balls (white); 3rd Contrast (C3) 2 balls (red). One pair each No.5 and No.8 knitting needles. Two stitch-holders. Bobbins.

Tension

20 sts and 26 rows to 4" over st st, using No.8 needles.

Note. When changing colors in the middle of a row, twist the color to be used (on wrong side) underneath and to the right of the color just used, making sure that both of the yarns are worked firmly at joins.

Use a separate ball of yarn for each section of color; wind yarn on bobbins or into smaller balls where it is necessary.

Back

Using MC and No.5 needles, cast on 110 sts.

Work in K1, P1 rib for 20 rows.

Change to No.8 needles.

Work in patt from Graph, inc one st at each end of first and foll 5th rows until there are 124 sts, then in foll 10th rows until there are 130 sts.

Cont straight in patt from Graph until 160th row has been worked.

Keeping colors correct as in last row, cast

off 43 sts at beg of next 2 rows.

Leave rem 44 sts on a stitch-holder.

Front

Work as for Back until 144th row of Graph has been worked.

Shape neck. 145th row. Patt 48 sts, turn.

Cont in patt from Graph on these 48 sts, dec one st at neck edge in foll alt rows until 43 sts rem.

Cont straight in patt until 160th row has been worked.

Cast off.

With right side facing, sl next 34 sts on a stitch-holder and leave. Join yarn to rem 48 sts and work to correspond with side just completed, reversing shapings and working from Graph for right side of neck.

Neckband

Using backstitch, join right shoulder seam. With right side facing, using MC and No.5 needles, knit up 108 sts evenly around neck, incl sts from stitch-holders.

Next row. Knit.

Work in K1, P1 rib for 21 rows.

Cast off loosely.

Using backstitch, join left shoulder and Neckband seam.

Sleeves

(Beg at armhole)
Tie a colored thread 79 rows down from each shoulder seam on Back and Front side edges.

With right side facing, using C1 and No.5 needles, knit up 158 sts evenly across armhole edge between colored threads.

Change to No.8 needles.

Next row. *P2tog, P3; rep from * to last 3 sts, P1, P2tog...126 sts.

Cont in patt from Graph, ending with 108th row, at the same time, dec one st at each end of every 3rd row until 56 sts rem.

109th row. Using C1, knit, dec one st at each end...54 sts.

110th row. Using C1, P1, P2tog, (P15, P2tog) twice, P14, P2tog, P1...50 sts.

Change to MC and No.5 needles.

Work in K1, P1 rib for 18 rows.

Cast off.

TO MAKE UP

Tie yarn ends tog, then sew in all ends. Using backstitch, join side and Sleeve seams. Fold Neckband in half to wrong side and slip-stitch in place.

Project by Libby Jones
Photography by Stuart Spence

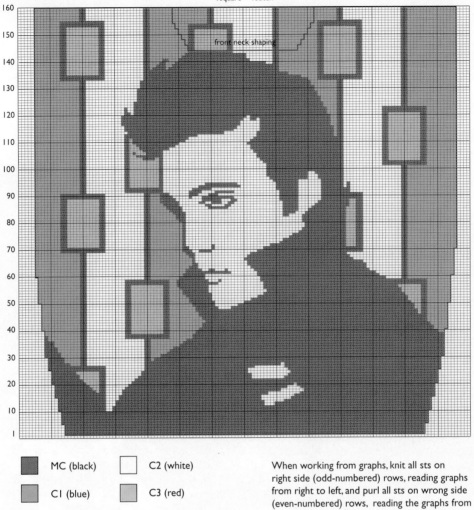

	MC (black)		C2 (white)
	C1 (blue)		C3 (red)

When working from graphs, knit all sts on right side (odd-numbered) rows, reading graphs from right to left, and purl all sts on wrong side (even-numbered) rows, reading the graphs from left to right.

SLEEVE

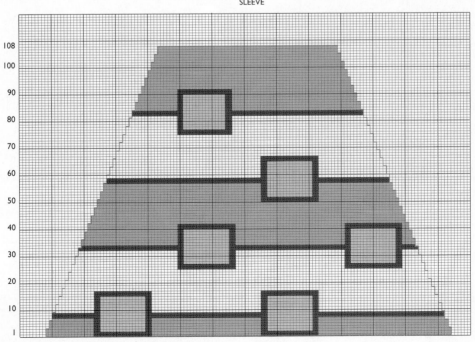

Festive Flair

Cornucopias

Make these pretty paper cones for next to no cost and in very little time — Christmas papers, cardboard, glue and cord or ribbon are all that is needed. Traditionally, cornucopias are a symbol of plenty associated with festivities.

MATERIALS

Compass, glue stick; Christmas wrapping paper; colored cardboard; clothes pegs; rubber bands; lengths of cord or ribbon.

METHOD

Using a compass, make a quarter circle pattern (we made several different sizes) adding a ¼″ allowance to one straight edge. Glue wrapping paper to wrong side of cardboard. Use pattern to cut shapes from cardboard. Trim allowance at pointed end and roll into cone shape, then glue allowance under opposite straight edge. Hold in place with a peg

and rubber bands until glue dries. Pierce holes at top edge on opposite sides, thread ribbon or cord length through and knot or tie ends into bows. Fill with chocolates or sweets.

Project by Judy Newman
Photography by Andre Martin

Everlasting Floral Pots

Colorful dried flowers will bring cheer to your home. Trim them with festive ribbons for a Christmas feel, then in the New Year, remove the bows and enjoy them for the rest of the year.

MATERIALS

Terracotta pot; dry Oasis (brown florist's foam); dried plant materials:
For red and white pot: red-dyed

broom, white larkspur and forest moss;
For wheat and lavender pot: wheat stalks, lavender, red mini-rosebuds; secateurs; ribbon.

METHOD

Cut Oasis block to fit and fill each pot. For red and white pot, cut larkspur to approximately 12″ lengths and push stems into Oasis around the back edge of the pot. Cut broom to 6″ lengths and fill the remainder of pot. Top Oasis with moss. For wheat and lavender pot, divide the Oasis into 3 sections across the width, marking each section by drawing a knife across the divisions. Cut wheat to 9″-12″ lengths and push into the back section of the pot. Cut lavender to 6″-8″ lengths and push into the middle section. Cut roses to 2″-4″ lengths and push into the front section. Decorate the pots with ribbon bows.

Project by Judy Newman
Photography by Andrew Elton

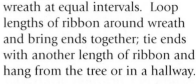

wreath at equal intervals. Loop lengths of ribbon around wreath and bring ends together; tie ends with another length of ribbon and hang from the tree or in a hallway.

Project by Judy Newman
Photography by Andre Martin
❖ *Indicates pattern on pattern pages*

Lavender Wreath

Christmas stars and hearts are a warm and cheering combination made extra special by the scent of lavender. You'll be surprised at how quickly and easily you can make this lovely wreath.

MATERIALS
Gold cardboard (or paint with gold folk art paint); PVA glue; dried lavender; fine cord; grapevine wreath; ribbon. (If you don't want to buy a wreath, you can easily make your own by twisting lengths of grapevine or willow around each other to form a circle.)

METHOD
Trace patterns for small heart and star ❖. Cut out shapes in cardboard. Pierce hole in top of shape. Apply glue to one side and sprinkle with lavender. To keep flat while drying, place under a heavy weight (book or brick). Thread cord through hole and knot in place. Tie shapes onto

Spicy Fabric Pomanders

Fill your home with the fragrance of Christmas. For the scent of cinnamon and cloves, give these spicy pomanders a squeeze. A small fabric bag contains stuffing and spices, with a cinnamon stick and bay leaves adding the finishing touch.

MATERIALS
Cotton Christmas prints; fine cord; polyester fiber filling; cloves; ground cinnamon; cinnamon sticks; PVA glue; bay leaves.

METHOD
Trace around a dinner plate to make a circular pattern. Ours were 8", 9" and 10" in diameter. Cut out fabric circles.

Run a gathering stitch around the circle, pull up slightly to ease in edge. Turn under ½" around the circle, stitch ½" from edge to make casing. Thread cord through casing using a safety pin. Pull up cord to form a pouch, insert a little fiber filling, add 1 teaspoon cloves and 1 teaspoon cinnamon, then fill with fiber. Insert cinnamon stick and tie in place with cord. Glue bay leaves on top.

Project by Judy Newman
Photography by Andre Martin

Patchwork Hearts

Scraps of Christmas prints and vibrant silks are stitched together for these hanging hearts — make them in plain patchwork or add beads and embroidery to create exquisite family heirlooms. Tie them onto a wreath, string them along the mantelpiece, or hang them on the front door to welcome guests.

MATERIALS FOR ALL HEARTS

2"-wide fabric strips (we used cotton Christmas prints and silk taffeta scraps); small amount of fusible interfacing; fabric for backing; polyester fiber filling; 16" length of ribbon.

EXTRA MATERIALS FOR BEADED HEART

Seed beads (red, green and gold); straw or beading needle; embroidery threads; three pebble beads (ours were red).

METHOD

Trace large heart pattern ❖. Stitch fabric strips together using a ¼" seam to make a fabric piece large enough to cut desired number of hearts. Fuse interfacing to wrong side of patchwork fabric. Cut out one heart shape from patchwork fabric and one from backing fabric for each heart. Staystitch between dots and at each point on heart by stitching ¼" from the edge. Place patchwork heart and backing right sides together and, using small stitches, sew, leaving opening between dots. Clip and trim seam allowance. Turn right side out, turn under seam allowance along opening.

Fill lightly with polyester fiber, stitch opening closed. Stitch ribbon at top point on backing.

BEADING (OPTIONAL)

Embroider seams with embroidery thread and stitch as desired — we used herringbone, chain and running stitch. Stitch seed beads along some patchwork seams using straw or beading needle and working a double stitch into the fabric every so often to secure beads if thread breaks. On one patchwork panel, stitch beads in flower clusters — first stitch a red bead for the center, then stitch five or six gold beads around it to form the flower petals.

Stitch three pebble beads at the bottom point and stitch three bead loops. For bead loops, bring needle and thread through pebble beads, then thread seed beads onto the thread until loop is desired length.

Then bring thread back up through the pebble beads and into fabric, taking a stitch to secure the strand. Repeat with different colored beads to make two more bead loops.

Project by Judy Newman
Photography by Andre Martin
❖ *indicates pattern on pattern pages*

Mini Christmas Tree

This miniature Christmas tree is easy to make and costs only a few dollars. Buy a polystyrene cone from a craft store and paint it with metallic gold acrylic paint (spray paint may react with the polystyrene). Spray some pine cones with gold paint and allow to dry. Arrange the largest in a layer around the bottom of the polystyrene cone. Use a hot glue gun to attach the cones to the polystyrene. When the glue is dry, continue with the next layer of cones, working your way up, using the smaller cones as you go. Add a small cone to the tree top and finish with a ribbon bow.

Project by Judy Newman
Photography by Cath Muscat

Gold Walnuts

Some of the nicest Christmas decorations are also the simplest. Add a little gold spray (we used a folk art spray paint) to walnuts in the shell and display them in beribboned baskets.

Project by Judy Newman
Photography by Andre Martin

Cinnamon Pomanders

Enjoy the fragrance of Christmas with spicy cinnamon pomanders, baked with a mixture of ground cinnamon and apple sauce. Tie them on the tree or hang them in a hall where they will send the scent of Christmas wafting through your home.

INGREDIENTS

2 cups ground cinnamon; 1 to 1½ cups smooth apple sauce; cookie molds; plastic drinking straw; narrow ribbon or cord; glitter glue or paint; craft glue or hot glue; tiny dried flowers (optional).

METHOD

Mix cinnamon with 1 cup of apple sauce to make a dry, crumbly mixture. Add more apple sauce, a little at a time, until you have a very firm dough (but not sticky). Sprinkle the mold with a little extra cinnamon and press in a tablespoonful of dough. Press firmly and use a knife to trim excess dough from back of mold. Tap side of mold sharply on a wooden chopping board to remove dough, and place on a baking tray. Repeat with remaining dough. Alternatively, roll dough and cut into shapes with cookie cutter. Using the straw, cut out a neat hole at top of pomanders to hold the hanging loop. Bake for about 2 hours in a very slow oven. After 1 hour, remove from baking tray, place directly on oven rack, continue cooking to dry out pomanders evenly. When pomanders feel dry and hard, remove from oven and cool on a rack. To decorate, tie ribbons through holes, paint with glitter paint as desired or glue on dried flowers. If the scent of your pomander starts to fade, refresh it by rubbing the back with sandpaper.

Makes 8 or 9 pomanders, depending on size of mold.

Project by Judy Newman
Photography by Andrew Elton

Handmade Crackers

Fill handmade crackers with surprises — sweets, novelties and tiny gifts.

MATERIALS

Cardboard rolls; crepe paper in colors to match your table setting; glue (we used a glue stick); cracker friction strips; strong thread; sweets, whistles, confetti, hats, riddles and other treats; ribbon.

Step 1. Cut one cardboard roll about 4″ long for the center of each cracker and two 2″-long pieces (these can be re-used for each cracker as they only shape the paper ends). Cut a length of paper 1″ wider than the circumference of the roll and about 11″ long. Center the long roll on the paper, with short rolls at each end. Roll paper around cardboard and glue in place on the center roll only. Insert the friction strip into cracker.

Step 2. Tie paper at one end of the center roll using strong thread. Fill with treats, then tie other end. Tie ribbon or bows over the thread, add other decorations if desired. Remove the short rolls at ends and use for the next cracker.

Project by Judy Newman
Photography by Cath Muscat

STEP 1

STEP 2

glue or a pin if you can't tie it on). You could also try the same technique using other favorites like gumnuts, dried banksia flowers, or decorative seed pods.

Pine Basket

Glue pine cones around the edge of a plain basket, then give it a generous spray of metallic gold paint. Fill your basket with Christmas flowers, nuts or tiny gifts.

Festive Fruit

For a spectacular display, spray some real or artificial fruit with metallic gold paint and arrange it on a side table with a candle or two.

Pine Cone Hangings

One of the most stylish and economical ways to decorate your home is by using natural materials collected from the garden or country roadsides — and these materials are also environmentally friendly. Pine cones are easy to come by and have long been a traditional Christmas favorite. So for a cheering display, gather them up, add a spray of gold folk art paint and attach a bright ribbon (use

All projects on this page by Judy Newman Photography by Cath Muscat

Golden Ivy

Explore your garden for Christmas craft materials. This glittering, gilded wreath is simply made from lengths of ivy twisted around each other to form a circle. No wiring is needed; just keep winding lengths of ivy until your wreath is the desired fullness. Spray it gold and tie a ribbon bow at the top.

Santa Stocking

Everyone will want one of these, and they are simple to make.

MEASUREMENTS

Width (from heel to toe): approximately 10". Length: approximately 14".

MATERIALS

Cleckheaton Country 8-ply (50g): 2 balls Main Color (MC, we used green); 1 ball 1st Contrast (C1, we used white); 1 ball 2nd Contrast (C2, we used red); small quantity 3rd Contrast (C3, we used black); small quantity 4th Contrast (C4, we used yellow); small quantity 5th Contrast (C5, we used pale pink). One pair No.5 knitting needles. One No.4 crochet hook. Knitter's needle for sewing seams and embroidery.

TENSION

22 sts and 30 rows to 4" over st st, using No.5 needles.
Note. Stocking may be worked using one of two methods. It may be knitted entirely in st st and the detail from graph embroidered on afterwards using knitting stitch embroidery. Alternatively, it may be worked throughout in Fair Isle. If working in Fair Isle, do not weave in colors but carry color/s not in use loosely across on wrong side of work.

Note. For 1st side:
Read right side rows (odd-numbered) from right to left and wrong-side rows (even-numbered) from left to right.

For 2nd side: Read right-side rows (even-numbered) from left to right and wrong-side rows (odd-numbered) from right to left (ie all right-side rows for 1st side have become wrong side for 2nd side and all wrong-side rows for 1st side have become right-side rows for 2nd side)

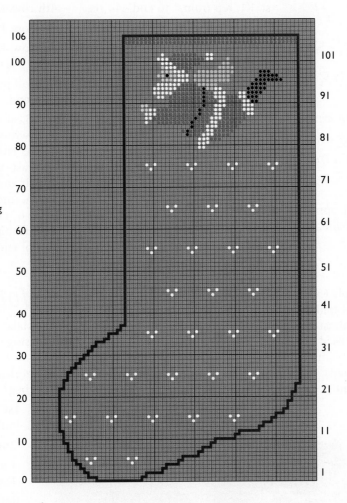

Second Side

Using MC and No.5 needles, cast on 11 sts.

1st row. (wrong side). Purl.

2nd row. Cast on 2 sts, knit to last st, inc one st in last st...14 sts.

3rd row. Cast on 4 sts, purl to last st, inc one st in last st... 19 sts.

4th row. Inc one st in first st, knit to last st, inc one st in last st...21 sts.

Cont as for 1st side, as placed in last 4 rows, until row 106 has been completed.

Change to C2 only.

Next row. (fold-line). Knit. Work 9 rows st st, beg with a knit row.

Cast off loosely.

It is important, however, that no color be carried across more than 7 sts and where this is necessary, it should be woven under and over color in use at center st. Always carry colors to ends of rows and catch in at side edge.

Always carry MC above other colors.

If Stockings are worked in Fair Isle, the size will vary slightly from stated measurements.

We used the first method (embroidery) to make our stocking.

First Side

Using MC and No.5 needles, cast on 11sts.

1st row. (right side). Knit.

2nd row. Cast on 2 sts, purl to last st, inc one st in last st...14 sts.

3rd row. Cast on 4 sts, knit to last st... 19 sts.

4th row. Inc one st in first st, purl to last st, inc one st in last st... 21 sts.**

Cont working from Graph , as placed in last 4 rows until row 106 has been completed, noting to inc, dec, cast-on and cast-off as indicated on Graph.

Change to C2 only.

Next row. (foldline). Purl. Work 9 rows st st, beg with a purl row.

Cast off loosely.

To make up

Embroider detail from Graph to both sides, reversing Santa motif on Second Side. Join side and foot seams. Fold 9 rows at top to inside and slipstitch loosely in position. Using C3 and No.4 hook, make a 6″ length of ch. Work 3 rows sc. Fasten off. Attach ends of ch to side of Stocking to form loop, as illustrated.

Project by Cleckheaton
Photography by Justine Kerrigan

183

Small Red Christmas Stockings

Wonderfully quick to knit, these little stockings are designed to hang on a tree.

MEASUREMENTS

Width (from heel to toe): approximately 3". Length: approximately 4½".

MATERIALS

Cleckheaton Country 8-ply (50g) balls: Main Color (MC) 1 ball (we used bright red); 1st Contrast (C1) small quantity (we used green); 2nd Contrast (C2) small quantity (we used berry red); 3rd Contrast (C3) small quantity (we used light brown); 4th Contrast (C4) small quantity (we used white). One pair No.2 knitting needles. One No.4 crochet hook. Knitter's needle for sewing seams. *Note.* One ball of each color wool will make approximately four stockings.

TENSION

26 sts and 38 rows to 4" over st st, using No.2 needles.

Stocking

(Worked in one piece, beg at foot.)
Using MC and No.2 needles, cast on 30 sts.
Next row. (wrong side). Purl.
Next row. K2, *inc one st in next st, K1; rep from * to end...44 sts.
Work 9 rows st st, beg with a purl row.
Shape top of foot. 1st row. K18, (K2tog) 4 times, K18... 40 sts.
2nd and alt rows. Purl.
3rd row. K16, (K2tog) 4 times, K16...36 sts.
5th row. K14, (K2tog) 4 times, K14...32 sts.
7th row. K12, (K2tog) 4 times, K12...28 sts.
Work 17 rows st st, beg with a purl row.
Knit 5 rows garter st.
Cast off loosely.

Holly Leaves

(Make 2)
Using C1 and No.2 needles, cast on 16 sts, noting to leave a 6" yarn end at beg.
1st row. (wrong side). P7, inc one st in each of next 2 sts, P7...18 sts.
2nd row. Knit.
3rd row. (Picot edge). K1, (yfwd, K2tog) 8 times, K1.
4th row. Knit.
5th row. Purl.
6th row. K7, (K2tog) twice, K7...16 sts.
Cast off purlways, leaving a 6" yarn end.
Fold Leaf in half at picot edge with wrong sides together. Using one 6" end, oversew cast-on and cast-off edges tog. Fold Leaf in half and oversew seamed edges tog on underside of Leaf. Using other 6" end, pull up ends of rows firmly and secure, leaving rem of end to fasten Leaf to stocking.

Holly Berries

(Make 2)
Using C2 and No.2 needles, cast on 12 sts firmly, noting to leave a 6" yarn end at beg.
1st row. (wrong side). Purl.
2nd row. Knit.
Cast off firmly purlways, leaving a 6" yarn end.
Roll up knitted strip from side to side, so that right side is facing outwards. Using 6" ends, oversew ends of rows in position, then thread end through outer edges and pull up to form a ball. Fasten off securely, leaving rem of thread at one end to fasten Berry to Stocking

Pine Cones

(Make 2)
Using C3 and No.2 needles, cast on 48 sts, noting to leave a 6" yarn end at beg.
Note. When turning, bring yarn to front of work, sl next st on right hand needle, take yarn back, then turn and proceed as instructed, to avoid holes in work.
1st row. K8, turn.

2nd and alt rows. Purl to end.

3rd row. K16, turn.

5th row. K24, turn.

7th row. K36, turn.

9th row. Knit across all sts to end. Change to C4.

10th row. (Picot edge). K1, *yfwd, K2tog; rep from * to last st, K1. Change to C3.

11th row. Knit.

Cast off, leaving a 6″ thread end.

Fold row above picot edge to wrong side and catch cast-off edge in position. Roll up strip so that right side is facing outward, beg with the longest set of row ends and noting to keep the cast-on edge sts level at base of Cone. Sew the short set of row ends at the base of Cone in position, then oversew all layers of Cone at center and tightly secure, leaving rem of end to attach Cone to Stocking.

TO MAKE UP

Join side and foot seams of Stocking. Attach Holly Leaves, Berries and Cones to Stocking, as shown. Using No.4 hook and MC, make a 4″ length of ch. Attach ends of ch to top of Stocking at side seam to form loop.

Project by Cleckheaton
Photography by Justine Kerrigan

Bread Dough Decorations

These decorations look wonderful, whether painted or plain. They're so simple to prepare all the family can share in the making.

MATERIALS

1 cup cooking salt, 1 cup warm water, 2 teaspoons cooking oil, 3 cups plain flour.

METHOD

Dissolve the salt in the water, mix in the oil. Mix the liquid into the flour. Turn the dough onto a floured surface and knead until pliable and plastic-like. Make decorations following the shapes we have provided ❖.

Cover a baking tray with aluminum foil, dull side up. Place decorations on the foil, at the back on bottom shelf of the oven, on the lowest temperature setting until hard (1½ to 2 hours). Long, slow baking prevents the decorations from burning, and dries them thoroughly.

Christmas Scents

Add a little spice with these cinnamon stick bundles. Simply tie sticks with gold cord and add a pretty spray of dried flowers. Display in bundles on a windowsill, or tie them on the tree.

Project by Judy Newman
Photography by Andre Martin
❖ indicates pattern on pattern pages

185

Scented Oranges

Scent your home with festive oranges.

Simply push cloves into oranges in heart, star and geometric patterns. Draw a heart and a star on paper, cut out and use as guides, pressing cloves around them.

Project by Judy Newman
Photography by Andrew Elton

Seasonal Potpourri

Your home will not only look festive but smell festive too.

INGREDIENTS

1 teaspoon orris root granules; 4 drops oil of cloves; 1 cup rose petals; ½ cup lavender; 2 teaspoons mixed spice; ⅓ cup star anise; ¼ cup bay leaves; cinnamon sticks; cedar roses; gumnuts; dried straw daisies.

METHOD

Combine orris root with clove oil, leave until oil is absorbed. In a bowl, combine rose petals, lavender, spice, star anise and bay leaves with oil and orris root, gently mixing with your hands. Add remaining ingredients and decorate with a few dried daisies.

Project by Judy Newman
Photography by Andrew Elton

Cherub-trimmed Tree

A delightful hanging for the door.

MATERIALS

1 large artificial pine branch (approximately 18″ long); weathered backing board (ours measures 24″ x 20″); hot glue gun and glue sticks; terracotta half pot; dried Spanish moss; 60″ of wide burgundy velvet ribbon; 60″ of wide gold metallic ribbon; 8 cherubs; 1 spray of artificial berries; 10 mini pine cones.

METHOD

Spread branch and shape into a tree. Attach to backing board using hot glue and leaving room for pot at base. Position pot over base of branch and glue in place. Fill pot with moss. Make a large bow using both ribbons and glue between base of tree and pot. Make small bows of each ribbon and arrange in tree with cherubs, gluing both in place. Pull berry spray apart, glue berries and pine cones on tree.

Project by Karen Rawolle
Photography by Andrew Elton

Rosebud Tree

A beautiful mini-tree for the table.

To make this tree of dried mini-rosebuds, fill a small terracotta pot with dry Oasis (brown florist's foam). Insert a cinnamon stick in center, fix with PVA glue. Cut dried rose heads, leaving 1″ stalks. Push roses into a small dry Oasis cone. Push covered cone onto cinnamon stick.

Project by Judy Newman
Photography by Andrew Elton

The Luxury of Gold Leaf

Gold leaf adds an extra glow when used instead of gold spray paint. You can tell the difference...

MATERIALS

Item to be gilded; acrylic sealer; poster paint (in a traditional reddish brown color); gold size (adhesive); gold leaf (from art supply shops); various brushes; soft cotton cloth. Gilding Kits are available which contain all you need.

PREPARATION

Ensure that the surface of the item to be gilded is clean. It may be painted or varnished but, if raw, it must be sealed using a good acrylic sealer. Acrylic paint primer can be used on timber in place of an acrylic sealer. After applying the sealer, sand lightly with fine sandpaper. The smoother the surface, the greater the brilliance of the gold leaf. Glass, papier-mâché or any painted surfaces don't require sealing.

Step 1. Paint item with poster paint and allow to dry. Repeat if necessary to give a good coverage.

Step 2. Apply size and allow it to dry until it is still sticky (it should feel tacky, but not actually wet).

Step 3. Cut gold leaf to a suitable size. Lay over item and gently smooth with fingertips until the area is covered. If there are gaps, go back and fill with small pieces of gold leaf. It's better to overlap slightly and, if the gold leaf breaks, patch it with small pieces.

Step 4. When the item you're working on is covered with gold leaf, rub surface gently with a cotton cloth to polish. Paint box with sealer and allow to dry for several hours. Antiquing mediums can also be applied to give an aged finish.

Project by Judy Newman
Photography by Valerie Martin

STEP 1

STEP 2

STEP 3

STEP 4

Gilded Stars

There's nothing like gold leaf to turn perfectly ordinary items into precious pieces. Terracotta, timber and papier-mâché — like these stars — are just some of the surfaces which can be turned to gold with a gilding kit.

Project by Christine Moss
Photography by Andrew Elton

Gilded Cards

These cards are embellished with gold leaf. Cut a heart or star from thin cardboard; retain cardboard with shaped hole as stencil. Take a blank card or cut and fold one from stiff paper. Position stencil on card. With a stencil brush,

apply gold size through cut-out onto card. Allow size to dry until clear but sticky. Place stencil over area and apply gold leaf over the stencil so it sticks to size. Rub gently with fingertip to fix gold leaf.

Project by Judy Newman
Photography by Andrew Elton

Gilded Box

Add luxury to a simple gift by presenting it beautifully. To gild a plain cardboard box, follow the step-by-step instructions on previous page.

Wrappings and Stamping

Brown paper packages tied up with...brown paper ribbons.

These stylish parcels are wrapped in hand-stamped paper featuring angels, hearts, fir trees, circles, stars and bands of green and red ink. We cut our stamps from inexpensive erasers or used what was handy — like a corn plaster for the thick circle and a button on a wire for the angels' haloes. Ties and tags are stamped to match.

Stamped Stationery

Enlist the help of the children to make your own range of Christmas cards and wrapping papers. All you'll need are some craft stamps, ink pads and plain white paper. And there's also a whole range of embossing powders, coloring pens and glitter powders to add extra pizazz. Why not stamp sheets of writing paper, too, and send some special Christmas letters this year?

MATERIALS
Plain white cards; gift boxes; paper; Christmas stamps; colored ink pads; felt coloring pens; glitter glue; small piece of sponge; embossing powder (this is optional).
Note. Brown wrapping paper or recycled papers are also very effective for craft stamping.

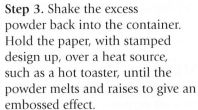

Step 1. Apply ink to stamps; if using tiny ink pads, dab pad onto stamp surface. Stamp paper, cards and boxes with stamps and red or green ink. Using felt pens, color sections of pattern. Add glitter glue highlights. Allow ink to dry. Dab just-damp sponge onto ink pad, then dab lightly on cards, paper.

Step 2. For an embossed effect: Stamp your designs using an embossing pad. Then sprinkle the stamped design with colored embossing powder.

Step 3. Shake the excess powder back into the container. Hold the paper, with stamped design up, over a heat source, such as a hot toaster, until the powder melts and raises to give an embossed effect.

Project by Robin Jaques
Photography by Valerie Martin

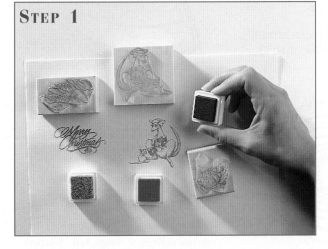

STEP 1

STEP 2

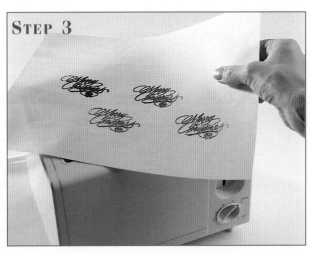

STEP 3

Quilled Cards

Roll your own colorful cards and pictures following our easy instructions.

Quilling is not a new craft. It dates back about 600 years when paper was wound around feathers (or quills) to create circular shapes and was used by religious orders to decorate holy books and boxes. Often the paper was gilded or colored to resemble precious metal filigree work.

GENERAL MATERIALS

Quilling tool or, as an alternative, use a tapestry needle; pre-cut paper strips; white, clear-drying glue; tweezers; several toothpicks; scissors; cards or heavy paper on which to mount quilled design.

The paper strips come in varying widths, and are available at craft shops in packets or kits.

METHOD

Step 1. Quilling shapes are made by winding paper around a quilling tool. Catch one end of the paper in the gap at the end of the tool and carefully wind the paper, making sure to keep it even as you roll.

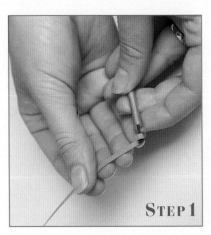

STEP 1

Step 2. After rolling the paper, release it from the quilling tool and let it expand as much as desired. Apply a dab of glue on the outside end to hold the roll. To position the rolled shapes on the card, hold the roll with tweezers, dip into clear-drying glue, then position on card.

STEP 2

Basic Shapes

Tight Roll. Wind paper around quilling tool, remove, then glue loose end.

Loose Roll. Make a tight roll and remove from quilling tool. Allow to unroll a little; glue loose end.

Teardrop. Make a loose roll. Pinch an edge of the circle between your thumb and index finger to form the shape shown.

Eye (Marquis). Make a loose roll. Place between thumb and index finger of both hands and pinch ends to form the shape shown.

Clown

MATERIALS

2 strips orange, 2 strips green, 3 strips yellow, 2 strips red, 1 strip of white ⅛″ quilling paper; 1″ length of yellow ⅓″ quilling paper.

Head — use half strip of white to make a loose roll. Press lightly between thumb and index finger to give oval shape.

Hair — fringe the ⅓″-wide paper, cut in half and glue to each side of head for hair.

Body — make loose roll from 1 strip of green.

Arms — (make 2) use half strip of

yellow to make a teardrop.

Legs — (make 2) use 1 strip of orange to make a teardrop.

Shoes — (make 2) use quarter strip of green to make eye (marquis) shape.

Balloons — use 1 strip each blue, yellow and red to make loose rolls.

Hat — make tight roll from 2″ strip of yellow.

Make teardrop from half strip of red; holding pinched end in finger, pinch other end to form triangle.

Glue all pieces into place on card. Draw on balloon strings with a marker pen.

Balloons

MATERIALS

5 strips of ⅛″-wide quilling paper in different colors; 5 x 8″ lengths of ¼″-wide satin ribbon in matching colors; toothpicks; blank card.

Balloons — make loose rolls using 1 full strip for each. Glue balloons into place on card. Hold ribbons, one on top of the other and in the same color order as for balloons, and tie a knot a third from lower ends. Glue knot to card (you may need craft glue to secure).

Use a toothpick to paint a line of glue from the knot to each balloon. Glue each matching ribbon in place. Fan out short ends of ribbons, trim ends and glue.

Dog

MATERIALS

2 strips grey; 2 strips black; 1 strip white; 1 strip red; small amount of green ⅓″-wide quilling paper; 2 x ⅓″-wide joggle eyes; 4″ of ¼″-wide red satin ribbon; fine black marker pen; toothpick;

blank card.

Body — use 1 strip of grey to make loose roll.

Head — use half strip of grey to make loose roll.

Ears — (make 2) make teardrop using ¼ strip of black. Bend pinched end over slightly to fit shape of head.

Muzzle — join 1″ of black to quarter strip of white. While glue is still damp, and starting from the black end, roll tightly to the join. Leave to dry, then make loose roll with white.

Feet — (make 2) use quarter strip of black to make a teardrop. Holding pinched end between thumb and index finger, pinch into triangle shape.

Ball — make loose roll from 1 strip of red. Glue all pieces into place on card. Note that the muzzle is glued on top of the head.

Cut thin strips of green to make grass. Use toothpick to

paint glue onto the card, then position grass over it.

Glue on eyes and bow. Use a marker pen to draw tail and hair on head.

Ducks

MATERIALS

3 strips of yellow ⅓″-wide quilling paper, small strips of green quilling paper; blue marker; blank card.

Mother Duck — ½ teardrop for the head and full strip teardrop for body. Turn up end of teardrop to form tail.

Ducklings — (make 2) ¼ strip teardrop for the head and ½ strip teardrop for body. Turn up tail as for mother duck.

Glue rolls into place on card.

Cut thin strips of green paper for reeds. Use a blue marker to draw in water.

Project by Anne Redman
Photography by Ashley Mackevicius

Country Cards

These cards have country charm — and look delightful. Use scraps of bright printed fabrics in heart or star shapes. Cut a heart and a star from paper first, then cut the fabric shapes around them using pinking shears. Glue onto a card and stitch a button in the center, leaving thread ends long.

Project by Judy Newman
Photography by Andrew Elton

Cards That Stand Out

A little ingenuity makes these gorgeous cards perfect partners for your wrapping paper.

MATERIALS

Wrapping paper with at least three pattern repeats that can be cut out; glue; silicone sealant; plain card or stationery; small scissors or scalpel; dark-colored felt pen; tweezers.

SOME TIPS

- Choose a wrapping paper with a design which has a repeating pattern that is easy to cut out.
- Don't use paper that has been creased.
- If making gift tags, you'll find a base layer plus only one other layer will be sufficient — and leave you plenty of paper for wrapping.
- Off-cuts suitable for cards can often be had from a friendly printer. We used writing paper, folded twice, to make a greeting card.

METHOD

If making your own card, cut and fold card-board to desired size.

The cut-out design is applied to the card in layers. If the first design can be cut as a rectangle, square or circle, it can be glued straight onto the front of the card.

Otherwise, carefully cut out around the edge of a motif with small scissors, or use a scalpel on a safe surface.

After cutting, you may notice a rough white edge to the paper cut-outs. Turn the motif upside down on scrap paper and, using the dark felt pen, carefully outline the edge to disguise the whiteness.

Carefully cut around the edge of motifs for second and third layers and color white edges as for first layer. Gently squeeze a dab of silicone in several places on the first layer and position second layer over silicone. Use the tweezers to adjust the position so the second layer sits exactly over the first. Very gently apply a small amount of pressure on the second layer, but don't push down flat. The height difference created by the silicone between the layers gives the card its 3D look.

Repeat precedure for third layer, positioning the third layer motifs exactly over the second layer.

The silicone will take about an hour to dry.

Project by Stella Robinson
Photography by Andre Martin

It's a Wrap

When you've finally bought all your gifts, don't let expensive paper break the budget. Here are some simple ideas for stylish wrapping.

1. Collect dried leaves, gumnuts or flowers from the garden and spray paint them with gold paint. Use hot glue or craft glue to fix them onto gifts

wrapped in plain white paper for a simple but stunning effect

2. Glue white or gold paper doilies over plain wraps. Tie with a length of ribbon and glue on some dried flowers, or simply add a ribbon bow.

3. Gold stickers over white typing-paper wrap look effective.

4. Wrap your gifts in white paper then hold a paper doily over it. Spray paint with gold paint to get a lacy gold pattern.

5. Plain wraps tied with a gold ribbon are beautifully finished with a generous ribbon bow or dried flowers glued on top.

6. Brown paper stamped with Christmas motifs looks great. The finishing touch is a string tie with gold bells knotted on each end.

Project by Judy Newman
Photography by Andrew Elton

Fabric Gift Tags

Delightful Christmas stationery need not be expensive — use your scraps of Christmas prints to make these gift tags. Cut out cardboard stars or small hearts using our trace-off patterns ❖ and use glue stick to attach to the wrong side of fabric. Cut around the shape using pinking shears and thread with a string or cord. When the presents are unwrapped, hang the tags on the tree!

Project by Judy Newman
Photography by Andre Martin

Beautiful Boxes

Silk flowers and pretty paint finishes make these boxes extra special.

Small Box

MATERIALS

Papier-mâché box; Matisse acrylic paint in Antique White and Antique Green; Matisse Cracking Medium; foam brush; PVA glue; mauve grosgrain ribbon; silk flowers.

METHOD

Paint box with Antique Green, allow to dry. Paint box with Cracking Medium, allow to dry until just tacky, leaving it no more than 12 hours. Apply a thick coat of Antique White, avoiding overworking the brush, as this will decrease the cracking effect. Allow to dry.

Glue loops of ribbon on to box lid. Cut flower heads and leaves from stems and arrange on top of ribbon. Glue in place.

Large Box

MATERIALS

Papier-mâché box; Matisse acrylic paint in Shell Pink and Antique White; foam brush; sea sponge; palette; silk roses; PVA glue.

METHOD

Paint box with Shell Pink, allow to dry. Dampen sponge with water then wring out. Dip in Antique White and dab onto palette to remove excess paint. Lightly dab onto box to apply soft color, repeating over the box until satisfied with the effect.

Cut the silk rose heads and leaves from the stems. Arrange them decoratively on the box lid, then glue in place.

Project by Judy Newman
Photography by Andrew Elton
❖ *indicates pattern on pattern pages*

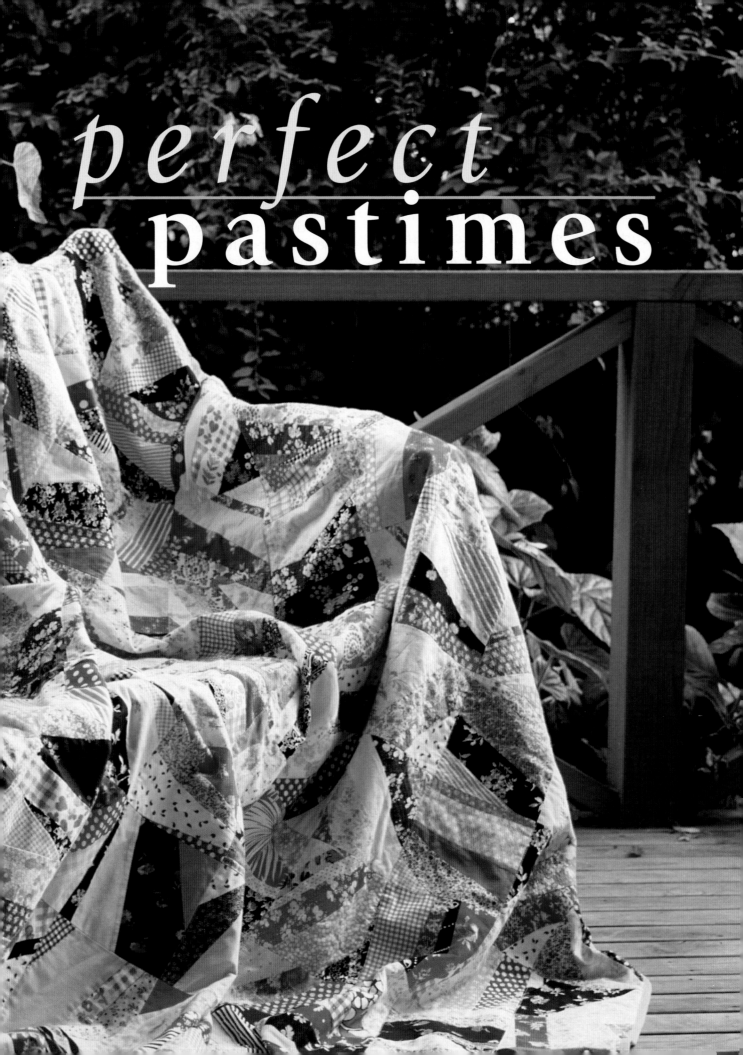

perfect
pastimes

Broderie Perse Appliqué Basket Picture

Make creative use of printed fabrics by cutting out motifs and stitching them onto new designs — an appliqué method which is known as broderie perse.

STEP 1

Traditionally, this technique was used to make the most of precious scraps of Chintz...and the idea is still a good one.

MATERIALS

Tracing, paper; pencil; assorted floral and printed fabrics, such as chintz and patchwork prints; scrap of checked fabric for basket; greaseproof paper; fusible webbing; 20″ x 18″ fine striped fabric for background; 20″ x 18″ fabric stabiliser (such as Stitch and Tear); threads to match fabrics.

FINISHED SIZE

16″ x 14″.

METHOD

Step 1. Cut out motifs — flowers, buds, leaves and butterflies or birds — from fabrics. Enlarge our basket pattern ❖ and cut out of checked fabric. Place motifs and basket shape face down on greaseproof paper, on ironing board.

Step 2. Place fusible webbing face down (paper side up) over motifs. Press using a dry, hot iron. Lift webbing; motifs will adhere to it and excess glue from webbing will remain on the greaseproof paper.

Step 3. Cut around each of the motifs and remove paper backing; motifs now have a coating of glue on wrong side. Center the

STEP 2

STEP 3

basket shape on the background fabric, approximately 4″ from the bottom edge, press in place. Position flowers, leaves and other motifs in a pleasing arrangement — try placing the larger motifs first, then smaller ones. When you are satisfied with your design, remove and set aside any motifs which overlap others. Press remaining motifs in place with a hot, dry iron. Pin fabric sta-biliser to wrong side of background fabric. Using matching threads, machine stitch around each motif with satin stitch (a close zigzag stitch). Reposition overlapping motifs, fuse in place and stitch in the same way; tear away fabric stabiliser.

Project by Christine Moss
Photography by Andrew Elton
❖ *indicates pattern on pattern pages*

Beaded Butterfly Cushion

Our gorgeous butterfly motif, worked in cross-stitch, is embellished with glass seed beads on this exquisite cushion.

MATERIALS

14" square of Permin linen, Twilight Blue, 11 threads to ½"; sewing thread; No.24 tapestry needle; 1 skein each DMC stranded thread in the following colors: 995 dark turquoise, 996 turquoise, 958 dark aqua, 959 aqua, 333 dark purple, 340 purple, 917 dark pink, 3607 pink, 310 black, 645 grey; Mill Hill glass beads: 3 packets seed beads in color 374, 1 packet frosted seed beads in color 62056, 6 packets frosted seed beads in color 3013; 28" x 45"-wide silk fabric;

1 skein trim, for inside edge of border (we used Au Ver A Soie Veralica Trim color 3337); 64″ fringe (we used Mulberry long cut); 16″ cushion insert.

FINISHED SIZE
16″ square plus 2″-wide fringe.
Note. 1″ seams used.

METHOD
Overcast the edges of linen to prevent fraying. Tack a horizontal and vertical center line through the fabric. Work each cross over 2 horizontal and 2 vertical threads of fabric using 2 strands of thread. Stitch using thread no longer than 18″.

Place middle butterfly in the center of linen, and work butterflies in rows 2 stitches apart horizontally, between wingtips, and 10 stitches apart vertically (at closest point), alternating the blue/green butterflies with pink/purple butterflies. Follow graph and key for colors. Use 2 strands of 310 (black) for backstitching antennae.

When stitching is complete, handwash your stitched piece using mild soap; do not rub, just squeeze the water through the fabric. Lie face down on a clean white towel and leave to dry. While fabric is still damp,

press dry with a medium hot iron. Trim fabric to 10″ square, for cushion center.

Cut two 17″ x 5″ pieces of silk for top and bottom borders and two 11″ x 4″ pieces for side borders. Stitch side borders to linen, then stitch top and bottom borders in place. Press seams away from linen. Hand stitch trim to inside border.

Cut 17″ square piece of silk for cushion back. Tack fringe around cushion front. Place front and back right sides facing, making sure fringe is enclosed. Stitch around the cushion leaving a 10″ opening on one side. Trim and neaten seams and turn right side out. Fill with insert and stitch closed.

Project by Rachel Dulson

Photography by Joseph Filshie

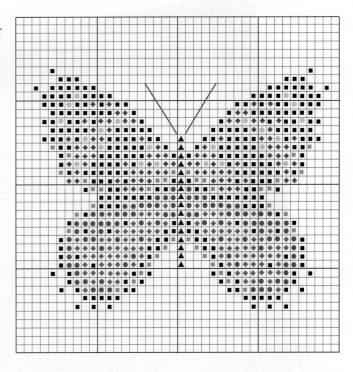

Purple/pink butterfly			Blue/green butterfly	
3013	bead	■	374	bead
62056	bead	▲	62056	bead
340	purple	◆	959	aqua
333	dark purple	●	958	dark aqua
3607	pink	●	996	turquoise
917	dark pink	◆	995	dark turquoise
645	grey	■	645	grey

199

Silk Ribbon Daisies

*If you haven't tried silk ribbon work,
you'll be surprised how easy it is
to learn.*

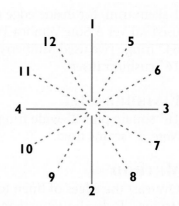

MATERIALS

16″ square blue fabric; embroidery hoop;
6yds of 4mm-wide silk ribbon in bright pink
(color 123); size 18 chenille needle
(pointed with large eye); DMC Perle 8
embroidery thread, in green 367; DMC
stranded thread, in yellow 725.

FINISHED SIZE

6″ x 4″.

METHOD

Daisies are positioned in a bunch, as desired.
Place fabric into embroidery hoop. Cut a
12″ length of ribbon. Thread chenille
needle with silk ribbon and work
petals in straight stitches,
following diagram.
Bring needle down at
flower center and keep
tension loose. Stitch
each flower by working
12 ½″-long stitches in a
circle. Work buds by
stitching up to half a
flower. Work stamens in
French knots with two
strands of yellow thread.
Work up to 5 French knots
to fill the center. Work
stems in green in single long
straight stitches from flower
to bottom of stem, adding
straight stitches through silk
at the base of buds. Tie stems
with a 6″ length of silk
ribbon looped into a bow.
Trim ends of ribbon. Frame as
desired.

Project by Merrilyn Heazlewood
Photography by Valerie Martin

String Of Hearts

A trio of patchwork hearts makes a pretty bedroom accessory. Fill each heart with potpourri or lavender, or use them as hanging pincushions for brooches.

MATERIALS

Small pieces of cotton fabric; sewing thread; needle; fiber filling; embroidery threads; seed beads; buttons; sequins and heart charms; 28" of ½"-wide ribbon.

METHOD

Make patterns for 3 hearts measuring 5", 4" and 3½", by following the directions below.

Cut fabrics into 2", 1½" and 1"-wide strips of various lengths. Using ¼" seam allowance, stitch together to form fabric pieces large enough to cut 3 hearts. Cut out 3 hearts from patchworked fabric and 3 from plain fabric, using patterns. Place each patchwork and plain heart together, with right sides facing, and stitch around, leaving an opening along one side. Turn right side out and fill with fiber (or lavender or potpourri); stitch opening closed.

Embroider over seams as desired, using herringbone, chain, feather, fly, lazy-daisy, or cretan stitch. Add single chain stitches or French knots to the embroidered seams. Stitch seed beads alongside embroidery or on fabric motifs and stitch buttons, sequins and charms in place. If desired, personal messages can be written with an ink pen. Place hearts along the ribbon and stitch in place. Tie a bow at the top of the ribbon.

FOLD

TO MAKE THE HEART PATTERN

Fold paper in half and measure desired length from point to point of heart. Draw a curve between points to give shape desired. Cut out and open to form pattern.

Project by Judy Newman

Photography by Andrew Elton

Crazy Quilt

You can easily make this unusual scrap quilt, using our instructions for the individual blocks. You can make your quilt any size.

MATERIALS

White lawn for backing squares (quantity depends on size of quilt); scraps of medium-weight cotton fabric; thread; fabric for backing; wide bias binding.

METHOD

Cut lawn into 9" squares (fabric A). To stitch patchwork, lay a scrap of fabric (fabric B) right side up, over one corner of the lawn, pin in place, see Step 1. Take the next piece of fabric (fabric C) and lay it face down along one diagonal edge of fabric B, see Step 2. Machine stitch a ½" seam. When fabric C is opened out the ends of the lawn square must be covered, see Step 3. Trim sewn edge and open fabric C right side out, press. Continue stitching pieces together until the base square (fabric A) is covered. Press and trim edges to same size as the base fabric, see Step 4. Make as many squares as required. To make up, join squares in strips, then join strips, matching seam allowances. Cut and join fabric for backing; make at least 2" larger than quilt. Tack backing and quilt top wrong sides together (no wadding is used). Machine quilt along all seams (use a walking foot or the dual feed on your machine). Trim corners into curves and bind edges of quilt with bias binding.

Project by Yvonne Line

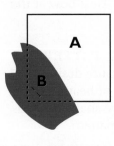

Step 1

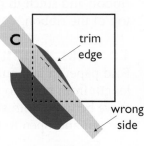

Step 2

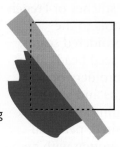

Step 3

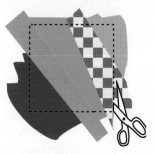

Step4

Rosy Cushion

Ribbonwork is one of the most exquisite of the Victoriana crafts. On our superb cushion we show a bunch of satiny blooms in dusky pink ribbon on a background of black and beige checks.

MATERIALS

80" x 1"-wide dusky pink and 80" x 1"-wide pale pink double-sided satin ribbon for roses; matching threads; embroidery needle; 10" square cream and black small-checked fabric; chenille needle (large eye and sharp point); 80" x ½"-wide pale green rayon ribbon, for leaves; DMC six-stranded embroidery thread, dull grey-green 646; 40" x 45"-wide cream and black large-checked fabric; 6yds x 1"-wide dusky pink double-sided satin ribbon, for piping and frill; 36" of piping cord; invisible thread; 10" zip.

FINISHED SIZE

12″ square, plus 4″-wide frill.
Note. Very soft ribbon works best when
making these ribbon roses.

Small ribbon roses

Peony roses

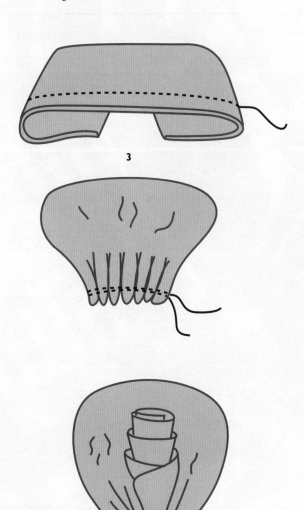

(Make one small and one very small.) Use
dusky or pale pink ribbon. Take a 10″ length
of ribbbon, cut with a straight edge at one
end. Fold the straight end over 3 or 4 times,
then stitch to secure to form bud. (See
diagram 1.) Fold ribbon away from you on
the diagonal, then take it halfway around the
bud, securing with stitches at the base.
Repeat, stitching each fold until ribbon has
been used and you have formed a rose.(See
diagram 2.) Conceal and secure the final
fold under the rose.

(Large roses in cushion center.) Make 2,
using darker ribbon for the center of one and
lighter ribbon for the center of the other.
Make ribbon roses as above and use as the
centers of the peony roses. Cut several 1″ to
3″ lengths of ribbon (the number depends
on how large you wish to make the rose);
each length will form a separate petal.
Gather each length of ribbon with short
running stitches to form a petal. (See
diagram 3.) Stitch each petal around the
center of the rose adding as many petals as
desired. (See diagram 4.)

Rosebuds

(Make 4.) Cut a 4″ length of ribbon for each rosebud. Fold length in half, forming a loop. At the halfway point between fold and raw edges, stitch a running thread through

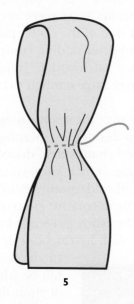

5

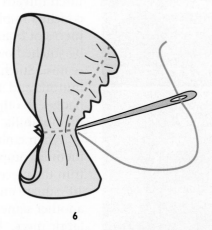

6

both thicknesses of ribbon, gather running thread and pull tightly. (See diagram 5.) Wind thread around gathers, stitch to secure. Fold raw edges up to running stitches and stitch to form a small bundle. Stitch a tiny running stitch around one edge of ribbon loop. (See diagram 6.) Tuck the ribbon bundle up inside the loop and pull the running stitches tightly to form a bud. Make sure the petals of the bud hide the ribbon bundle well and stitch to secure.

Cushion centre

Stitch the two peony roses on the small check fabric square for cushion center, placing them side by side diagonally in middle. Arrange roses each side of the larger ones and 2 rosebuds side by side in 2 corners of the square.

Make leaves by threading a chenille needle with green rayon ribbon and making a single straight stitch. Stitch stems with very large stem stitches using 6 strands of embroidery thread.

TO ASSEMBLE CUSHION

Use ½″ seam allowances. Cut two 13″ squares of large cream and black checked fabric for front and back. Pin pink double-sided satin ribbon around piping cord and tack close to cord. Pin covered piping cord to edges of center square, placing all raw edges together. Using zipper foot, machine stitch close to piping.

Take seam allowances on center square to wrong side and tack center square over cushion front.

Using a zipper foot and invisible thread, stitch in the ditch between piping and center square.

Cut 8 ½″-wide bias fabric strips and piece together to measure 3yds in length. With right sides facing, join short ends. With wrong sides facing, press fabric in half lengthwise. Open out fabric and pin one edge of satin ribbon next to center fold, joining on the bias where necessary. Stitch ribbon in place.

Fold fabric in half lengthwise again and stitch two rows of gathering threads along raw edges. Pull up threads and, with all raw edges aligned, pin frill to cushion front, easing gathers, stitch in place. With right sides facing, stitch cushion front to back, enclosing frill and leaving an opening on one side for zip. Turn right side out; stitch zip into side opening.

Project by Kaye Pyke

Photography by Andrew Elton

205

Family Heirloom Cushion

Here's a clever technique which allows you to transfer photocopied images to fabric. Use the transferred images to create family heirlooms — a keepsake cushion, framed picture or memory quilt.

MATERIALS

Photo transfer on fabric; scraps of brocade, silk, satin fabrics; thread; embroidery threads; braid; old buttons, badges or memorabilia; polyester fiber filling; cords; 4 tassels.

METHOD

Cut one or two corners from the photo transfer to give a five-sided shape. Cut a triangle from a fabric scrap and lay one side of it along the photo piece, with right sides facing and aligning raw edges. Stitch, using a ¼" seam, flip the piece over to the right side and press. Cut another scrap piece and stitch onto the next side of the center piece in the same way. Continue adding fabric pieces using this crazy patchwork technique, until you have a piece large enough to cut a 10" square.

Embroider over the seams using stitches and threads as desired, e.g. herringbone stitch, detached chain stitch, double feather stitch, couching, French knot, cretan stitch. Work some embroidery stitches in double rows for a more decorative effect and combine stitches such as French knots and chain stitches with herringbone or cretan stitch. Seed beads can be added to rows of embroidery, textured threads can be couched in place and pieces of braid can be stitched over seams. Stitch on buttons and add badges or other memorabilia.

When embellishment is complete, trim the piece into a 10" square and cut another same-size fabric piece. With right sides facing, stitch around, leaving an opening on one side. Turn right side out and fill with fiber; stitch opening closed. Stitch cords in place around the edge and stitch tassels to each corner.

STEP 1

STEP 2

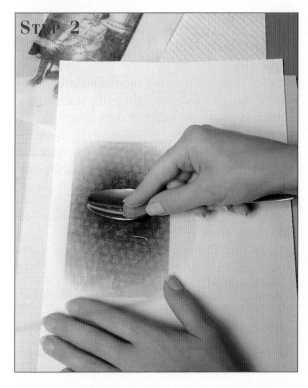

STEP 3

Step-By-Step Transferring

MATERIALS

Photocopies of your photographs (copied just before transferring); pure gum turpentine (from hardware and art supply stores); cotton fabric (voile, batiste or organza work well); cotton wool; paper towel.

Step 1. Choose a clear photograph with good light and dark contrast and photocopy it just before transferring (within 12 hours). The quality varies with photocopiers — the best result will be obtained on a 'mono-compo-nent' machine. If you don't have access to one of these machines, use the machine available and test the results. Small- to medium-sized photographs will be easier to handle during the transfer process.

Step 2. Place the cotton fabric on paper towel on a smooth surface and lay the photocopy face down on it. Using a cotton ball soaked with gum turpentine, gently rub the paper until it is saturated. When you have used enough liquid, the image will be clearly visible. Starting from the center, rub the back of the paper with a spoon, in a circular direction. Rub only the parts you wish to transfer — you can create an oval or circular area, if you want. Avoid moving the paper against the fabric, as this will cause smudges.

Step 3. Remove the paper to reveal the transferred image and allow to dry. The image can be colored to blend with other fabrics by painting with a pale wash of thinned acrylic paint (folk art paint is suitable). Transfers can be washed by hand using a mild soap.

Project by Denise Lawler

Photography by Andrew Payne

Cottages and Pathways Quilt

This lovely design makes an appealing quilt when stitched in muted shades.

Quantities listed are for 45"-wide fabrics.

MATERIALS
104" beige print, for background; 64" assorted medium-dark prints, for roofs and squares in pieced blocks, sashing and border; 40" medium-dark print, for border; 28" assorted medium-light prints, for walls, chimneys and squares in pieced blocks and sashing; 28" dark print, for windows, doors and binding; 8" contrast dark print, for windows and doors; 8' x 76" wadding; 16' backing fabric; clear monofilament thread, for machine quilting.

FINISHED SIZE
90" x 65"
Note. Cutting measurements include ¼" seam allowances. This quilt is ideal for rotary cutting methods (using a cutting mat and rotary blade cutter), if desired.

METHOD
Cottage blocks
(make 18)
For each cottage, use one medium-dark print for the roof, a medium-light print for the walls and chimney, and the dark prints for doors and windows. (Alternate these dark prints so that some cottages have the dark print for the door and the contrast dark print for the windows, while other cottages have the reverse).

Cutting out
Refer to the Cottage Block diagram; for each block, cut:

A (background): one 2" square.

B (chimney): one 2" x 1½" rectangle.

C (background): one 7" x 2" rectangle.

D (roof): one 9½" x 3½" rectangle.

E (veranda roof): one 9½" x 2" rectangle.

F (walls): four 2" x 1¼" rectangles.

G (windows): two 2" squares.

H (walls): two 4¼" x 2⅕" rectangles.

I (door): one 4" x 2" rectangle.

Lay out pieces of each cottage before sewing. Using a ¼" seam allowance, sew pieces together following the construction diagram. Trim blocks so that they are exactly 9½" square.

Pathway blocks

(make 17)
Cutting out
Cut center squares (J) from assorted

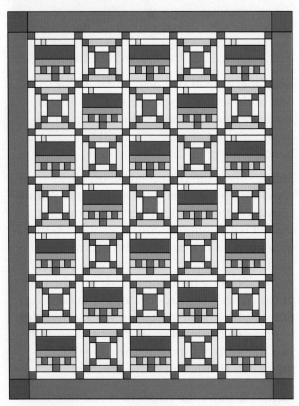

Cottages Block

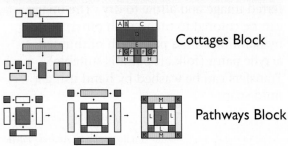

Pathways Block

medium-dark prints and corner squares (K) from both medium-dark and medium-light prints. Refer to Pathway Block diagram and for each block, cut:

J (center square): one 3 ½" square.
K (corner squares): eight 2" squares.
L (background): four 3 ½" x 2" rectangles.
M (background): four 7" x 2" rectangles.

Using a ¼" seam allowance, sew block pieces together following the construction diagram. Trim blocks so that they are exactly 9½" square.

QUILT ASSEMBLY

From background fabric for sashing strips, cut 82 rectangles, each 9½" x 2". From assorted medium-dark and medium-light prints for corner squares, cut 48 squares, each 2". Join blocks together with sashing strips between, making 7 rows with 5 blocks in each. Join remaining sashing strips to corner squares (making 8 rows of 5 strips and 6 squares) and sew these strips between each row of blocks.

From border fabric, cut 8 strips 40" x 5" wide; join strips together in pairs to make top, bottom and side borders approximately 80" in length.

Measuring quilt through the center (rather than at the edges) to determine its true dimensions, cut and join border strips to correct length. Sew side borders to quilt. From medium-dark print, cut four 5" squares. Join corner squares to ends of remaining border strips, and sew

borders to top and bottom of quilt.

Cut and join backing fabric to make a rectangle approximately 90" x 85". Sandwich wadding between wrong sides of quilt top and backing. Fasten layers together with safety pins or baste together. Mark quilting lines with chalk in a diagonal grid 2" apart, then machine quilt using monofilament thread. Trim excess wadding and backing.

From dark print for binding, cut 8 strips, each 45" x 3" wide. Join strips together in pairs and press in half lengthwise with wrong sides together.

To bind quilt sides, pin a binding strip to each quilt edge with all raw edges together, stitch in place. Fold binding over to wrong side, slipstitch folded edge into stitching. Trim excess binding at ends. Bind top and bottom edges in the same way, folding under the binding at corners.

Project by Margaret Rolfe
Photography by Ross Coffey

Floral Quilt

This quilt was inspired by a lovely old nineteenth century English quilt.

Quantities listed are for 45"-wide fabrics. Where assorted fabrics are required, buy 8" pieces as each will yield 6 squares. We have indicated which fabrics should be light, medium and dark in color; following this is essential to achieve the shading in our quilt.

MATERIALS

24" light floral fabric for center square (this is the key fabric in the quilt and other fabrics should be chosen to complement its colors); 48" assorted light florals; 2½yds assorted medium florals; 1¾yds assorted dark florals; 1½yds border-print fabric (or substitute a large print); 28" contrast fabric for binding; thread; 7yds backing fabric; 100" square of wadding; quilting thread for hand quilting or neutral colored thread for machine quilting.

FINISHED SIZE

90" square (approx).
Note. Measurements include ¼" seam allowances. This quilt is ideal for rotary cutting methods, if desired.

METHOD

Cutting out

From light fabric for center square, cut one 20" square and eight squares 7".

From assorted light fabrics, cut 36 squares 7" (making a total of 44 light squares).

From assorted medium fabrics, cut 64 squares 7".

From dark fabric, cut 28 squares 7".

From assorted dark fabrics, cut 16 squares 7"; re-cut each square across the diagonal to yield two half-square triangles (a total of 32 triangles for the sides of the quilt).

From assorted dark fabrics, cut one square 8"; re-cut the square across both

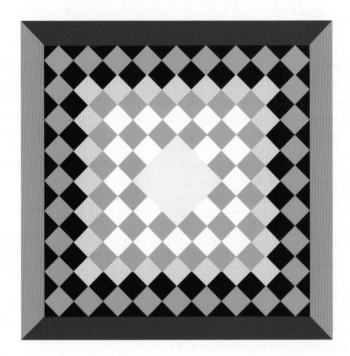

diagonals to yield four triangles for the corners.

From border fabric, cutting lengthwise down the fabric, cut eight strips, each approximately 5″ wide or width of printed border pattern.

From fabric for binding, cutting widthwise across the fabric, cut nine strips, each 46″ x 3″.

ASSEMBLY

Lay out squares around large center square, making a chequerboard pattern of lights and darks as illustrated in diagram. Arrange side and corner triangles appropriately.

Starting from one corner and working in diagonal rows, join pieces together to form strips (do not join center square yet).

Press seam allowances together to one side, pressing each row in the opposite direction to the previous row.

Sew the rows together, stitching the center square into the three central rows of strips. Staystitch around the edge of the quilt so that the bias edges do not stretch.

Join border strips together in pairs to make 4 long strips. Stitch border strips to the sides of the quilt, matching centers of quilt edges and borders and leaving excess at each end for mitering corners. At the corners, stitch only to the point where the seam allowances cross, then reverse stitch; DO NOT stitch into the seam allowances. Press seams towards outer edge.

Miter corners by marking a 45-degree angled line onto the wrong side of each border strip, then pin and stitch along the marked lines.

Trim seam allowances at the mitered corners and press seams open.

Cut and piece backing fabric to make a 2¾yd square. Lay backing right side down, smooth wadding on top; lay quilt top on wadding with right side up. Tack layers or fasten together with safety pins. Using chalk, mark a diagonal grid of lines 1½″ apart all over the quilt, with every fourth line falling in a seam. Quilt by hand or by machine.

Take one of the nine binding strips and cut it into quarters. Join two full strips with one quarter strip to make one 96″ length. Repeat with remaining strips, making four long strips in all. Fold strips in half lengthwise and press.

With all raw edges together, pin and stitch strips to two opposite sides of the quilt. Trim excess wadding and backing. Fold binding to the back and pin in place. Stitch remaining two binding strips to quilt. Trim excess binding, wadding and backing.

Fold binding to the back of the quilt; folding under the corners neatly; hand stitch in place.

Project by Margaret Rolfe
Photography by Ross Coffey

Knitting and Crochet Notes

Use only the yarns specified for each pattern; other yarns may give unsatisfactory results. Yarn quantities are based on average requirements and are therefore approximate.

TENSION

Correct tension is essential. If your tension is not exactly as specified in the pattern, your garment will be the wrong size. If you have more stitches than stated, use larger needles. If you have less stitches than stated, use smaller needles.

GENERAL ABBREVIATIONS

Alt: alternate; **beg:** beginning; **cont:** continue; **dec:** decrease, decreasing; **foll:** following, follows; **inc:** increase, increasing; **incl:** including, inclusive; **patt:** pattern; **rem:** remain/ing; **rep:** repeat; **tog:** together;

KNITTING ABBREVIATIONS

K: knit; **P:** purl; **rnd/s:** round/s; **sl:** slip; **st/s:** stitch/es; **st st:** stocking stitch (knit all sts on right side of work, purl all sts on wrong side of work); **inc:** increase (usually knit into front and then into back of next st, thus making one stitch); **lp/s:** loop/s; **M1:** make 1 — pick up loop which lies before next st, place on left hand needle and knit into back of loop; **0:** (zero) — no sts, rows or times; **psso:** pass slip stitch over; **sp/s:** space/s; **rev st st:** reverse stocking stitch (purl all sts on right side of work, knit all sts on wrong side of work); **tbl:** through back loop; **yrn:** yarn round needle; **yfwd:** yarn forward (bring yarn under needle, then over into knitting position again, thus making one stitch).

CROCHET ABBREVIATIONS

Ch: chain; **sc:** single crochet; **crab st:** work as for sc, noting to work from left to right instead of from right to left so that sts are worked backwards; **tr:** treble; **hdc:** half double crochet; **lp/s:** loops; **sl:** slip; **sp/s:** space/s; **st/s:** stitch/es; **dc:** double crochet; **dtr:** double treble; **yoh:** yarn over hook; **picot:** 4ch, sl st back into last dc; **rep:** repeat; **rnd/s:** round/s.

KNITTING STITCH EMBROIDERY

In knitting stitch embroidery a completed stitch looks like a 'V'.

Step 1. When working from right to left, bring needle from back of work through the centre of the stitch below the one to be covered, then insert from right to left under both strands of the stitch above the one to be covered.

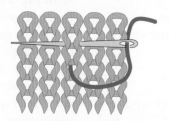

step 1

Step 2. Bring needle back to the start of the stitch and through to the back. Carry yarn loosely across wrong side of work to the position for the next stitch. Be

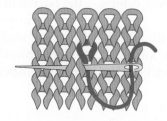

step 2

careful not to pull the stitch too firmly and you'll find it will cover the existing stitch entirely.

Note: When working from left to right, note to insert the needle from left to right under both strands of the stitch above the one to be covered.

Pompoms

Cut 2 pieces of cardboard in a circle, using the following sizes as a guide for small, medium or large pompom:

3″ in diameter with a 1″ diameter hole for a small pompom;

4½″ in diameter with a 1½″ diameter hole for a medium pompom;

6″ in diameter with a 2″ diameter hole for a large pompom.

Hold both circles of cardboard together and wind the yarn round and round the cardboard until the center hole is completely filled — small pompom should take approx half a ball; medium pompom 1 ball and large pompom 2 balls. Place the point of a pair of sharp scissors between the 2 pieces of cardboard and cut around, keeping scissors between circles of cardboard all the time.

Place a length of wool in the fold, and wrap this around pompom between the cardboard. Knot very firmly, removing cardboard. Trim pompom to round shape.

Stitches

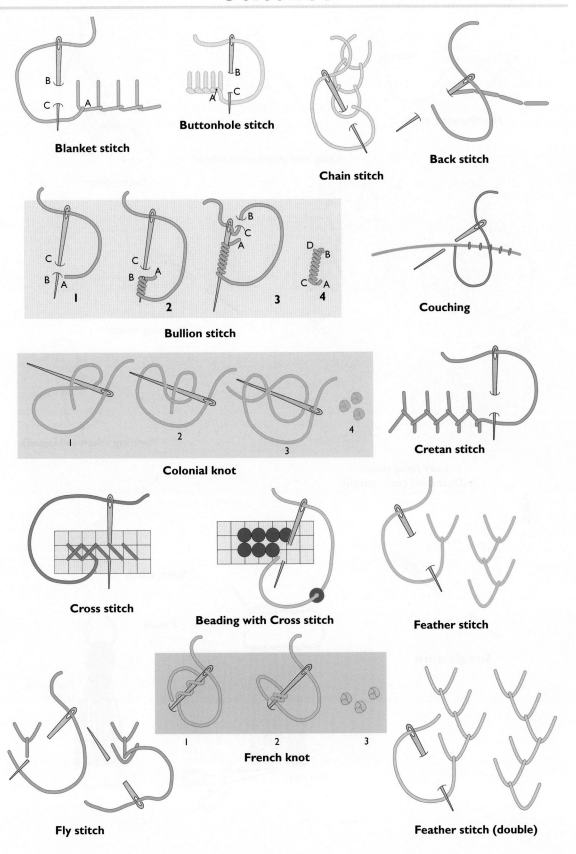

Blanket stitch

Buttonhole stitch

Chain stitch

Back stitch

Bullion stitch

Couching

Colonial knot

Cretan stitch

Cross stitch

Beading with Cross stitch

Feather stitch

Fly stitch

French knot

Feather stitch (double)

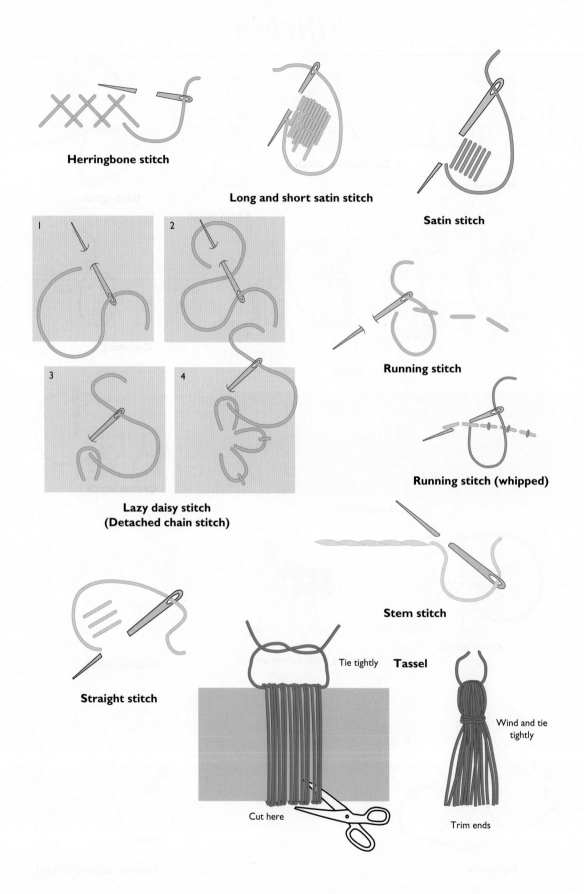

Herringbone stitch

Long and short satin stitch

Satin stitch

1

2

3

4

**Lazy daisy stitch
(Detached chain stitch)**

Running stitch

Running stitch (whipped)

Stem stitch

Straight stitch

Tie tightly   **Tassel**

Wind and tie
tightly

Cut here

Trim ends

Patterns

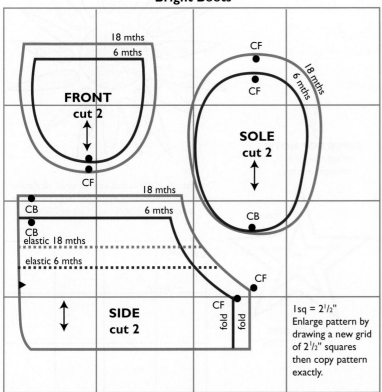

Bright Boots

18 mths
6 mths

FRONT
cut 2

CF

CF

CF

SOLE
cut 2

18 mths
6 mths

CB

18 mths
6 mths

CB
CB

elastic 18 mths
elastic 6 mths

CF

CF

fold
fold

SIDE
cut 2

1 sq = 2½"
Enlarge pattern by
drawing a new grid
of 2½" squares
then copy pattern
exactly.

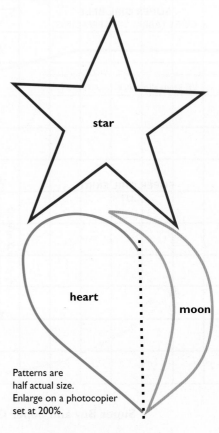

star

heart

moon

Patterns are
half actual size.
Enlarge on a photocopier
set at 200%.

Teaser and Squeaker

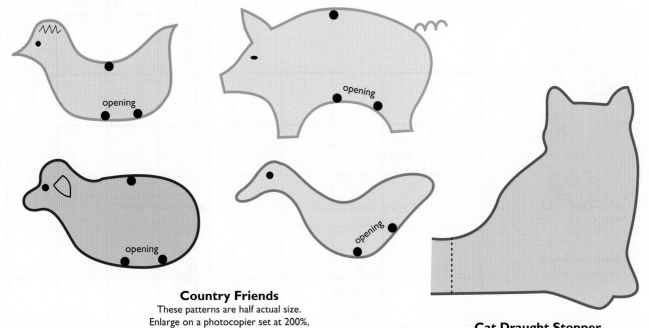

opening

opening

opening

opening

Country Friends

These patterns are half actual size.
Enlarge on a photocopier set at 200%,
then add a ¼" seam allowance.

Cat Draught Stopper
Pattern – 25% of actual size

215

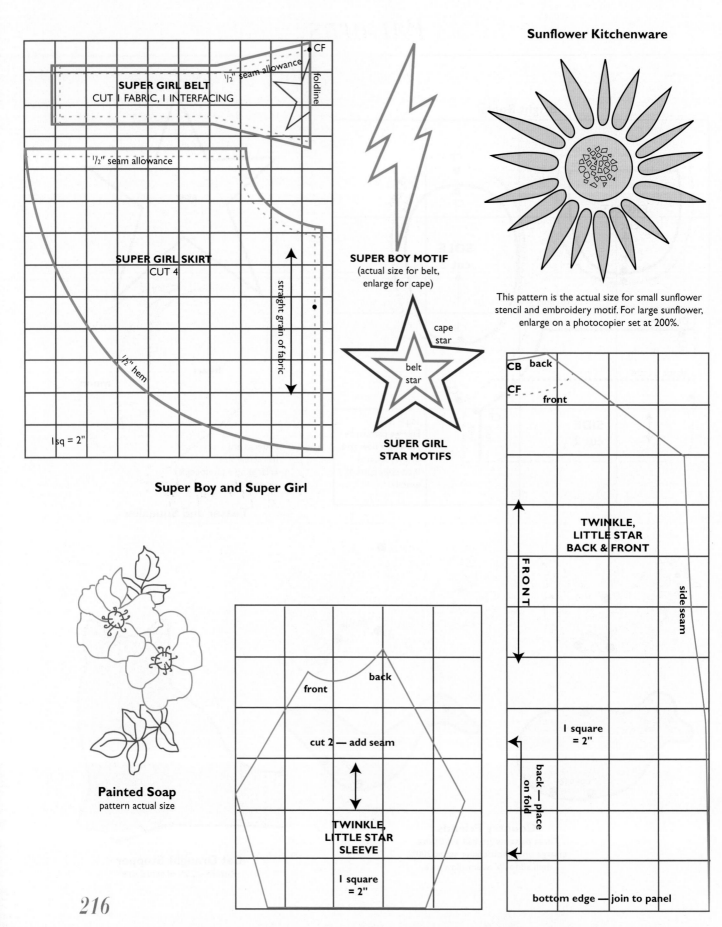

SUPER GIRL BELT
CUT 1 FABRIC, 1 INTERFACING

½" seam allowance

CF

foldline

½" seam allowance

SUPER GIRL SKIRT
CUT 4

straight grain of fabric

½" hem

1 sq = 2"

Super Boy and Super Girl

SUPER BOY MOTIF
(actual size for belt,
enlarge for cape)

cape
star

belt
star

**SUPER GIRL
STAR MOTIFS**

Sunflower Kitchenware

This pattern is the actual size for small sunflower stencil and embroidery motif. For large sunflower, enlarge on a photocopier set at 200%.

CB back

CF

front

**TWINKLE,
LITTLE STAR
BACK & FRONT**

FRONT

side seam

1 square
= 2"

back — place
on fold

bottom edge — join to panel

Painted Soap
pattern actual size

front   back

cut 2 — add seam

**TWINKLE,
LITTLE STAR
SLEEVE**

1 square
= 2"

216

Twinkle, Twinkle, Little Star Sleeping Bag

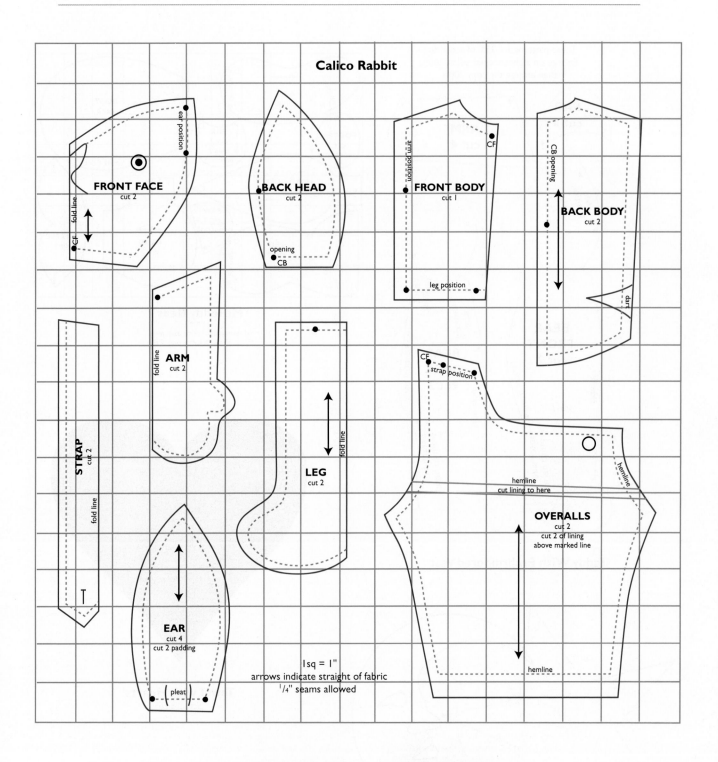

Calico Rabbit

FRONT FACE
cut 2

ear position

CF fold line

BACK HEAD
cut 2

opening
CB

arm position

CF

FRONT BODY
cut 1

leg position

CB opening

BACK BODY
cut 2

dart

fold line ARM
cut 2

STRAP
cut 2

fold line

LEG
cut 2

fold line

CF

strap position

hemline
cut lining to here

hemline

OVERALLS
cut 2
cut 2 of lining
above marked line

hemline

EAR
cut 4
cut 2 padding

(pleat)

1 sq = 1"
arrows indicate straight of fabric
¼" seams allowed

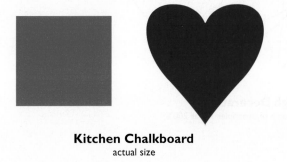

Kitchen Chalkboard
actual size

217

These patterns are 25% of actual size. Enlarge on a photocopier set at 200%, then enlarge the copy 200%.

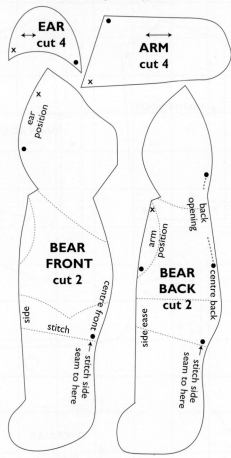

Teddy With Embroidered Vest

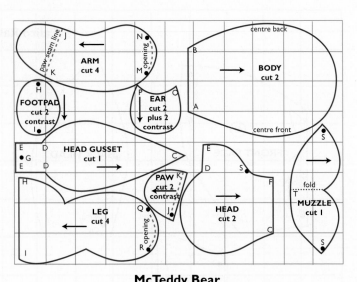

McTeddy Bear
1 sq = 2"
1/4" seam allowance on each piece
follow arrows for direction of pile

Towel with Hearts
actual size

Bread Dough Decorations
Half actual size, enlarge on a photocopier set at 200%.

218

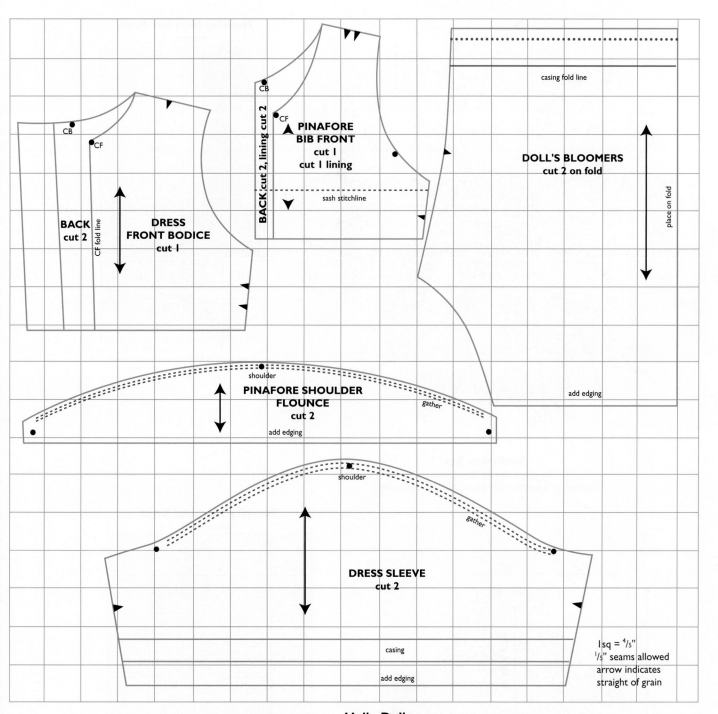

BACK
cut 2

CF fold line

**DRESS
FRONT BODICE**
cut 1

CB

CF

BACK cut 2, lining cut 2

CB

CF

**PINAFORE
BIB FRONT**
cut 1
cut 1 lining

sash stitchline

casing fold line

DOLL'S BLOOMERS
cut 2 on fold

place on fold

add edging

**PINAFORE SHOULDER
FLOUNCE**
cut 2

shoulder

gather

add edging

shoulder

gather

DRESS SLEEVE
cut 2

casing

add edging

1 sq = ⁴/₅"
¹/₅" seams allowed
arrow indicates
straight of grain

Hello Dolly

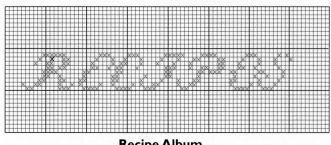

Recipe Album

219

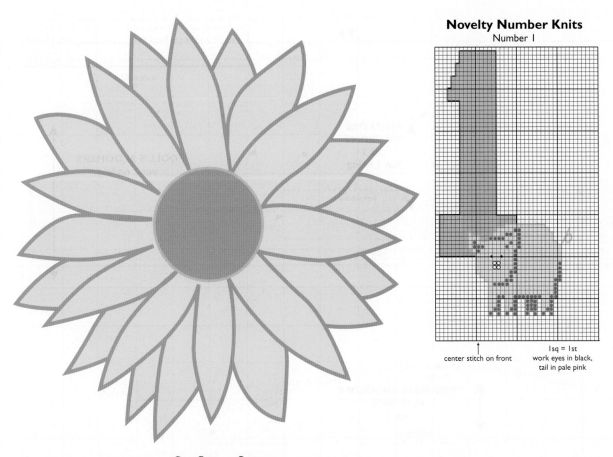

Novelty Number Knits
Number 1

center stitch on front

1sq = 1st
work eyes in black,
tail in pale pink

Sunflower Set
Use actual size for apron appliqué,
enlarge on a photocopier set at 200% for pot holder.

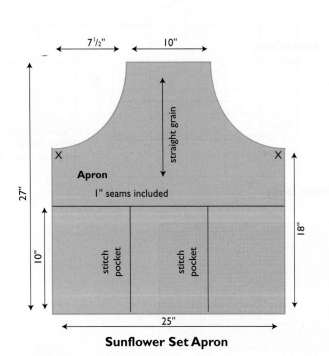

7½"   10"

straight grain

Apron

1" seams included

27"

10"

18"

stitch pocket

stitch pocket

25"

Sunflower Set Apron

Novelty Number Knits
Number 4

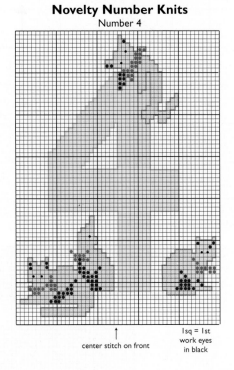

center stitch on front

1sq = 1st
work eyes
in black

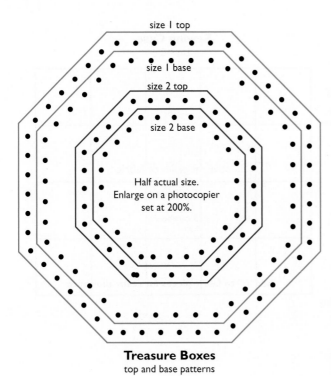

size 1 top

size 1 base

size 2 top

size 2 base

Half actual size.
Enlarge on a photocopier
set at 200%.

Treasure Boxes
top and base patterns

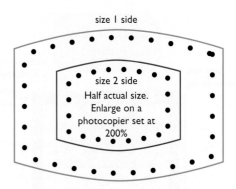

size 1 side

size 2 side
Half actual size.
Enlarge on a
photocopier set at
200%.

Treasure Boxes
side patterns

Novelty Number Knits
Number 3

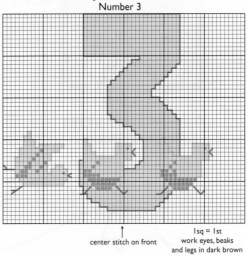

↑
center stitch on front

1sq = 1st
work eyes, beaks
and legs in dark brown

Novelty Number Knits
Number 5

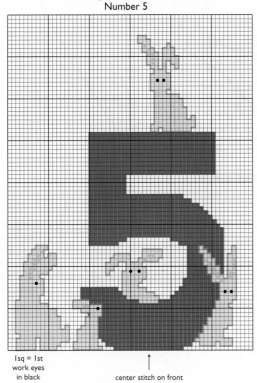

1sq = 1st
work eyes
in black

↑
center stitch on front

Novelty Number Knits
Number 2

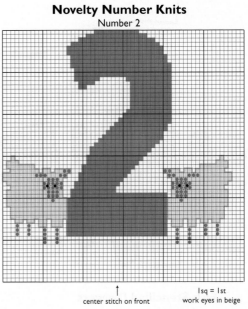

↑
center stitch on front

1sq = 1st
work eyes in beige

221

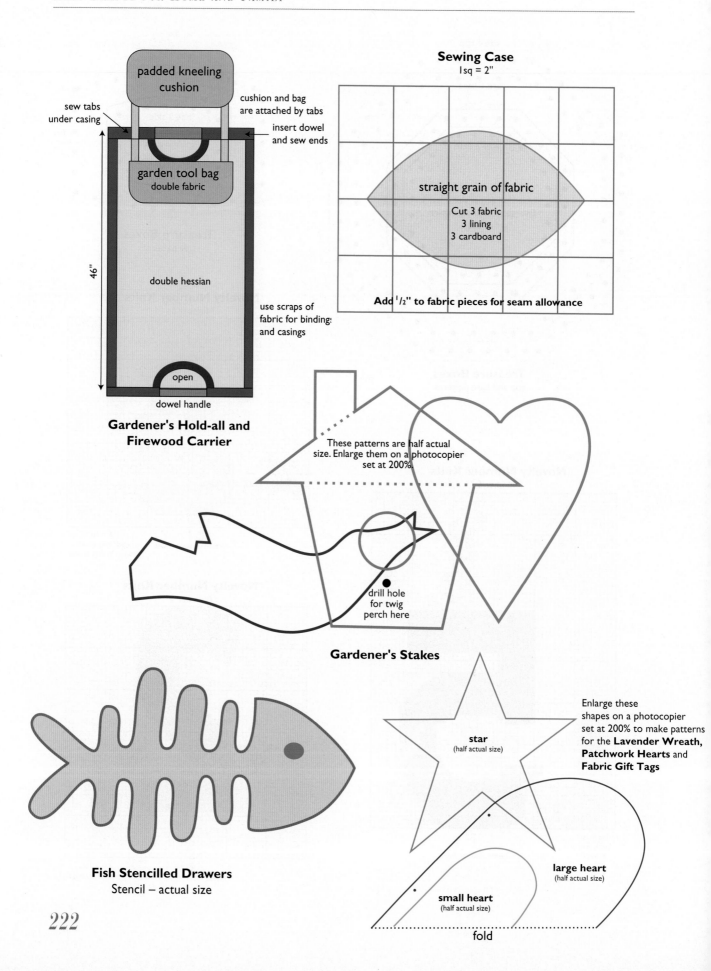

padded kneeling cushion

sew tabs under casing

cushion and bag are attached by tabs

insert dowel and sew ends

garden tool bag
double fabric

46"

double hessian

use scraps of fabric for bindings and casings

open

dowel handle

Gardener's Hold-all and Firewood Carrier

Sewing Case
1 sq = 2"

straight grain of fabric

Cut 3 fabric
3 lining
3 cardboard

Add ¹/₂" to fabric pieces for seam allowance

These patterns are half actual size. Enlarge them on a photocopier set at 200%.

Gardener's Stakes

drill hole for twig perch here

Fish Stencilled Drawers
Stencil – actual size

star
(half actual size)

Enlarge these shapes on a photocopier set at 200% to make patterns for the **Lavender Wreath, Patchwork Hearts** and **Fabric Gift Tags**

large heart
(half actual size)

small heart
(half actual size)

fold

222

Catnip Mouse

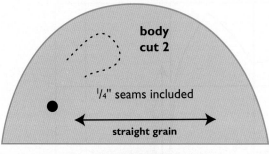

body
cut 2

¹/₄" seams included

straight grain

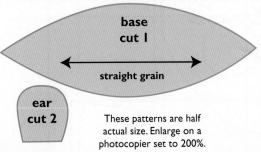

base
cut 1

straight grain

ear
cut 2

These patterns are half
actual size. Enlarge on a
photocopier set to 200%.

**Checked Bedroom Set
Make-up Bag**

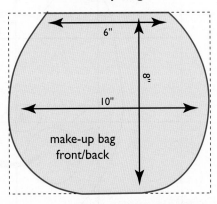

6"

8"

10"

make-up bag
front/back

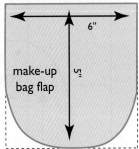

6"

5"

make-up
bag flap

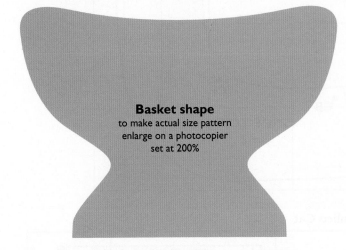

Basket shape
to make actual size pattern
enlarge on a photocopier
set at 200%

Paper-cut Shelf Liner

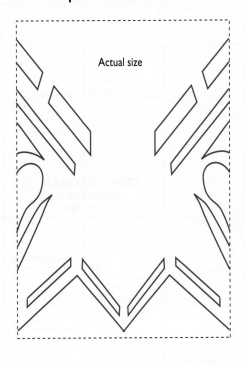

Actual size

Broderie Perse Appliqué Basket Picture

Kitchen Set Mitt

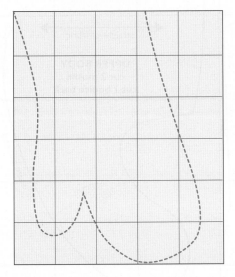

1 square = 2"

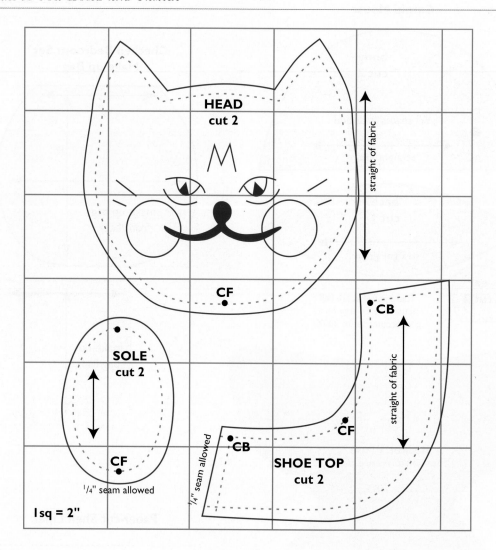

HEAD
cut 2

SOLE
cut 2

CF

SHOE TOP
cut 2

CB

CF

CB

CF

¹/₄" seam allowed

¹/₄" seam allowed

1 sq = 2"

straight of fabric

straight of fabric

Calico Cat

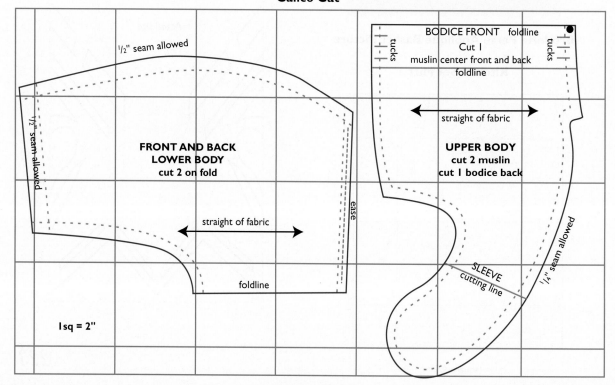

¹/₂" seam allowed

**FRONT AND BACK
LOWER BODY
cut 2 on fold**

¹/₂" seam allowed

ease

foldline

straight of fabric

BODICE FRONT   foldline
Cut 1
muslin center front and back
foldline

tucks

tucks

straight of fabric

**UPPER BODY
cut 2 muslin
cut 1 bodice back**

¹/₄" seam allowed

SLEEVE
cutting line

1 sq = 2"

Calico Cat

Stockists

Most of the materials used in the projects in this book are easily found in craft and hobby stores. However, some items may be a little harder to find.

PANDA/CLECKHEATON yarns are distributed by
Plymouth Yarns Co. Inc.
PO Box 28
Bristol PA 19007
website: http://www.plymouthyarn.com

COATS/SPENCER CROCHET COTTON for information
concerning availability, contact
Coats & Clark
30 Patewood Drive
Greenville
SV 29615 USA
Ph: 864 234 0331
Fax: 864 675 5609

DMC THREADS are distributed by
DMC Corporation
10 Port
Kearny
South Kearny NJ
07032-4688 USA
Ph: 973 589 0606
Fax: 973 589 8931

Index of Projects

Treasures for Tots 6

Heirloom Shawl 8
Bright Boots 11
Angel Birth Memento 12
Christening Bonnet 14
Quick-Knit Shawl 16
Edged Bib 17
Flannel Edging 17
Cot Sheet Set 18
Wrist Rattle 19
Teddy Frame 20
Butterfly Rug and Crib String 22
Teddy Blanket and Bear 24
Teaser and Squeakers 25
Jungle Jingler, Sheet and Quilt 26
Traditional Pompom Hat 28
Eye-Catching Pompom Hat 30
Socks and Singlet 31
Touch-and-Feel Playmat 32
Country Friends Mobile 34
Twinkle, Twinkle Little Star Sleeping Bag 35

Charming for Children 36

Rabbit in Liberty Duds 38
Teddy with Embroidered Vest 39
Calico Cat 40
Country Cousin 41
Three Bears 42
Hello Dolly 48
Fairyland Fantasies 50
Paper Beads 53
Priscilla Pig 54
Drawstring Bags 55
Double Delight (sweater and doll) 56
Tie-Dyed Casual Clothes 60
Kiddy's Indoor Cubby 62
Novelty Number Knits 64

Simple Summer Dress 67
Scrunchies Holder and Box 68
Charm Bracelets 69
Fancy Dress for Kids 70

Gorgeous Gifts 72

Terracotta Pot Candles 74
Stylish Make-up Purse and Glasses Case 74
Découpage Floral Tray 75
Bejewelled Pots and Platter 76
Travellers' Aid 76
Clever Tea-cosy 77
Sunflower Set 78
Towels with Hearts 79
Knitted String Bag 79
Kitchen Chalkboard 80
Towel Trims 80
Painted Soap 81
Recipe Album and Matching Tea Towels 81
Découpage Box 82
Practical Work Apron 83
Victorian Sewing Case 84
Seaside Key Holder and Box 84
Treasure Boxes with Crochet Lace Trim 85

Great Gardeners' Goods 86

Matching Gloves and Kneeling Pad 88
Rose Swag 89
Herb Hangers 89
Gardener's Set 90
Firewood Carrier 92
Gardener's Hold-all 93
Pressing Flowers 94
Key Holder with Pressed Flowers 95
Say It In Flowers 95
Pressed in Paper 95
Herb Pictures 96

Pressed Flower Picture 96
Drying Flowers 97
Dried Flower Basket 97

Hearth & Home 98

Simple Cushions 100
Fabulous Frame 101
Fish Printed Cushion 102
Country Chest and Frame 104
Make It Easy Tableware 105
Sunny Drawers and Vase 106
Kitchen Set 108
Bathroom Set 110
Checked Bedroom Set 112
Mirror and Tissue Box Cover 115
Sunflower Kitchenware 116
Paper-cut Shelf Liner 117
Transformed Chair 118
Rag-Rolled Frames 120
Fern Spattered Tinware 122
Fish Stencilled Drawers 124
Doona Cover and Pillowcase 126
Pinboard 127
Pleated Paper Lampshade 128
Cat Draught-Stopper 129

Fete Favourites 130

Float Candles 132
Beeswax Candles 132
Fabric-Covered Pots 132
Shell Candles 132
Découpaged Soaps 133
Drawstring Bags 133
Juggling Balls 133
Storage Jars 133
Patchwork Jar Cover 134
Floral Bookmark 135
Lace Lavender Ball and Bolster 135
Bath Crystals 136
Marbled Stationery 136
Photograph Frames 136

Fridge Magnets 137
Beaut Bangles 137
Herb Bath Sachets 137
Catnip Mouse 138
Heart Key Rings 138
Ribbon Streamers 138
Unusual Pincushions 139
Rosette Headbands 139
Ponytail and Baby Bows 139

Nicest Knits and Classic Crochets 140

Tartan Traveller's Rug 142
Lacy Cotton Tunic 143
Tea-time Trimmings 146
Timeless Tunic 148
Hooked on Colour 150
Tartan Rug in Tunisian Crochet 153
A Pretty Heirloom Cloth 155
Embroidered Vest 156
Fisherman's Rib Sweater 158
Twin Chic 160
Classic Cables for Cosy Comfort 162
His 'N' Her Jumper 165
Shore Favourites 168
King of the Knit Parade 171

Festive Flair 174

Cornucopias 176
Everlasting Floral Pots 176
Lavender Wreath 177
Spicy Fabric Pomanders 177
Patchwork Hearts 178
Mini Christmas Tree 179
Gold Walnuts 179
Cinnamon Pomanders 179
Handmade Crackers 180
Festive Fruit 181
Golden Ivy 181
Pine Cone Hangings 181
Pine Basket 181

Santa Stocking 182
Small Red Christmas Stockings 184
Bread Dough Decorations 185
Christmas Scents 185
Scented Oranges 186
The Luxury of Gold Leaf 187
Gilded Stars 188
Gilded Cards 188
Gilded Box 188
Wrappings and Stampings 188
Stamped Stationery 189
Quilled Cards 190
Country Cards 192
Cards That Stand Out 192
It's a Wrap 193
Fabric Gift Tags 193
Beautiful Boxes 193

Perfect Pastimes 194

Broderie Perse Appliqué Basket Picture 196
Beaded Butterfly Cushion 198
Silk Ribbon Daisies 200
String of Hearts 201
Crazy Quilt 202
Rosy Cushion 203
Family Heirloom Cushion 206
Cottages and Pathways Quilt 208
Floral Quilt 210